THE KENNEDY

CONTRACT

★　　　★　　　★

The Mafia Plot to Assassinate the President

John H. Davis

HarperPaperbacks
A Division of HarperCollinsPublishers

For Sohodra

HarperPaperbacks *A Division of* HarperCollins*Publishers*
10 East 53rd Street, New York, N.Y. 10022

Cover photo of JFK courtesy of the Bettmann Archives
Cover photos of all others courtesy of AP/Wide World Photos

First printing: August 1993

Printed in the United States of America

HarperPaperbacks and colophon are trademarks of HarperCollins*Publishers*

❖ 10 9 8 7 6 5 4 3 2 1

Also by John H. Davis

The Bouviers: Portrait of an American Family

Venice

The Guggenheims: An American Epic

The Kennedys: Dynasty and Disaster

Mafia Kingfish: Carlos Marcello and the Assassination of John F. Kennedy

Mafia Dynasty: The Rise and Fall of the Gambino Crime Family

CONTENTS

★

Contents

CHAPTER 1

The Allegation of
Frank Ragano

In the fall of 1991 Frank Ragano, a noted criminal defense attorney, who had represented Florida Mafia boss, Santos Trafficante, Jr., for twenty-seven years, and International Brotherhood of Teamsters Union boss, Jimmy Hoffa, for fifteen, and had been a counselor to Carlos Marcello, boss of the Gulf Coast underworld, sent a manuscript of his autobiography to his friend, New York crime reporter Nicholas Pileggi, for editorial advice.

Pileggi had first met Ragano in 1966 when he covered for his newspaper the legendary Mafia sitdown in the La Stella Restaurant in Queens, New York, attended by thirteen of the nation's most powerful Mafia leaders, including Santos Trafficante, Jr. and Carlos Marcello. The thirteen mobsters had been arrested for "consorting with known criminals." Ragano had represented Trafficante at the bail hearing, and in the process had gotten to know Pileggi. The two men had remained friends ever since.

Nicholas Pileggi, who, in the meantime, had written *Wiseguy—Life in a Mafia Family,* and the screenplay for the film *Goodfellas,* waded through Ragano's long, rambling manuscript without encountering anything particularly arresting, until he was over three quarters through it. Then, suddenly, what he was reading leapt off the pages and momentarily stunned him. Frank Ragano was admitting to having been a firsthand witness to the plotting of the assassination of President John F. Kennedy by Jimmy Hoffa, Santos Trafficante, Jr., and Carlos Marcello. It was as if Ragano had buried a time bomb at the end of a mountain of words.

Upon recovering from the shock of this unexpected revelation, Pileggi showed the manuscript to his friend, Jack Newfield, a former friend and biographer of Robert F. Kennedy, now a columnist for the *New York Post*. Intrigued, Newfield got in touch with Ragano and after interviewing him in Tampa over the course of several days, broke Ragano's story in the *Post* on January 14, 1992. The article was an immediate sensation causing a stream of articles on the allegation to appear in papers and magazines throughout the nation and prompting former chairman of the House Select Committee on Assassinations, Congressman Louis Stokes, to call for an official investigation of Ragano's claims.

In his interviews with Newfield, Ragano alleged that he was a witness to an assassination plot among Hoffa, Trafficante, and Marcello and had actually carried a message in February 1963 from Hoffa to Trafficante and Marcello urging them to kill the president.

Specifically Ragano told Newfield that in January 1963 he met with his client, Jimmy Hoffa, at the Teamsters' splendid five-story glass and white-marble headquarters in Washington, D.C. Hoffa was fretting under two federal indictments brought against him by Attorney General Robert F. Kennedy who had mounted the most extensive attack on organized crime in the nation's history. Hoffa was in a rage. He was aware that Kennedy had established an entire division within the Justice Department charged with the sole task of investigating and prosecuting him. The "get Hoffa Squad" it was called. According to Hoffa's sources, Kennedy would not rest until he put him behind bars.

Frank Ragano, at the time, was about to fly to New Orleans to meet with two other beleaguered associates of Hoffa's, Santos Trafficante, Jr., former boss of the mob's rackets in Havana, Cuba, and currently boss of the Florida underworld, and Carlos Marcello, supreme boss of the underworld in the Gulf Coast states of Mississippi, Louisiana, and Texas.

Trafficante was smarting under a federal investigation of his criminal empire in Florida at the time and was angered that his wife had recently been subpoenaed before a grand jury. Marcello, like Hoffa, was suffering under two federal indictments brought against him by Robert Kennedy, one of which threatened to result in his permanent deportation.

To Ragano's surprise Hoffa told him that inasmuch as he was going to New Orleans to meet with Trafficante and Marcello he could deliver to the two men a message from him to kill President Kennedy. "This has to be done," Hoffa told Ragano, as if he were aware that Trafficante and Marcello had already been contemplating such an action, which, in fact, was the case.

According to Ragano, Hoffa was convinced the Mafia could accomplish anything and get away with anything. As an example, Ragano told Jack Newfield that once Hoffa was able to get the Mafia to do the seemingly impossible. Hoffa had become enraged when singer Sammy Davis, Jr., who was scheduled to perform at a Teamsters' national convention in Miami, suddenly called him to cancel because he had accepted an invitation to appear on the *Ed Sullivan Show*. Hoffa had called Ragano and asked him to urge Trafficante to get Davis to change his mind. Trafficante then called mobster Joe Fischetti about it and Fischetti told him he would take care of the matter. "When Sammy flew down on the next plane, Hoffa was convinced the mob could accomplish anything it wanted," Ragano told Newfield.

Ragano flew to New Orleans in February and met with Marcello and Trafficante over lunch at the Royal Orleans Hotel. When he delivered Hoffa's message to them, Marcello and Trafficante looked at each other and didn't say a word. According to Ragano, "They didn't laugh. They were dead serious. They looked at each other in a way that made me feel uncomfortable. It made me think they already had such a thought in mind."

Several weeks later, Ragano met with Hoffa again in Washington and, in response to Hoffa's questioning, told him he had given the two Mafia leaders the message. Hoffa then expressed absolute confidence that Marcello and Trafficante would get the job done.

On November 22, 1963, Ragano was about to leave his office to give a lecture at a legal seminar at the Tampa County Courthouse when a lawyer burst in and told him about the assassination of President Kennedy.

A few minutes later Jimmy Hoffa called Ragano. "Have you heard the good news?" he asked. "They killed the sonofabitch. This means Bobby is out as attorney general. Lyndon will get rid of him."

Ragano admitted to Jack Newfield that he, too, felt pleased at the news of Kennedy's murder. He and Hoffa had been battling the young attorney general for the past two and a half years. Now, in retrospect, Ragano feels great shame. "I had crossed the line of professionalism," he told Newfield. "I got too close to my clients. Their enemies had become my enemies."

The night of November 22, 1963, Santos Trafficante invited Frank Ragano to dinner at the International Inn in Tampa. When Ragano and his nineteen-year-old girlfriend and future wife, Nancy, arrived, Trafficante embraced them warmly. Ragano had never seen the normally taciturn Santos so effusive. "Our problems are over," he told Ragano. "I hope Jimmy is happy now. We will build hotels again. We'll get back into Cuba now."

Once at the table, Trafficante launched into a tirade against the slain president then proposed a toast. Turning to Ragano and his future bride, he raised a glass and said: "To your health and John Kennedy's death."

Nancy Ragano, a college student at the time, was horrified at what Trafficante had just said. She had just come from her campus where the students were crying over what had happened in Dallas. Unable to take it, she ran out of the restaurant, leaving Frank and Santos alone.

Frank Ragano saw Carlos Marcello in New Orleans around two weeks after the assassination. Trafficante had asked him to go down and see how Carlos was doing. Ragano found the Louisiana boss angry because he had not yet received the three-million-dollar loan he had requested from the Teamsters Central State pension fund. Ragano observed that Carlos "looked like the cat who ate the canary. "He had a smug look on his face, and said: 'Tell Jimmy he owes me, and he owes me big!'"

According to Jack Newfield, Ragano believes that unlimited access to the $500 million Teamsters pension fund might have been an additional incentive for Marcello and Trafficante to accomplish the assassination. By the fall of 1963, Ragano told Newfield, Trafficante had already received millions in Teamster pension fund loans from Hoffa and expected more. Marcello had asked Hoffa for his first loan—three million dollars—and had let him know he also expected more to come.

After the assassination Frank Ragano did not see Jimmy Hoffa until late December in Washington. At their meeting Hoffa confided to Ragano: "I'll never forget what Carlos did for me." At the time Ragano claims, he thought Hoffa might have been referring to his intercession on Hoffa's behalf with a witness who was in a position to give damaging testimony against him at his trial. "It was only years later,"

Ragano told Newfield, "after Trafficante's deathbed confession to me in 1987, that I realized Hoffa's expression of gratitude was in relation to the Kennedy assassination."

Ragano told Newfield that Hoffa never met either Trafficante or Marcello face-to-face. Ragano was always the designated go-between. "Trafficante and Marcello always wanted to be able to truthfully testify before a grand jury that they had never actually met Hoffa," Ragano told Newfield.

Frank Ragano claims no further knowledge of the assassination plot other than what he told Jack Newfield about being an unwitting intermediary between Hoffa, and Trafficante and Marcello in their plan to kill the president. He makes no claim to knowing how Lee Harvey Oswald or Jack Ruby were involved in the crime. He does, however, have reason to believe that Carlos Marcello was "the central planner of the assassination."

Trafficante never talked about the Kennedy assassination with Ragano again, after their dinner in Tampa the evening of November 22, 1963, until he was approaching death in 1987. Suffering from heart disease, he knew that his end was near and wanted to get a few regrets off his chest to his friend of twenty-seven years.

It was about two weeks before his death that Trafficante summoned Ragano to his bedside and said: "You know, Frank, Carlos screwed up. We should have killed Bobby, not Giovanni."

After Jimmy Hoffa's disappearance and presumed death in 1975, and Trafficante's death in 1987, Frank Ragano felt his obligation of maintaining confidentiality as their attorney had ended. "The privilege ends at the grave," Ragano told Jack Newfield, adding that none of the conversations he related to him involved criminal cases in which he had represented Hoffa and Trafficante.

What does Nicholas Pileggi, the man ultimately responsible for Frank Ragano going public, think of Ragano's allegation? In March 1992, Pileggi told me that he believed Ragano is "absolutely credible. If anyone knew what was going on between Hoffa, Trafficante, and Marcello in 1963 he did." Pileggi went on to say that "the mob figured if Kennedy put Hoffa in jail it would lose access to the huge Teamsters pension fund. Greed, as well as revenge, was undoubtedly a powerful motive for the mob."

Frank Ragano is the highest level person to come forward claiming knowledge of the conspiracy to assassinate President Kennedy. As such his allegation deserves attention. Is there any corroboration for Ragano's assassination scenario?

It so happens there is. In 1979 the House Select Committee on Assassinations released a final report on its two-year investigation of the assassination of President Kennedy. In it the committee concluded that President Kennedy had "probably been killed as a result of a conspiracy" and named Jimmy Hoffa, Santos Trafficante, and Carlos Marcello as the most likely individuals behind the conspiracy.

I discussed Ragano's allegation with G. Robert Blakey, former Chief Counsel of the House Select Committee on Assassinations, and he told me that he believes Ragano's story is the "most plausible and logical explanation of the assassination." In 1979 Blakey and his congressional committee had concluded that Hoffa, Trafficante, and Marcello had the motive, means, and opportunity to carry out the assassination and now Frank Ragano has ratified that conclusion. Blakey, who knows Ragano, believes his allegation rings true and that Ragano, at this stage in his life, does not have a motive to lie.

A considerable body of circumstantial evidence does, in fact, exist pointing to the possible complicity of Hoffa, Trafficante, and Marcello in the Kennedy assassination, but before we set it forth and evaluate it, it is necessary to consider the historical context in which the assassination took place.

CHAPTER 2

★

The Secret Wars
of the Kennedys

The assassination of President Kennedy
took place in the midst of two largely secret wars the
Kennedy brothers were waging concurrently, one
against organized crime, the other against Fidel
Castro's Cuba—and was directly related to both.

The war against organized crime was largely
Attorney General Robert Kennedy's pet operation, but
it was carried on with the full backing of his brother,
the president.

Robert Kennedy also played a major role in the struggle to overthrow Fidel Castro, code-named Operation
Mongoose, but it was essentially an effort carried on by
the CIA in alliance with the Cuban exiles. Again, the

campaign had the full backing of President Kennedy.

By the time the Kennedys came to power, organized crime and its pawns in organized labor, like Jimmy Hoffa and the Teamsters Union, had become enormously powerful and arrogant. During the thirty years from 1931 to 1961, organized crime had grown from a handful of feuding families in New York and Chicago making a precarious living from illegal liquor, loan-sharking, and gambling, to a huge brotherhood of twenty-two families, operating in every major city in the country, numbering 5,000 "made" members and 50,000 to 100,000 associates, with an aggregated income in excess of that of the ten largest industrial corporations of the United States combined.

The Mafia bosses, inebriated with their power, and essentially unchallenged by the federal government, had become arrogant and spoiled. They thought they could get away with anything and usually did. More often than not, law enforcement authorities and corrupted state and local governments had actually aided and abetted their advance.

Paradoxically, J. Edgar Hoover himself had aided and abetted their advance. For years the FBI chief had refused to admit the Mafia even existed. In the absence of pressure from the FBI, organized crime had grown largely unchecked from 1930 to 1961. It was attorney general Robert F. Kennedy who finally forced Hoover to face up to organized crime and the menace it represented. Even then the FBI director confronted the Cosa Nostra with extreme reluctance.

What was behind this strange attitude on the part of the nation's number one crimefighter?

In recent years it has come to light that, in all probability, J. Edgar Hoover had been corrupted and neutralized by the powerful New York mobster, Frank Costello, known in his heyday as "the prime minister of the underworld."

That a relationship between Hoover and Costello did, in fact, exist was confirmed to me in an interview with William G. Hundley, former head of the Organized Crime and Racketeering Division of the Justice Department under Attorney General Kennedy.

The cement of that relationship was, according to Hundley, Hoover's addiction to race track betting. Costello supplied Hoover with hot tips on fixed races that enabled the FBI Director to make considerable amounts of money betting at the track. In return for these favors Hoover would refrain from pursuing some of Costello's friends, such as Carlo Gambino and Carlos Marcello, among others.

The accession of the Kennedys to power brought a radical change in the relationship between the federal government and the Mafia families. Under the Kennedys there were to be no compromises with the Mafia. It was to be all-out war. This was the first time in U.S. history that the executive branch of the government was to lead the fight against organized crime.

After the debacle of the failed Bay of Pigs invasion, President Kennedy's Cuba Study Group came to the conclusion that "there can be no long-term living with Castro as a neighbor" and the President accepted this conclusion. Accordingly, in the summer of 1961, the Kennedys launched a massive campaign to overthrow Fidel Castro, which was named Operation Mongoose. Robert Kennedy asserted he wanted to invoke "the terrors of the earth" against Castro.

Complicating the Kennedy wars against the Mafia and Castro was the strange and sinister alliance with certain Mafia bosses that the CIA had entered into, unbeknown to the Kennedys, for the purpose of assassinating the president of Cuba. The CIA's mob allies were all major targets of Robert Kennedy: Sam Giancana, Johnny Rosselli, Santos Trafficante, and Carlos Marcello.

The CIA-Mafia murder plots against Castro unwittingly placed the Kennedy brothers on the same side as the Mafia in their mutual struggle to overthrow Castro. Being in alliance with the Mafia on one hand and going after them on the other put the Kennedy brothers in a perilous position. The double cross is a cardinal sin of the Mafia code, one punishable by death without trial.

The secret wars of the Kennedys were further complicated by the fact that President Kennedy had entered into a relationship with a Mafia boss's girlfriend. She was Judy Campbell and her lover was Chicago boss, Sam Giancana, one of the mafiosi the CIA had hired to kill Castro. As if that were not enough to fuel an intrigue both President Kennedy and Attorney General Kennedy had affairs with the actress Marilyn Monroe, which were being monitored by Jimmy Hoffa's wireman, Bernard Spindell. The possibilities for blackmail inherent in the CIA's alliance with the Mafia and in the Kennedy brothers' liaisons with Marilyn Monroe and others were obvious.

How much did John and Robert Kennedy know about the CIA's plots to assassinate Castro? From the 1975 Senate Intelligence Committee's report on the plots, it appears that the Kennedys were most definitely aware that an attempt on Castro's life was going to be made in connection with the 1961 Cuban exiles' invasion, but there are no records indicating they knew that Mafia leaders were involved in the plotting. However, Judy Campbell has stated that President Kennedy knew Giancana was involved in the plot and may have been using her to communicate with the Chicago boss.

Whatever the case, it is against this backdrop of plotting against Castro and unrelenting pursuit of organized crime by Robert Kennedy that the assassination scenario painted by Frank Ragano unfolded.

CHAPTER 3

The Evidence Against
Jimmy Hoffa

"We own de Teamsters"
—CARLOS MARCELLO
*(Taped remark to FBI undercover agents Joe Hauser,
Mike Wachs, and Larry Montague, 1979)*

James R. Hoffa, son of a poor
Indiana coal driller of Pennsylvania Dutch lineage,
dropped out of school at the age of sixteen, and went
to work in a warehouse unloading railroad cars at
thirty-two cents an hour. The working conditions
were intolerable and the young Hoffa, a scrappy
fighter, vowed he would do something about them
someday. At eighteen he rebelled against the warehouse management and organized his fellow workers
into a union, winning them substantial benefits. A
born labor organizer, he eventually joined the
International Brotherhood of Teamsters and worked

his way up to the top, becoming president of the union in 1957 at the age of forty-four. With single-mindedly determination, Hoffa proceeded to build the Teamsters into the most powerful labor union in the world, a huge 1.5 million-member organization with a "war chest" of $500 million. His major achievement was negotiating the precedent-setting National Master Freight Agreement, guaranteeing Teamsters uniform wage and benefit conditions across the country. On the way up the Teamsters' ladder, Hoffa befriended many gangsters, often using their muscle to advance through the ranks and force recalcitrant trucking companies to unionize. In so doing, the labor organizer became a labor racketeer.

It was in 1957 that Hoffa first ran afoul of the man who would be his nemesis, Robert Kennedy. The thirty-one-year-old Kennedy, whose father had established trust funds worth $10 million for him, had become chief counsel of the Senate McClellan Committee that was conducting an investigation of organized crime and corruption in labor unions. Hoffa would be called to appear before the committee as a witness.

When Hoffa and Kennedy first met, Hoffa told Kennedy, "I do to others what they do to me, only worse."

To which Kennedy replied, "Maybe I should have worn my bulletproof vest."

In his book *The Enemy Within,* Robert Kennedy wrote:

> *The Teamsters Union is the most powerful institution in this country—aside from the United States government itself. In many major*

metropolitan areas the Teamsters control all transportation . . . between birth and burial the Teamsters drive the trucks that clothe and feed us and provide the vital necessities of life . . . Quite literally, your life—the life of every person in the United States—is in the hands of Hoffa and his Teamsters . . . But though the great majority of Teamsters officials and Teamsters members are honest, the Teamsters Union under Hoffa is often not run as a bona fide union. As Mr. Hoffa operates it, this is a conspiracy of evil.

The inevitable clashes between the young chief counsel and Teamsters official came early in the McClellan committee hearings. Robert Kennedy recalled one of his early encounters with Hoffa in his book, *The Enemy Within*:

I noticed that he was glaring at me across the counsel table with a deep, strange, penetrating expression of intense hatred. I suppose it must have dawned on him about that time that he was going to be the subject of a continuing probe—that we were not playing games . . . There were times when his face seemed completely transfixed with this stare of absolute evilness.

What particularly bothered Kennedy about Hoffa was his connection with organized crime. He had found that Hoffa had created several phony local unions and had put in charge of these "paper unions" officials who were connected with such notorious Mafia figures as Johnny Dioguardia (Johnny Dio) and Anthony "Ducks" Corallo. It did not take Kennedy long to figure out that if the Mafia was in association with the Teamsters it was in a position to paralyze the nation. All the Mafia would have to do would be to pressure Hoffa into calling a national Teamsters' strike and the entire country would come to a standstill.

Once Robert Kennedy assumed office as attorney general, he pursued Jimmy Hoffa with relentless persistence, vowing to get him at any cost. In the words of Monroe Freedman in an article he wrote for the *Georgetown Law Journal*: "When Kennedy became Attorney General satisfying this grudge [against Hoffa] became the public policy of the United States."

In an unprecedented move Attorney General Kennedy ordered an entire unit of the Justice Department devoted solely to pursuing Jimmy Hoffa and the Teamsters. Known as the "get Hoffa squad," the unit obtained its first indictment against Hoffa on May 18, 1962, accusing him of receiving $1 million in illegal payments through a trucking company, the Test Fleet Corporation, he had set up in his wife's name. It was not long after this that Hoffa began discussing plans to assassinate Robert Kennedy, and his brother, the president.

Edward Grady Partin, a Teamsters official from Louisiana, who had connections with Carlos Marcello, was a witness to these discussions. He told the following story to federal investigators of the Justice Department:

> *One day in mid-summer of 1962, in the Teamsters headquarters in Washington, D.C., I was talking with Jimmy Hoffa in his office. We were alone when he asked my help in a scheme to kill Attorney General Robert Kennedy—and he was willing to chance killing Kennedy's kids to do it.*

As nearly as I can remember his exact words, he said: "You know anywhere you can get hold of a plastic bomb?" I told him that, hell, I don't even know what a plastic bomb was and what did he want it for?

He said, "Well, somebody needs to bump that sonafabitch off." I asked what sonofabitch and he said he meant the Attorney General. Then he got to thinking more about it and talking about it. He said, as well as I recall the order of it, "You know I've got a run-down on him . . . His house sits here, like this, and it's not guarded . . . " Jimmy was making a kind of diagram with his fingers and I remember being surprised about the Attorney General's house not being guarded. Then Hoffa said, "He drives alone in a convertible and swims by himself. I've got a .270 rifle with a high power scope on it that shoots a long way without dropping any. It would be easy to get him with that. But I'm leery of it; it's too obvious."

He wasn't quite ready to give up thinking about the rifle, though, because then he asked, "Do you know where I could get a silencer for it?"

But then he went on thinking it out some more, and he said, "What I think should be done, if I can get hold of these plastic bombs, is to get somebody to throw one in his house and the place'll burn after it blows up. You know, the s.o.b. doesn't stay up too late."

According to Partin, Hoffa went on to tell him Robert Kennedy "has so many enemies now they wouldn't know who had done it." He also told Partin "the ideal setup would be to catch him somewhere in the South, where it would look like some of the segregation people had done it."

To verify Partin's accusations, the Justice Department appointed an investigator, Hawk Daniels, to monitor phone calls between Hoffa and Partin. Daniels, who later became a Louisiana judge, testified "there were two telephone calls monitored by me. They originated with Partin and terminated with Hoffa on the other end of the line. Partin brought up the subject of the plastic explosives and told Hoffa he had obtained the explosive Hoffa wanted. Hoffa then said: 'We'll talk about that later,' as if he were well aware of what Partin was talking about."

Later, in 1978, Partin testified that Hoffa intended to kill the President as well as his brother. Hawk Daniels concurs. "I think Hoffa fully intended to carry the threats out," he stated, "I really think he had the capability. It was a question of how and when, not a question of whether he had doubts as to the necessity of eliminating at least Bobby Kennedy and possibly his brother also."

According to Frank Ragano, it was in January 1963, that Jimmy Hoffa told him to contact Santos Trafficante, Jr. and Carlos Marcello in New Orleans and tell them to assassinate President Kennedy.

If this is true Hoffa must have been in touch with Marcello and Trafficante about assassinating the President sometime between his discussion with Edward Partin in August 1962 and January 1963.

As we shall see there is reliable evidence that Marcello discussed a plot to assassinate President Kennedy in late September 1962, and a few weeks later an FBI informant reported to the Bureau that Trafficante had apparent foreknowledge of a plot to kill the President.

CHAPTER 4

The Evidence Against Carlos Marcello

Carlos Marcello's life was typical of that of the Mafia bosses who rose to great power and riches in the fifties. Clawing their way out of dire poverty, they accumulated vast sums of cash, mostly from the violent drug trade, until they were in a position to buy politicians, control labor unions, and exercise considerable influence in their communities. During the late forties and throughout the fifties they were able to operate without the interference of the U.S. government. Indeed, as we have already indicated, the director of the Federal Bureau of Investigation, J. Edgar Hoover, steadfastly maintained that organized crime, the Mafia, did not exist. For Marcello it was clear, unopposed sailing until he ran up against McClellan committee chief counsel, Robert Kennedy. The five-year struggle between Kennedy and Marcello was not resolved until the assassination of President Kennedy in 1963.

Carlos Marcello's rise from the swamps and bayous of the Mississippi Delta to become in 1947 the undisputed boss of the Gulf Coast underworld has become legendary in Louisiana where he has joined the early nineteenth-century pirates, Jean and Pierre Lafitte, in the state's pantheon of colorful villains.

One of seven sons of impoverished Sicilian immigrants, Giuseppe and Luigia Minacore, who came to New Orleans from Palermo via Tunisia in 1910, the diminutive Carlos soon emerged as the leader in the family, despite the fact that his height never exceeded five feet two inches. At an early age his father assigned him the task of carting the family farm's produce to the French Market in New Orleans, which was then controlled by local Mafia boss Sam "Silver Dollar" Carolla.

The Mafia had been in existence in New Orleans since 1869, making it the oldest Mafia family in the United States. "The First Family of the Mafia" it was called. In 1890 the family gained national attention when several of its members murdered Chief of Police David Hennessy and were, in turn, lynched by a mob of two thousand irate citizens who broke into the parish prison and shot some of the mafiosi dead and strung others up on trees and lampposts outside, causing a diplomatic incident between Italy and the United States that was eventually resolved by President Benjamin Harrison agreeing to have the government pay $25,000 in reparations to the Kingdom of Italy.

At the age of fourteen, young Carlos dropped out of school and became a street punk, a mugger, in New Orleans, committing petty robberies for small change. At age eighteen, he left the family farm on the West Bank of the Mississippi River, rented a room in the French Quarter for two dollars a week, and began planning burglaries of stores and banks using juveniles as his accomplices. At nineteen, the *New Orleans Times-Picayune* was describing him as "a criminal mastermind," a "fagin" who recruited "baby bandits" to carry out his crimes. For one of these crimes, the robbery of a grocery store, young Carlos was caught, tried, convicted, and was sent off to Angola State Prison to serve a sentence of from nine to twelve years. After serving four years, his father, Joseph Marcello, was able to get the puppet successor to the powerful Huey Long, Governor O. K. Allen, to issue a pardon for his son and soon Carlos was back on the streets.

Carlos' next venture was the purchase of a bar for "coloured people" called The Brown Bomber, which he ran with his brother Pete. There Carlos sold liquor to underage blacks and used the bar as a front for the sale of marijuana. Arrested in 1938 for selling twenty-three pounds of marijuana to an FBI undercover agent, Carlos was fined $76,830 and sentenced to a year in the Atlanta Federal Penitentiary. Again his father exerted pressure on Governor Allen, and Carlos ended up paying a fine of only $400 and serving only nine months of his sentence.

From these experiences Carlos learned that politicians could be manipulated and bought. One day Carlos would boast:

> *I got connections, yeah. I know everybody from fucking Grand Isle all the way to Raceland, man . . . Yeah it's really somethin' to see . . . I got two Italian boys. They state representatives. It takes time to get where I'm at. To know all dese people— governors, businessmen, the attorney general. They know me.*

On his discharge from the Atlanta penitentiary, Carlos joined the crime family run by Sam "Silver Dollar" Carolla. Before long Carolla entered into a deal with a powerful mobster from New York, Frank Costello, to allow Costello to install a thousand slot machines in the New Orleans metropolitan area. Chosen to distribute the machines was Carlos Marcello, regarded as an up and coming "capo" at the time. One thing led to another and soon Carlos found himself in partnership with Costello, "Dandy Phil" Kastel, and Meyer Lansky to run a huge illegal gambling casino on the outskirts of New Orleans, the Beverly Country Club. Carlos was made manager of the club and was awarded 12.5 percent of the profits.

During this period Carlos began getting more and more involved in the burgeoning drug trade. Mexican marijuana, Colombian cocaine, and heroin from Sicily was making its way into the port of New Orleans in large quantities and soon Carlos became Louisiana's major distributor of illegal drugs. It was wartime and contraband of every kind was reaching New Orleans' mob-controlled waterfront. The black market was flourishing. During the war Carlos was able to lay away enormous amounts of cash and make substantial investments in real estate, assembling a 6,400 acre estate on the West Bank of the Mississippi, among other holdings. By the end of the war Carlos Marcello had become a very rich man.

When "Silver Dollar" Sam was deported to Sicily in 1947, Marcello was chosen boss of the oldest crime family in the United States. Now his control embraced not only the whole of Louisiana but also Dallas and Houston and Galveston and much of southeast Texas, Texarkana and Hot Springs in Arkansas, and the Mississippi Gulf Coast all the way to Mobile, Alabama. Carlos Marcello had arrived.

A year before he was named boss, Carlos attended the Mafia summit called by Lucky Luciano in Havana, Cuba. There he sat down at the same table with all the titans of organized crime in the United States, Lucky Luciano, Meyer Lansky, Carlos Gambino, Santos Trafficante, Frank Costello, Sam Giancana, Vito Genovese, and Albert Anastasia. Marcello was awarded points in one of the mob-controlled casinos and was cut in on the sizeable flow of drugs that was being routed through the island nation. From then on Carlos would do a good deal of business in Cuba acquiring real estate and gambling concessions through his friend, Meyer Lansky, with whom he was already in partnership in New Orleans. Lansky also awarded Marcello one third of the drugs that came through Cuba.

After becoming boss of the Gulf Coast underworld in 1947, Carlos established his headquarters in the Town and Country Motel on the highway leading from New Orleans to the International Airport. He was assisted there by his brothers Joseph and

Anthony and two of his top lieutenants, Joseph Poretto and Nofio Pecora. Frances Pecora, Nofio's wife, became Carlos' secretary and the head of a huge call-girl ring embracing southeast Texas and the Gulf Coast of Mississippi in addition to New Orleans and environs.

From this nerve center Marcello planned his ever-expanding criminal operations including, many people believe, the assassination of President Kennedy. In 1979 an FBI undercover agent, Larry Montague, who was working on an FBI sting operation against Marcello, gained admittance to this underworld sanctum sanctorum and noted a sign on the inside of Marcello's office door. It read:

THREE CAN KEEP
A SECRET
IF TWO ARE DEAD

Yes, things had gone very well for Carlos Marcello. In thirty years he had risen from the mud flats and swamps of the Mississippi bayou to become boss of a vast criminal empire whose racing wire and bookmaking empire alone was netting him $500 million a year. People from all over the country were seeking him out, for advice, to obtain investment capital, and to obtain influence in the Louisiana state government, whose political machinery he had come to control.

As might be expected all this power went to the head of the diminutive, all but illiterate, school dropout, who had never even bothered to become a citizen of the United States. People who knew Marcello during the fifties speak of his colossal ego, his arrogance, his feelings of invulnerability. Marcello strutted around southern Louisiana as if he were the center of the universe. He was the boss. Who was the president of the United States compared to him? Louisiana, once ruled by Napoleon Bonaparte, had a way of producing powerful dictators, for example, Governor Huey Long, the legendary "Kingfish," who ruled the state as an absolute monarch from 1928 to 1935 when he was felled by an assassin's bullet.

Yes, it was clear sailing for Carlos Marcello until he ran up against a young, idealistic attorney by the name of Robert Kennedy in a Senate hearing room in 1959.

Robert Kennedy had been briefed on Carlos Marcello by the head of the New Orleans Crime Commission, Aaron Kohn, a former FBI agent and assistant to J. Edgar Hoover. Kohn had traveled to Washington for the briefing. For days Kohn reeled off the litany of Marcello's crimes to the thirty-one-year-old chief counsel of the McClellan committee. Kohn told Kennedy of the many murders Marcello had ordered for which he was never charged. He told him how vast the Marcello brothers' bookmaking network was. He told him about the crimes of Marcello's brothers, how Peter Marcello was involved in "repeated acts of violence and brutality." Kohn talked at great length about the corrupt political climate that gave the Marcellos protection in Louisiana. He explained Carlos' method of making his victims disappear: taking the body to his swampland estate, dumping it into a tub of lye, letting it decompose, then pouring the liquid remains into the swamp.

Carlos Marcello's appearance before the Senate McClellan Committee had been occasioned by the discovery on November 14, 1957, by the state police in Apalachin, New York, of a huge secret conclave of over sixty leaders of Mafia crime families from every major city in the country. At first the committee had concentrated on corruption in organized labor, causing the downfall of Teamsters leader Dave Beck and seriously challenging his immediate successor, Jimmy Hoffa. Now, as a result of the Apalachin discovery, the committee turned its attention to the leaders of organized crime.

Before Robert Kennedy's grilling of Carlos Marcello, Aaron Kohn addressed the committee. He presented a short history of the Louisiana Mafia and went on to describe the full range of Marcello's illegal activities, asserting that the Marcellos would soon attain almost total control of the political machinery and law enforcement apparatus in Louisiana. Kohn named as Marcello's principal associates his brothers Joseph, Vincent, and Anthony; Joseph Civello, his deputy in Dallas, and Joseph Poretto and Nofio Pecora, his two top lieutenants in New Orleans.

Four years and ten months later the names Anthony Marcello, Vincent Marcello, Joseph Civello, Nofio Pecora, and Joseph Poretto would turn up on FBI reports within days of the Kennedy assassination in connection with allegations made to the FBI by informants about the murder of the President.

Committee counsel Robert Kennedy and committee members, including Senator John F. Kennedy, confronted a cocky, defiant Carlos Marcello from a dais high above the spectators, press, and witnesses in the spacious marble-walled Senate hearing room on March 24, 1959.

To all of Kennedy's sixty-six questions Marcello

responded in his inimitable slow Sicilian-Louisiana drawl: "I decline to answer on the ground it may intend to incriminate me."

At one point committee member Senator Sam Ervin interrupted the questioning to observe: "I would like to know how you have managed to stay in the United States for five years, nine months, and twenty-four days after you were found ordered deported as an undesirable person? Can you give me any information on that point?"

"I wouldn't know," said Marcello.

Senator Mundt of South Dakota then suggested that the chair "direct a letter to the attorney general inquiring as to why this deportation has not been implemented and that the attorney general's letter be made a part of the record when he replies."

Robert Kennedy remembered Senators Ervin's and Mundt's admonitions when he took office as Attorney General of the United States in January 1961.

In his book, *The Enemy Within,* Robert Kennedy had written "If we do not attack organized criminals with weapons and techniques as effective as their own, they will destroy us."

Once ensconced in his office in the Justice Department Kennedy decided on a swift, sudden, audacious attack on Marcello using weapons and techniques as effective as Marcello's own. Legal niceties never meant much to Marcello. When he wanted a man to disappear he threw his body into a tub of lye and spilled the decomposed remains into his swamp. Kennedy would not let legal niceties stand in the way of getting rid of Marcello. He would ambush the Louisiana Mafia boss and, in one bold stroke, throw him out of the country.

Accordingly on the morning of April 4, 1961, eleven days before the abortive Bay of Pigs invasion of Cuba, Robert Kennedy had agents of the Immigration Naturalization Service abduct Carlos Marcello from the INS office in downtown New Orleans where, as an alien, Marcello had gone for his required trimonthly check-in, and whisk him to the airport where an INS passenger plane and a cordon of police were waiting to fly him out of the country and deposit him in Guatemala.

Marcello later called the operation a "kidnapping." As he told reporters, he didn't even have time to cash a check, pack a toothbrush, or call his wife. It was all over in less than an hour.

There followed a two-month ordeal in Central America that saw Marcello expelled from Guatemala to El Salvador, and then thrown out of El Salvador to Honduras, during which time Marcello was compelled to trek for eight hours and seventeen miles along a dusty, pitted, jungle road near the El Salvador–Honduran border in 100 degree heat. During the ordeal Marcello collapsed several times suffering three broken ribs. Finally, after a long downhill trek along a trail thick with underbrush, Marcello arrived at a provincial airport where he hired a small plane to take him to the Honduran capital, Tegucigalpa.

Various accounts of how Marcello made his illegal reentry into the United States have been set forth— by commercial airline to Miami or by private plane, piloted by David Ferrie, to New Orleans—but the House Select Committee on Assassinations discovered by wiretap the true way. Marcello flew back on a Dominican Air Force jet probably obtained by Santos Trafficante, Jr. who was a good friend of the Dominican dictator Rafael Trujillo. Whatever the case, Marcello managed to slip back into the country without either customs or immigration officials detecting his arrival.

Sources in Louisiana have said that from the moment of Marcello's reentry, he swore vengeance against Robert Kennedy for what had befallen him. The "kidnap deportation" had been a deeply humiliating experience, an unprecedented affront to his pride and dignity. According to the Sicilian-Mafia code by which Marcello lived, his honor and respect could only be restored by inflicting on his tormenter the ultimate penalty.

That tormenter had, in the meantime, struck back at Marcello's return by getting a federal grand jury to indict Carlos for illegal reentry and getting the Internal Revenue Service to slap an $835,396 tax lien against Carlos and his wife. Then on July 11, 1961, the INS ruled Marcello was an undesirable alien and once again ordered him deported.

Marcello's attorneys appealed the new deportation order, but on December 30, 1961, a five-member Board of Immigration Appeals upheld the deportation order. A month earlier Robert Kennedy had announced the indictment of Marcello by a federal grand jury in New Orleans on charges of conspiracy and perjury. Thus by year's end Carlos was under two federal indictments and faced deportation from one moment to the next.

Carlos Marcello's honor was now on the line. Robert Kennedy was threatening to destroy everything he and his family had built up during a half-century of struggles in Louisiana. It would not be long now before his hatred of Robert Kennedy could no longer be contained. It was in this menacing atmosphere that Carlos would occasionally lose his head and, in a sudden outburst of rage, would give out hints of what he was going to do about Robert Kennedy.

One such incident occurred in July 1962 at a hunting-and-fishing camp Marcello owned on Grand Isle near the Gulf of Mexico. One weekend when Carlos and some of his family and friends were at the camp fishing and swimming, a black caretaker was startled to overhear the boss launch into a tirade over Robert Kennedy in front of a group of friends gathered at an outdoor picnic table.

"Don't talk about dat sonofabitch Bobby to me!" Marcello yelled. "You know he's driving my wife fuckin' crazy. All Jackie do is cry all night thinkin' Kennedy is goin' to throw me outa the country again . . . Bobby is drivin' my daughters crazy too. They don't want to lose their Daddy . . . Well, I'll tell you boys they ain't goin' to lose their ole man. No, Sir. 'Cause I gotta plan. You wait an' see if that sonofabitch Bobby Kennedy is gonna take me away from my wife an' kids."

Things were coming down to the wire with Carlos Marcello. The pressures on him were overwhelming: two federal indictments; threat of deportation from one moment to the next; IRS lien of $835,396 against his and his wife's assets. Key figures in his gambling operation, Ed Levinson and Gilbert Beckley, were under indictment. Attempts at a political solution to his problems failed. His efforts to get Frank Sinatra to intervene with the Kennedys on his behalf boomeranged with the effect of intensifying Robert Kennedy's efforts to prosecute him. Some of his closest associates, Jimmy Hoffa, and Santos Trafficante, Jr., were coming under attack by the attorney general. President Kennedy had replaced the Director of Bureau of Narcotics. The new director had announced a crackdown on Carlos Marcello. The attorney general was compelling schools to desegregate, an abhorrent development to the bigoted, violently racist Marcello. Unless he acted now Marcello faced utter ruination: imprisonment, loss of all his assets, perhaps permanent deportation.

By late summer of 1962 Carlos Marcello felt trapped and resolved to do something to extricate himself from the intolerable situation the attorney general had put him in. He decided to have President Kennedy assassinated. But why the President when it was his brother Bobby who was persecuting him? Because, Marcello reasoned, if he had Bobby killed the President would use all the power at his command to find out who was behind his brother's murder. Knowing who his brother was pursuing, the President would immediately suspect Hoffa and Marcello. He had already received a report of Hoffa's threats against his brother. Now he would have the Justice Department crack down harder than ever on the two men who he knew were closely allied to one another. Killing Robert Kennedy would only spell doom for Carlos Marcello.

But if Marcello had the president killed he would neutralize the attorney general who derived his great power from his brother, the president. Knowing full well that both Lyndon Johnson and J. Edgar Hoover detested Robert Kennedy, Marcello was sure they would pay little heed to the attorney general after the President was assassinated, which, of course, turned out to be the case.

Carlos Marcello outlined his plan to kill President Kennedy at a meeting that took place in a farmhouse at Churchill Farms—his 6,400 acre swampland property on the West Bank of the Mississippi. Present at the meeting, which took place in September 1962, were Carlo Roppolo, a close personal friend from Shreveport, Louisiana, Edward Becker, an acquaintance of Roppolo from Las Vegas, Nevada, and Jack Liberto, a hulking bodyguard, who was Carlos' personal barber. Roppolo and Becker were seeing Marcello about a business deal. They wanted Marcello's support because he was so powerful in Louisiana it was virtually impossible to establish a new business in the state without Carlos' help.

The four men were drinking scotch and eating antipasti in the farmhouse kitchen when Becker mentioned reading something in the papers about Bobby Kennedy's plans to deport Marcello.

At this Carlos' mood changed abruptly. He jumped up from the table, and reverting to Sicilian, shouted *"Livarsi 'na pietra de la scarpa!"* *[Get the stone out of my shoe!]* "Don't worry about that little Bobby sonofabitch," Marcello ranted, "he's goin' to be taken care of. I got plans . . . "

Marcello, still standing, went on. "You know what they say in Sicily: If you want to kill a dog, you don't cut off the tail, you cut off the head." He explained that you had to think of President Kennedy as a dog and Attorney General Kennedy as the dog's tail. "The dog will keep biting you if you only cut off its tail."

Marcello went on, "but if the dog's head is cut off the dog will die, tail and all."

Sitting down, Marcello then told his visitors that he had made up his mind that President Kennedy had to go, but that he would have to arrange his murder in such a way that his own men would not be identified as the assassins. No, he would have to use, or manipulate, someone not connected with his organization into a position where he would be immediately blamed by the police for the job. He had already thought of a way to set up a "nut" to take all the heat "the way they do in Sicily."

Edward Becker testified to having witnessed Carlos Marcello state his plans to have President Kennedy killed before the House Select Committee on Assassinations in 1978 and the committee concluded that his testimony was credible.*

The question remains: Did J. Edgar Hoover receive a report of Marcello's threat? There is good reason to believe he did. Edward Becker was in partnership with ex-FBI agent, Julian Blodgett, in a private investigative agency in Los Angeles that did contract work with the Los Angeles FBI field office. In his testimony before the House Assassinations Committee, Becker said that he "might have informed" Julian Blodgett of Marcello's plans to assassinate President Kennedy. If he did, in fact, inform Blodgett of Marcello's plans

---

*I also interviewed Ed Becker exhaustively on February 18, 1987. In that interview Becker told me that what struck him most was that Marcello seemed very serious about his intention to kill John Kennedy and that he had the distinct feeling Carlos had already discussed his plans with someone else.

then Blodgett, who was in daily contact with the FBI, most assuredly would have notified the Bureau of such plans and Hoover would, in due course, learn of them.

There is no record of Hoover having acted to warn the Kennedy brothers or the Secret Service of the Marcello contract on the president's life. So, in the event that Hoover did know about Marcello's plans, and did nothing to prevent them from being carried out, Hoover was guilty of being an accessory to the murder of the president.

A week or so after Edward Becker overheard Marcello threaten the life of John F. Kennedy, it appears that Marcello might have confided his plans to his close associate, Santos Trafficante, for toward the end of September 1962, an FBI informant in Miami, the wealthy Cuban exile, José Alemán, heard Trafficante express apparent foreknowledge of the assassination.

The circumstances were as follows. Alemán, the son of a former Cuban cabinet minister, was active in the Cuban exiles' movement to overthrow the new revolutionary regime of Fidel Castro and was a friend of the Mafia boss, Santos Trafficante, who the CIA had recruited to assassinate the Cuban dictator. At the time Alemán met with Trafficante in Miami, he was anxious to negotiate a loan to finance a large condominium development he was planning to build in Miami and was hoping Trafficante could help raise the funds through his good friend, Jimmy Hoffa.

Trafficante and Alemán met to discuss the loan in

Miami's Scott Bryant Hotel, which Aléman owned. Aléman told Trafficante he needed $1.5 million and that Jimmy Hoffa had already provisionally cleared the loan which, if made, would come out of the Teamsters pension fund. Now he needed Trafficante to put in a good word for him with Hoffa to clinch the deal.

When Hoffa's name came up in the conversation, Trafficante digressed a bit from discussing the loan to complain how badly the Kennedys were treating his friend. Referring to President Kennedy, Trafficante remarked:

> *Have you seen how his brother is hitting Hoffa, a man who is not a millionaire, a friend of the blue collars? He doesn't know that this kind of encounter is very delicate . . . Hoffa is a hardworking man and does not deserve it. Mark my word, this man Kennedy is in trouble, and he will get what is coming to him.*

At this Aléman took issue with Trafficante, telling him that he thought Kennedy was doing a good job, was well liked, and would probably be reelected.

To which Trafficante responded emphatically: "No, José, you don't understand me. Kennedy's not going to make it to the election. He is going to be hit."

Aléman later testified that Trafficante made it clear to him that he was not guessing about the killing; rather he was given the impression that he knew Kennedy was going to be killed . . . Aléman was given the distinct impression that Hoffa was to be principally involved in the elimination of Kennedy.

Aléman doubled as an FBI informant. After the meeting with Trafficante he went to the FBI field office in Miami and reported Trafficante's remarks on the Kennedys and Hoffa to the agents on duty, George Davis and Paul Scranton, including Trafficante's belief that John F. Kennedy would be assassinated before the next presidential election. The agents then reported the assassination plan to their superior, Miami Special Agent-in-Charge Wesley G. Grapp, who, in turn, sent the information by AIRTEL to Hoover in Washington.

If Hoover had not been informed of the Marcello contract, which is unlikely if Becker had told Julian Blodgett about it, he now knew Santos Trafficante was aware of a contract on President Kennedy's life. This was troubling indeed. However, Hoover saw no need to inform the Kennedy brothers, or the Secret Service, of the assassination plot. Now the director of the FBI was most definitely an accessory to the impending murder of the president.

On September 29, 1962, not long after Marcello outlined his plan to kill President Kennedy to Edward Becker, and Trafficante had expressed foreknowledge of the assassination plan, Louisiana Teamsters official, and aide to Jimmy Hoffa, Edward Partin, informed Justice Department aide to Robert Kennedy, Walter Sheridan, that Hoffa was formulating a plan to assassinate the attorney general. The information was relayed to Robert Kennedy, who, in turn, told the President about it. According to then-Washington Bureau Chief of *Newsweek,* Ben Bradlee, President Kennedy told Bradlee about the plot one evening over dinner and expressed deep concern over it.

We come to February 1963, the month in which Frank Ragano alleged he carried a message from

Jimmy Hoffa to Santos Trafficante and Carlos Marcello in New Orleans telling them he wanted them to kill President Kennedy.

If we are to believe Frank Ragano, a hint of some conspirational activity involving Marcello, who Ragano believed was the principal planner of the assassination, would be dropped sometime in the months immediately following Ragano's meeting with Trafficante and Marcello in February 1963.

The first hint that we are aware of came in April: an apparent instance of foreknowledge of the impending assassination was expressed to an FBI informant by an associate of Carlos Marcello.

Eugene De Laparra was a young ex-Marine working part-time in a New Orleans bar and restaurant owned by Bernard Tregle, an associate of the Marcellos. Tregle's establishment, the Lounnor Restaurant, known also to its customers as Tregle's Bar, was located on Airline Highway not far from the Town and Country Motel, Marcello's headquarters. According to Aaron Kohn, the Marcellos had backed Ben Tregle's bar and restaurant for years since they were prime locations for their slot machines, pinball machines, and jukeboxes. Tregle also maintained a horse book that was connected to the Marcello gambling network, and he was the owner of several racehorses.

One day in April 1963, as De Laparra was going about his chores in Tregle's Bar, he overheard a conversation between Ben Tregle and Norman Le Blanc, a horse trainer, and someone referred to as "the professor," about what seemed to be a plot to assassinate President Kennedy.

According to De Laparra, Tregle and his friends

were looking at an advertisement in a detective magazine for a foreign-made rifle that sold for $12.95. Tregle stated to all present, including De Laparra: "This would be a nice rifle to buy to get the President. There is a price on the President's head, and other members of the Kennedy family. Somebody will kill Kennedy when he comes down South."

De Laparra, who also worked as a groom at the New Orleans Fairgrounds racetrack, took care of one of Vincent Marcello's racehorses and doubled as an informant for the FBI. In his original allegation De Laparra observed that "Vincent Marcella [sic], New Orleans racketeer" was a close friend of Tregle's and a financial backer of Tregle's businesses, who traveled regularly to Dallas.

In February 1967, De Laparra furnished the FBI with additional information at the time New Orleans District Attorney Jim Garrison was launching his reinvestigation of John Kennedy's assassination. In this second version of his original allegation, De Laparra told the FBI that one day while he was working in Tregle's Bar, Tony Marcello, a brother of Carlos, came into the bar to service the pinball machines and, at a certain point, announced to Ben Tregle and others at the bar: "The word is out to get the Kennedy family." Whereupon Ben Tregle repeated Tony Marcello's remark, using slightly different language, to some people in the back room.

One evening about the time Eugene De Laparra heard Ben Tregle remark about a plot in the works to assassinate President Kennedy, a visitor to New Orleans from Darien, Georgia, Gene Sumner, was having dinner with business associates at the Town and Country Motel restaurant. There, in Carlos Marcello's headquarters, the visitor witnessed something suspicious that, six months later, he believed might have been connected, in some way, to the assassination of President Kennedy. The Georgian noticed a young couple enter the restaurant and sit down two tables away from where he was sitting. Soon a man he thought was the owner of the restaurant entered the room and sat down at the young couple's table. After chatting with the couple briefly, he reached into his pocket, pulled out a big wad of bills and passed them to the man under the table. A few minutes later the couple left the restaurant without ordering any food or drinks.

The man from Georgia thought he had witnessed something suspicious, but gave little thought to it until he saw pictures of John F. Kennedy's accused assassin in the newspapers and on television in the days following the assassination. It was then that the Georgian became convinced beyond any doubt that the man he had seen take the money from the restaurant owner seven months before had been Lee Harvey Oswald.

When, three days after the assassination, the Georgian voiced this belief to the police and was asked if he knew anything about the owner of the restaurant, he replied that he knew nothing of his "background, associates, or activities."

What the visitor from Georgia did not know was that the man he presumed was the owner of the restaurant was, in reality, the manager, Joe Poretto, who was also one of Carlos Marcello's top lieutenants. In all likelihood, it was probably because the Georgian did not know anything about "the background, associates, or activities" of the man he thought was the owner of the restaurant that he had been willing to stick his neck out and declare to the police and the FBI he had seen Poretto pass a wad of bills to the President's alleged assassin.

The man from Georgia told the police, and later the FBI, that he believed his visit to the Town and Country Motel took place in April 1963. It was on April 24 that Lee Harvey Oswald left Dallas by bus and moved into his uncle Charles Murret's New Orleans apartment the following day. It was also on April 24 that the White House announced that President Kennedy would make a trip to Texas in November.

Charles "Dutz" Murret had served as Lee Harvey Oswald's surrogate father during his youth, since Lee's father had died two months before he was born. At the time Oswald moved in with Murret in April 1963, Murret was a prosperous bookmaker in the Marcello gambling network. He worked under one of the most notorious gamblers in the New Orleans underworld, Sam Saia, who Aaron Kohn testified "had the reputation of being very close to Carlos Marcello."

In 1979 the FBI ran an undercover sting operation against Carlos Marcello that eventually netted the Mafia boss. One of the FBI's undercover operatives in the sting was Joseph Hauser, a convicted swindler who was in the witness protection program. For several months in 1979 Joe Hauser saw Carlos Marcello practically every day. During the course of the sting operation, Hauser got Marcello to admit that he knew Oswald's uncle, "Dutz" Murret, and that Oswald had worked as a runner and collector for his uncle's book-making operation in New Orleans during the summer of 1963. That operation, Marcello explained, was located in Sam Saia's Felix Oyster House in the French Quarter, not far from Pete Marcello's Sho-Bar on Bourbon Street.

Some confirmation of Oswald's association with Marcello's gambling network comes from FBI informant Eugene De Laparra. De Laparra told the FBI that Ben Tregle operated a horse book and that Tregle knew Lee Harvey Oswald.

Did Oswald have any other connections to the Marcello organization in the summer of 1963? It so happens he had many. Sometime in July he went to work part-time in a private detective agency, Guy Banister Associates, run by ex-FBI agent Guy Banister at 544 Camp Street in New Orleans. Banister was vehemently anti-Castro and was actively financing various groups of Cuban exiles desirous of overthrowing Castro in partnership with Carlos Marcello, who had lost all his concessions in Havana as a result of Castro's revolution. Banister also did investigative work for Marcello.

According to Guy Banister's secretary, Delphine Roberts, Lee Harvey Oswald was given assignments by Banister and was given a room in Banister's suite of offices where he kept a store of pro-Castro leaflets and placards. It now appears reasonably certain that Banister employed Oswald to act as a pro-Castro activist, demonstrating for Castro on the streets of New Orleans, in order to build an image as a communist supporter of Fidel Castro. It also appears reasonably certain that Carlos Marcello backed these activities financially.

Thus Lee Harvey Oswald was being supported by Carlos Marcello through Guy Banister throughout the summer of 1963. How else could Oswald have rented an apartment for himself and his wife and daughter? He had no job and no source of income other than unemployment insurance.

Enter David Ferrie, the man many researchers believe played a key role in the assassination conspiracy. David Ferrie was a complex, bizarre individual. Brilliant, erratic, idealistic, and compulsive, he was an expert pilot, a competent research chemist, an aggressive homosexual, an amateur psychologist and practicing hypnotist, a militant anti-Castroite, a bishop of the Orthodox Old Catholic Church of North America (an offshoot of the Roman Catholic Church, not recognized by the Vatican), and a victim of alopecia, a rare disease that causes the loss of all head and body hair.

Since March 1962, Ferrie had been working for Carlos Marcello's New Orleans attorney, G. Wray Gill, as an investigator. In 1963 Ferrie was assigned to help prepare Marcello's defense against conspiracy and perjury charges brought against him by Attorney General Kennedy. By the summer of 1963, Ferrie was meeting regularly with Gill and Marcello at Marcello's Town and Country office.

During the same period Ferrie was also meeting regularly with a former cadet in a Louisiana Civil Air Patrol squadron he once commanded in New Orleans, Lee Harvey Oswald. Not long after Oswald returned to New Orleans in April 1963, he ran into Ferrie, perhaps through their mutual associations with the Marcello organization. The two then entered into a most mysterious relationship, seeing each other off and on in a variety of unusual circumstances.

Once a soldier of fortune, Ferrie had run guns to his idol of the fifties, Fidel Castro, when the Cuban revolutionary was raiding Cuban president Fulgenico Batista's forces from the Sierra Maestra. Then after Castro announced he was a Marxist and aligned his nation with the Soviet Union he turned against his idol and piloted bombers to Cuba on sabotage raids on behalf of various groups of Cuban exiles. After the Bay of Pigs fiasco, Ferrie turned against President Kennedy with such fanaticism that once the New Orleans chapter of the Military Order of World Wars had to halt a vehemently critical address Ferrie gave on Kennedy's Cuban policy. Ferrie once wrote the Secretary of Defense a letter stating, among other things "I want to train killers, however bad that sounds. It's what we need." It was during this period that Ferrie joined the violently anti-Castro Cuban Revolutionary Front, an organization principally financed by Carlos Marcello.

In addition to being employed by Carlos Marcello's attorney, Ferrie was also employed as an investigator by Guy Banister Associates. Witnesses reported seeing Oswald, Ferrie, and Banister together in the summer of 1963 at Banister's offices.

It was in mid-July that Oswald got into a fistfight with a group of vehemently anti-Castro Cuban exiles as he was distributing pro-Castro literature on Canal Street, at the instigation of Guy Banister. The fracas resulted in Oswald's arrest and imprisonment for disturbing the peace. Appealing to the Murrets to get him out of jail, he was finally rescued by "an old friend of the family," one Emile Bruneau, who put up his bail and paid his fine, enabling Oswald to go free.

Years later investigators for the House Select Commitee on Assassinations discovered that Emile Bruneau had been closely associated with two of Marcello's major associates, Nofio Pecora and Joseph Poretto. Poretto, of course, was the man the FBI informant from Darien, Georgia claimed to have observed passing money to Lee Harvey Oswald in the Town and Country restaurant.

Still another connection between Oswald and the Marcello organization was New Orleans attorney, Clem Sehrt. Marguerite Oswald, Lee Harvey's mother, had known Sehrt since childhood but had not seen the lawyer for years until she sought him out for legal advice about her son's desire to join the Marines in late 1956, when he was under the legal age for becoming a Marine. Marguerite Oswald wanted Sehrt to find a way to alter her son's birth certificate. Sehrt apparently obliged.

Later Sehrt became very close to Louis Rousell, a corrupt New Orleans financier, who enjoyed a close personal relationship with Carlos Marcello. During the late 1950s a police investigation revealed that two Louisiana Supreme Court justices were receiving regular payments from Louis Rousell.

In December 1978, the House Select Committee on Assassinations learned that Sehrt, just before he died, told a close and reliable associate that "some party had contacted him soon after the Kennedy assassination to request that he go to Dallas to represent the accused assassin, Lee Harvey Oswald." Sehrt did not tell his associate who had requested this legal representation, taking his secret to his grave. Was it his friend Carlos Marcello?

That Oswald had innumerable contacts with the

Marcello organization in New Orleans is well established. But what about Oswald's killer, Jack Ruby? Did he also have dealings with Marcello's men? And to what extent did Carlos Marcello have influence in Dallas?

For at least a decade there had been a tacit understanding among the leaders of the major Mafia families that Texas was the Marcellos' territory. Next to New Orleans the most important city in the invisible empire of Carlos Marcello was Dallas. The Marcello gambling syndicate in Texas numbered several hundred bookmakers handling gross revenues in the hundreds of millions of dollars. In 1963 the Marcellos' slot machines could be found in almost every city in Texas, especially in Dallas.

Carlos and his brothers owned hotels and restaurants in Dallas and Houston and the family's Pelican Tomato Company did a huge business in Texas, illegally importing large quantities of tomatoes over the border from Mexico. Vincent Marcello traveled frequently to Dallas, together with his brother Sammy to oversee the family's slot-machine business and other gambling interests.

The growth of Carlos Marcello's influence in Texas throughout the fifties would not have been possible without the cooperation of powerful Texas politicians. It is impossible for a Mafia crime family to operate successfully in a given area without the protection of those who hold high public office. Marcello secured the protection and cooperation of Texas politicians through Carlos' Texan bagman, Jack Halfen, who contributed a healthy percentage of the Marcellos' illegal profits to the political campaigns of Houston Congressman Albert Thomas, Associate Justice of the

Supreme Court Tom Clark, and U.S. Senator Lyndon B. Johnson.

It has been estimated that the Marcello-Halfen group contributed at least $50,000 a year in illegal gambling profits to Lyndon Johnson. In return for this support Senator Johnson helped kill in committee all anti-rackets legislation that could have harmed the interests of Carlos Marcello and Jack Halfen.

In 1963, thanks in part to Vice President Lyndon Johnson, Marcello was able to operate freely in Dallas. That freedom was purchased also by substantial payments to the Dallas police force. Marcello's criminal operations in Dallas were overseen by his Dallas deputy, Joe Civello, ex-convict, gambler, narcotics smuggler, liquor dealer, Italian-food-products importer, suspected murderer, and long-time friend.

Joe Civello had represented Marcello at the 1957 Mafia conclave in Apalachin, New York. A few days after he returned to Dallas from the conclave he was observed having dinner with a Dallas police officer, Sergeant Patrick T. Dean, who once admitted that the Dallas Police force "had no trouble with the Italian families." Six years later Sergeant Dean was in charge of basement security when an associate of Joe Civello's, Jack Ruby, entered the basement of Dallas Police Headquarters and murdered Lee Harvey Oswald in front of over seventy armed police officers.

Operating at a level below Joe Civello were two more friends of the Marcellos, Joe and Sam Campisi, owners of the Egyptian Lounge restaurant, a notorious hangout of the Dallas underworld. Joe Campisi was considered Marcello's number two man in Dallas. In 1978 Joe Campisi told investigators of the House Select Committee on Assassinations that he used to play golf with Vincent and Anthony Marcello and would often go to the racetrack with two or three of the brothers. Joe Campisi was the first to visit Jack Ruby after he was jailed for murdering Lee Harvey Oswald.

Jack Ruby occupied a position in the Dallas underworld several rungs below those occupied by Joe Civello and the Campisi brothers. Owner of a Dallas striptease nightclub, Ruby also functioned as a minor narcotics dealer, bookmaker, slot-machine operator, and pimp; he functioned in those capacities only at the sufferance of Carlos Marcello. Joseph Nellis, a former assistant counsel for the 1951 Senate Kefauver Committee on organized crime, now an attorney in private practice in Washington, D.C., has observed that in 1963 no one could have operated in the fields of gambling and narcotics in Dallas, as Ruby did, without Marcello's permission.

Records indicate that in 1963 Jack Ruby was in contact with at least three associates of Carlos Marcello as well as three of his brothers. Frank Caracci was a mid-level operative in the Marcello organization who owned and managed several striptease joints in New Orleans' French Quarter. Heavily involved in gambling operations in Texas and Louisiana, Caracci was friendly with Joe Civello and the Campisi brothers in Dallas and was on close terms with several of the Marcello brothers in New Orleans. FBI reports indicate that between June and October 1963, Jack Ruby visited one of Caracci's French Quarter nightclubs, telephoned another several times, and met with Caracci personally on at least one occasion. Ruby was in close contact with another Marcello-affiliated nightclub operator, Harold Tannenbaum, an associate of

Marcello's number three man, Nofio Pecora. Between May and November 1963, Ruby made at least eighteen calls to Tannenbaum, ostensibly about the nightclub business. On October 30 Ruby made one of his most suspicious calls of the month to Nofio Pecora, at the Tropical Court Motel in New Orleans.

As for the Marcello family, there is evidence Jack Ruby knew at least two of Carlos' brothers, perhaps as many as four. In 1963 Pete Marcello owned and operated the Sho-Bar, a strip joint and B-girl operation on Bourbon Street. Records indicate that between June and October 1963 Jack Ruby made at least two calls to the Sho-Bar and paid at least one visit to the club. Ruby probably also knew Vincent Marcello. Vincent was president and co-owner with Carlos of the Jefferson Music Company, Louisiana's largest slot-machine and jukebox distributor, and was heavily involved in the slot-machine business in Dallas. Since Ruby could have rented his slot machines only from the Marcellos it is almost certain he knew Vincent Marcello and perhaps his brother and partner, Sammy Marcello.

One thing is certain. Due to their many mutual contacts, and the fact that Ruby could not operate in Dallas without Carlos Marcello's permission, it is safe to say that Carlos was fully aware of Jack Ruby's presence in Dallas and aware also of Ruby's friendship with officers of the Dallas police force.

It is now known that Jack Ruby was on a first-name basis with at least seventy, perhaps a hundred, officers of the force and delighted in doing favors for them. He would bring boxes full of deli sandwiches to the officers on duty at headquarters. He would co-sign loans for officers hard up for cash. He would pro-

vide them with free drinks at his nightclub and
arrange free after-hours dates for them with his sexi-
est strippers. Once a week he would have police
officers' night at his Carousel Club. When, on the
weekend of November 23, 1963, it became necessary
to silence President Kennedy's accused assassin, who
was being held in custody in the Dallas Police
Headquarters, those who had reason to silence him
knew precisely to whom they could turn.

The story now returns to Carlos Marcello and David
Ferrie, who was known in the Cuban exiles community as "the master of intrigue."

After Lee Harvey Oswald left New Orleans for
Mexico City in late September, Oswald's eccentric
friend David Ferrie began meeting with Carlos
Marcello on a regular basis, ostensibly to help plan
Marcello's defense against the charges the federal
government had brought against him at the instigation of Robert Kennedy.

During October, Ferrie met with Marcello several
times at the Mafia boss's office in the Town and
Country Motel and traveled to Guatemala on business
for Marcello twice, from October 11 to 18, and from
October 30 to November 1, presumably on missions
having to do with Carlos' forged Guatemalan birth
certificate and passport, one of the important issues in
Carlos' upcoming trial. Then, in November, while the
case of the *United States v. Carlos Marcello* was being
tried in federal court, Ferrie, by his own admission,
spent the weekends of November 9, 10 and 16, 17 isolated with Marcello at Carlos' 6,400 acre swampland
property on the West Bank, Churchill Farms. These

were the first two weekends before the assassination of President Kennedy.

They were an odd couple, Marcello and Ferrie. Ferrie was highly educated. Marcello, as we know, dropped out of school when he was sixteen. Carlos was eminently pragmatic, while Ferrie was driven by sudden enthusiasms and, as one writer put it, "wild idealisms." But they had a lot in common also. Both men were imaginative schemers and both possessed an unusual ability to persuade people to do their bidding. Politically, Marcello and Ferrie were both right-wing extremists, militantly segregationist and anti-Communist. Sharing an intense desire to overthrow Castro, both worked hard on behalf of the Cuban exiles.

What the two had most in common was detestation of the Kennedy brothers. We know how much Marcello hated John and Robert Kennedy. As for Ferrie, an FBI report observed that Ferrie was "publicly and privately vitriolic about President Kennedy, and had stated, on occasion, that Kennedy 'ought to be shot.'"

David Ferrie told the FBI that the reason why he met with Carlos Marcello over the two weekends before the assassination of President Kennedy was to discuss strategy for Marcello's trial, which was in progress at the time.

But Marcello was represented by three able attorneys, G. Wray Gill of New Orleans, Mike Maroun of Shreveport, and Jack Wasserman of Washington, D.C. What was Marcello doing with David Ferrie at the isolated farmhouse at Churchill Farms? There was no telephone at the vast swampland estate. No office equipment. Wouldn't it have made more sense to discuss legal strategy at the Town and Country Motel where Marcello and Ferrie could get the other attorneys on the phone?

What strategy might Marcello and Ferrie have discussed in the farmhouse on Churchill Farms over the weekend of November 16, 17? On October 5 the Dallas papers had announced that President Kennedy would visit Dallas in November and Lee Harvey Oswald moved into a boarding house as Mr. O. H. Lee. On October 16 Lee Harvey Oswald started working at the Texas School Book Depository overlooking Dealey Plaza. On October 14 Secret Service Agent Winston Lawson had decided upon the route President Kennedy's motorcade would take in Dallas: it would pass through Dealey Plaza via Main Street, not too far from the Texas Book Depository where Lee Harvey Oswald worked.

Were these developments discussed between Carlos Marcello and David Ferrie the weekend of November 16, 17? It should be noted that on those dates Oswald dropped from sight entirely. His whereabouts on those days remains a mystery to this day. Was he with Marcello and Ferrie at Churchill Farms?

Whatever the case, the disturbing fact remains that on the weekend of November 16, 17 a Mafia boss who had discussed a plan to kill the president of the United States was meeting with a man "who had stated on occasion that 'Kennedy ought to be shot,'" and who was a friend of the man who would be accused on November 22 of assassinating the President.

Late on the night of November 20, 1963, two days before the assassination of President Kennedy,

Lieutenant Francis Fruge of the Louisiana State Police picked up an injured woman from the roadside near Eunice, Louisiana, and brought her to the East Louisiana State Hospital in Jackson. The woman's name was Rose Cheramie and she was known to be a prostitute and a heroin addict.

On the way to the hospital, Cheramie told Lieutenant Fruge that she had been making a "drug run" from Miami to Houston with two Italian male companions. They had stopped at a roadside bar and restaurant. She had gotten a little high and her companions had abandoned her. The owner of the restaurant then threw her out of his place. While she was trying to hitch a ride, she was grazed by a car and slightly injured. Shortly thereafter Fruge picked her up from the roadside.

On the way to the hospital at Jackson, Cheramie informed Fruge that her two male companions from Miami had told her that after a stop in Houston they were going on to Dallas where they would kill President Kennedy on November 22.

Cheramie further elaborated to Lieutenant Fruge that "word was out in the underworld that Kennedy would soon be killed."

Fruge did not pay much attention to Cheramie's ramblings about an impending Kennedy assassination at the time, but, two days later, after he was notified of the assassination, he went to the hospital in Jackson to interview her again.

At the hospital, Fruge was told by two of the doctors caring for Cheramie, a Dr. Bowers and a Dr. Victor Weiss, that she had told them on November 21 that Kennedy would be assassinated in Dallas the following day.

After speaking with Cheramie again about her prediction, now come true, Lieutenant Fruge reported Cheramie's apparent foreknowledge of the Kennedy assassination to the Dallas Police. The Dallas Police, in turn, told the Louisiana State Police that they were not interested, that they already had their man, a "commie nut" named Lee Harvey Oswald who they already knew had acted alone in killing the president.

In 1978 the House Assassinations Committee interviewed both doctors who had treated Cheramie on November 20 and 21, 1963, and had heard her prediction that President Kennedy would be assassinated in Dallas on November 22, and concluded that both doctors were telling the truth about Cheramie's assertions.

In a 1988 television documentary marking the twenty-fifth anniversary of the death of President Kennedy, produced by Jack Anderson, one of the doctors who had treated Rose Cheramie at the East Louisiana State Hospital on November 21, 1963, Dr. Victor Weiss, was interviewed for the first time on television. According to Dr. Weiss, Rose Cheramie was absolutely sure Kennedy was going to be assassinated in Dallas on Friday, November 22. Dr. Weiss added that Cheramie had indicated to him that "word was out in the New Orleans underworld that the contract on Kennedy had been let." Although Dr. Weiss did not recall whether Cheramie specifically mentioned the name Carlos Marcello, he quickly inferred at the time that by the expression "New Orleans underworld" Cheramie was referring to the Marcello organization.

The question has frequently been raised by critics of the notion that Marcello was behind the Kennedy assassination that Marcello would never have attempted such a crime because he lacked the apparatus to cover it up.

But Marcello knew he possessed an elaborate apparatus to cover it up. First of all, he had the principal investigator of the assassination "just where he wanted him." We now know that J. Edgar Hoover had been corrupted by Carlos' good friend, mobster Frank Costello. Hoover could not move against Marcello for many reasons. For one, it would anger Frank Costello and deprive him of the favors he received from the mobster. For another, it would come to light during the grand jury investigation that Hoover had bungled the investigation of Marcello. Three, Marcello had enough on Attorney General Kennedy and Lyndon Johnson to be able to control them. Four, the CIA would not have moved against Marcello for fear the existence of the top secret CIA-Mafia plots to assassinate Fidel Castro would come to light in an eventual investigation. Marcello and Trafficante had both been involved in those plots. Five, it could conceivably come to light *that Hoover had been well aware of the Marcello contract on Kennedy's life and had done nothing to prevent it from succeeding, making him an accessory to the President's murder.*

In the last analysis Marcello knew that Hoover would not move against him for fear that a thorough investigation of the assassination of President Kennedy might result in his own implication in the crime.

CHAPTER 5

The Evidence Against
Santos Trafficante, Jr.

Santos Trafficante, Jr., the urbane boss of the Florida underworld, was a Mafia prince. His father Santos, Sr., had been boss of the Tampa-St. Petersburg Mafia from 1930 to his death in 1954 when he bequeathed his crown to his favorite son.

Santos, Sr., who was born in Sicily, and came to the United States in 1914, settling in Tampa, Florida, succeeded Ignaccio Antinori as boss of the local Mafia family, which was one of the oldest in the nation.

Ignaccio Antinori had been heavily involved in narcotics. He had set up a drug pipeline that went from Corsica and Marseilles to Cuba to Tampa. Santos

Trafficante, Sr. had inherited this narcotics operation and had expanded it substantially. He had also been very much involved in illegal gambling and dreamed of expanding into Cuba. Cementing a close relationship with Lucky Luciano early in his career, Santos, Sr,. enjoyed the respect of his Mafia peers.

Santos, Sr., occasionally performed acts of "benevolent terrorism" for the Sicilian community in Tampa, one of which touched the Ragano family. One of Ragano's sisters, Rose, had a violent husband who periodically beat her. At a certain point Frank's father reached the limits of his patience with his son-in-law and he went to Santos Trafficante, Sr., for help. The Mafia boss obliged by having the offender's legs broken and issuing a warning that the next time he molested Rose he would be killed. According to Frank Ragano, Rose's husband got the message and never harmed her again. The incident was the genesis of the respect Ragano felt for the Trafficantes. When Santos, Jr., needed an attorney Frank Ragano was delighted to serve him.

Santos, Jr., grew up in an affluent household, attended high school, and acquired a degree of polish that would distinguish him from other mobsters. After high school, his father sent him to New York to serve an apprenticeship under Carlo Gambino who had built his crime family into the richest and most powerful one in the nation.

In time, Santos, Jr., acquired a reputation for cunning and ruthlessness. He was the one Mafia leader Meyer Lansky would not cross. Frank Ragano, his attorney for twenty-seven years, has characterized him as "polished," "brilliant," "wise and intelligent beyond belief."

Santos, Jr., received his first big assignment from his father in 1946 when he was sent to Havana to establish a presence in casino gambling and to supervise the Cuban link in the narcotics pipeline. He took up residence in Cuba that same year and remained there until 1959, the year of the Castro coup d'état. After his father's death in 1954, Santos, Jr., became one of the most powerful men in Cuba, establishing close personal relationships with Meyer Lansky, who had become "King of the Casinos," and with the obliging Cuban dictator, Fulgencio Batista. Lansky gave Traffcante control of the Sans Souci and large shares of the Capri, the Hilton, and the old Hotel Commodoro. While in Cuba, Trafficante got to know Carlos Marcello, who had received favors from Batista and was doing considerable business in Havana.

Life was sweet for the mob in the Havana of the fifties. They were able to operate their fourteen casinos, their nightclubs and bordellos, with the full encouragement of the government. The profits from casino gambling and narcotics trafficking were enormous. The future appeared limitless. Then it all came to an abrupt end.

Fidel Castro, victorious in his uprising against Batista, took over the government on January 1, 1959. After a period of accommodation that lasted about nine months, Castro confiscated all the casinos and expelled the mobsters who owned and operated them from the island. Santos Trafficante, Jr., was jailed in the Trescornia detention camp.

According to gambler Lewis McWillie, who worked at the Tropicana casino, and British journalist John Wilson Hudson, who was also detained at Trescornia, Jack Ruby, who once ran guns to Castro, visited Trafficante at Trescornia. Ruby was probably acting as a mob courier at the time.

Eventually   Trafficante   was   released   from

Trescornia, largely through negotiations with the Cuban government conducted by his attorney, Frank Ragano. He returned to Tampa and immediately established relations with the communities of Cuban exiles in Tampa and Miami.

Meanwhile Trafficante's friend, Carlos Marcello, who had lost everything in Havana, was financing a branch of the Cuban Revolutionary Council, a group of militant Cuban exiles with headquarters in Miami, whose delegate in New Orleans was Sergio Arcacha Smith, a man described in an FBI report as "one of the more conspirational of the Cuban exiles leaders." Among those working for Arcacha Smith was David Ferrie, suspected by many of playing a key role in the conspiracy to assassinate President Kennedy. According to an FBI report of April 1961, Marcello had offered Smith a deal whereby he would make "a very substantial donation" to the Cuban Revolutionary Council in return for large concessions in Cuba after Castro's eventual overthrow, and a promise of Cuban citizenship.

When the CIA-sponsored Cuban exiles' invasion of Cuba at the Bay of Pigs failed, Trafficante and Marcello became furious at the Kennedy administration and began stepping up their support of various Cuban exiles groups in New Orleans and Miami, determined to win Cuba back at any cost.

Reacting to their sudden, and, in some cases, disastrous loss of revenue, Meyer Lansky, representing the Mafia bosses, had put out a million-dollar contract on Castro's life.

Meanwhile the CIA had determined to eliminate Fidel Castro by assassinating him. The decision had been made by CIA director, Allen Dulles, at the end of the Eisenhower administration.

By September 1960, CIA officers Sheffield Edwards and Richard Bissell had agreed on a plan to assassinate Castro in alliance with Mafia leaders, John Rosselli, Sam Giancana, and Santos Trafficante, Jr.

The first CIA-sponsored attempt to assassinate Castro, utilizing its Mafia allies to carry out the execution, occurred just before the disastrous invasion of the CIA-trained Cuban exiles at the Bay of Pigs in April 1961. The idea was to destroy the morale of the Cuban armed forces before the invasion by eliminating their commander-in-chief. For reasons that remain obscure the assassination attempt failed, as did the Bay of Pigs invasion. Further attempts by the CIA, in alliance with Giancana, Rosselli, and Trafficante, and unnamed Cubans also came to naught. As relations between the United States and Cuba grew worse and worse, the Mafia and the frustrated Cuban exiles grew more and more hostile to both Castro and the Kennedy administration.

Although the Kennedy brothers were behind the effort "to get rid of Castro," as Robert Kennedy once phrased the initiative in a memorandum, they did not learn of the alliance of the CIA and the Mafia until over a year after taking office. Robert Kennedy, who had mounted the most intensive campaign against the Mafia in the nation's history, understood the seriousness of the situation immediately, displaying considerable anger at the CIA for hiring the Mafia to do its dirty work, but he failed to make sure the CIA-Mafia alliance would be discontinued.

The CIA-Mafia plots to assassinate Castro continued to unfold, mostly because of the efforts of Johnny Rosselli who even went on daring commando raids off the Cuban coast. According to Frank Ragano,

Trafficante took no part in them. He just strung the CIA along. Apparently he felt it would be just too difficult and dangerous to ambush Castro. The Cuban dictator was reportedly protected day and night by a cadre of some three hundred armed bodyguards.

Meanwhile the Kennedy brothers had created Operation Mongoose, a coordinated secret CIA-led attack on Cuba involving intelligence collection, propaganda, sabotage, guerilla strikes, and assassination.

Soon the CIA's special Mongoose unit, Task Force W, under the direction of William K. Harvey, established a huge nerve center on the campus of the University of Miami, code-named JM/WAVE, which had some four hundred men working for it in Washington and Miami; maintained over fifty business fronts in Florida, a small navy of high-speed vessels, and an air force; and employed over two thousand Cuban agents, the whole at a cost of $100 million a year. The JM/WAVE station soon became one of Florida's largest employers and the second-largest CIA station in the world after the CIA headquarters in Langley, Virginia.

Trafficante, thought of as still active in the CIA-Mafia plots, was a welcome visitor to the JM/WAVE station and it is believed he went to the installation regularly to check up on the effort to undermine Castro.

Trafficante was in a difficult position in regard to the U.S. government. On the one hand he was ostensibly cooperating with the government in the effort to overthrow Castro, on the other hand he was feeling heat from the Justice Department. By 1962 Robert Kennedy's men had Trafficante and his crime family under intensive investigation.

An FBI bug planted in a Miami restaurant overheard Trafficante complaining about how federal agents were harassing his Cuban lottery offices and bookmaking establishments:

> *Let me tell you this. This is what happens to me. Now I don't give a fuck about the S and the Government. I know when I'm beat, you understand?*
>
> *I got a numbers office in Orlando. They grab everybody, forty or fifty people. Forty or fifty thousand in bond. They have no evidence, but when they get through it costs thousands.*
>
> *I got another office in St. Cloud, Florida. You can't even find St. Cloud on the fuckin' map, but the fuckin' "G" found it.*
>
> *Kennedy's right-hand man, he goes through the fuckin' nigger town. Must have been 2,000 niggers, and makes a fuckin' big raid over there.*
>
> *Just a start, any fuckin' place that they found a phone connection in there from Tampa.*

A transcript of the tape is sent by AIRTEL to J. Edgar Hoover, who takes note of Trafficante's displeasure over Attorney General Kennedy's crackdown.

It was around this time that Trafficante's Detroit friend, Jimmy Hoffa, was outlining a plan to assassinate the Kennedy brothers to Edward Partin. At the same time his New Orleans friend, Carlos Marcello, was telling Edward Becker of his plans to have President Kennedy killed.

As we have already indicated, there is evidence that Trafficante was in touch with his friends in Detroit and New Orleans and was aware of their plans to assassinate President Kennedy for he clearly expressed apparent foreknowledge of the assassination to the Cuban exiles leader and FBI informant, José Aléman, in September 1962:

No Jose, you don't understand me. Kennedy is not going to make it to the election. Kennedy's going to be hit.

If we are to believe Frank Ragano, things came to a head a few months later in February 1963. It was then that Ragano, at the instigation of Jimmy Hoffa, met with Marcello and Trafficante at the Royal Orleans Hotel in New Orleans and told the two Mafia chieftains that Hoffa wanted them to assassinate President Kennedy when he came south. It will be recalled that when Ragano told Trafficante and Marcello that Hoffa wanted Kennedy killed the two men "didn't laugh. They were dead serious. They looked at each other in a way that made me feel uncomfortable. They made me feel they already had such a thing in mind."

What Trafficante then did to further the progress of the plot is unknown. There is a chance the two men who were driving with Rose Cheramie, from Miami to Dallas, to assassinate Kennedy were sent by Trafficante, but we do not know their identities. Another possibility is that the three Corsican drug smugglers author Steve Rivele and British television producer Nigel Turner claim were hired by the American Mafia to kill Kennedy, were hired by Trafficante since he maintained the closest ties to the Corsican Mafia of any American godfather. But since Rivele's and Turner's scenario is based wholly on the questionable testimony of two notorious convicted French drug dealers, it cannot be considered anything more than a conjectural hypothesis at this time.

Ragano said in his allegation that he believed Carlos Marcello was "the central planner of the assassination." Perhaps Trafficante acted in an advisory role, helping Marcello formulate a plan.

The next we hear of Trafficante is on the evening of November 22, 1963. Kennedy has been assassinated in Dallas. Trafficante has invited Ragano and his nineteen-year-old fiancee, Nancy, to dinner at Tampa's International Inn. He is jubilant. He greets his guest warmly. Nancy describes him today as "a perfect gentlemen," "well mannered and well read." But he horrifies her during dinner by toasting the death of President Kennedy. In tears, she gets up from the table and runs out of the restaurant.

Trafficante and Marcello then turn up together about three years later at the big Mafia sitdown at the La Stella Restaurant in Queens, New York. A photograph taken of them having lunch with Ragano and three other mobsters shows an obviously self-satisfied Marcello and a smug Trafficante. The nightmares Bobby Kennedy and the Justice Department had visited upon them are long over. During the three years since the assassination both men have prospered greatly. They are no longer under federal investigation. Only Jimmy Hoffa is still in trouble. He will go to jail in 1967.

But before going to jail Hoffa will reward his two friends in the South. He would make generous "loans" to them both from the Teamsters Central States pension fund, presumably in payment for the Kennedy assassination.

In 1968, at the height of the Vietnam War, Trafficante journeyed to Singapore, Hong Kong, and South Vietnam in an effort to secure new sources of heroin for Mafia distributors in the United States. Since the 1950s, the

Corsican Mafia, with which the Trafficantes, father and son, had done business for years, was buying large quantities of heroin from the so-called Golden Triangle of Burma, Thailand, and Laos, and shipping it out through Vietane and Saigon. Trafficante was evidently successful in his dealings with the Corsican Mafia in Vietnam for FBI reports indicate that he prospered greatly in the 1970s and as a result fell under intense investigation by the Internal Revenue Service.

In the early seventies a beleagured Johnny Rosselli, facing deportation proceedings, came forward and presented his version of the Kennedy assassination to the Washington columnist Jack Anderson. According to Rosselli, Fidel Castro became aware of the CIA-Mafia plots to assassinate him and may have formed an alliance with Trafficante to turn the tables on the U.S. president and assassinate *him*.

Rosselli told Anderson that the assassination was the work of Cubans associated with Santos Trafficante. Lee Harvey Oswald was recruited as a decoy. He may have fired at the President, but the shot that killed Kennedy was fired from the front by a Cuban in Trafficante's employ, implying a shot from the grassy knoll. When Oswald was captured by the Dallas Police, the Mafia had him killed by their man in Dallas, Jack Ruby.

In 1975 Rosselli was called by the Senate Intelligence Committee (the Church Committee) to testify on what he knew about the CIA-Mafia plots to assassinate Castro. In his two secret appearances before the committee, Rosselli opened up and told the good senators all he knew about the plots. Then, at a top secret hearing held on April 23, 1976, in a suite at the Carroll Arms Hotel in Washington, Rosselli told representatives of the committee and Senator Richard Schweiker all he claimed he knew about the Kennedy assassination, indicating he believed Cubans associated with Castro and Trafficante were behind the crime. Senator Schweiker then asked him whether he knew about Trafficante meeting Jack Ruby in Havana, and Rosselli told him he knew about the meeting, that Ruby and Trafficante knew each other.

On July 28, 1976, Johnny Rosselli was abducted, murdered, dismembered, and his body stuffed into a fifty-five gallon steel oil drum and dumped in Dumfoundling Bay off Miami.

It was never conclusively determined who the murderer, or murderers, were, but a Mafia informant later told investigators that he believed a Trafficante associate lured Rosselli onto a yacht, where, while sitting on a deck chair, he was garroted from behind, had his legs sawed off, was crammed into an oil drum, and thrown into Dumfoundling Bay. Clearly Rosselli had talked too much.

On February 22, 1977, in a front-page article in *The New York Times,* Nicholas Gage wrote that "two men known to have personal knowledge of the circumstances of the murder provided solid information that Mr. Rosselli was killed by members of the underworld as a direct result of his testimony before the Senate Committee."

A year later, the House Select Committee on Assassinations, which investigated the crime, came to suspect that Trafficante had a hand in the killing.

The House Select Committee on Assassinations interviewed Santos Trafficante on March 16, 1977. He was asked if he had known or discussed information that President Kennedy would be assassinated. The Florida boss declined to answer, citing his constitutional right to avoid self-incrimination.

The Assassinations Committee questioned Trafficante again on September 28, 1978, this time in public session and under a grant of immunity. Trafficante categorically denied ever having discussed any plan to assassinate President Kennedy. However, he did admit to having participated in a CIA plot to assassinate Fidel Castro.

José Aléman also testified before the Assassinations Committee in closed session in March 1977. Aléman stated that Trafficante had made it clear to him that he was not guessing that the president was going to get killed. Rather Trafficante did in fact know such a crime was being planned. Aléman further stated that Trafficante had given him the distinct impression that Hoffa was principally involved in planning the presidential murder.

In September 1978, prior to his appearance before the Assassinations Committee in public session, Aléman reaffirmed his earlier account of the alleged meeting with Trafficante in September 1962. Nevertheless, Aléman informed the committee staff that he feared for his physical safety and was afraid of a possible reprisal from Trafficante or his organization. In this testimony Aléman changed his professed understanding of Trafficante's comments. Aléman repeated under oath that Trafficante had said Kennedy was "going to be hit," but he then stated that it was his impression that Trafficante may have only meant the President was going to be hit by "a lot of Republican votes," in the 1964 election, not that he thought he was going to be assassinated.

In its final report the House Assassinations Committee noted Trafficante's predisposition to participate in a murder contract against President Kennedy:

> *Santos Trafficante's stature in the national syndicate of organized crime, notably the violent narcotics trade, and his role as the mob's chief liaison to criminal figures within the Cuban exiles community, provided him with the capability of formulating an assassination conspiracy against President Kennedy . . . In testimony before the Committee, Trafficante admitted participating in the unsuccessful CIA conspiracy to assassinate Castro, an admission indicating his willingness to participate in political murder.*

Subsequent to his testimony before the House Assassinations Committee José Aléman, suffering a number of financial reversals, became convinced that his 1978 congressional testimony against Trafficante had ultimately caused his financial ruin and had marked him and his family for the rest of their lives.

Tormented by these thoughts, Aléman went berserk on the morning of August 1, 1983 and, in a wild rampage, opened fire on everyone in his house and then after the SWAT team arrived and he had exchanged fire with them, shot himself in the temple, dying instantly.

Aléman's surviving relatives later told the press that he had been consumed with fear because of his 1978 testimony before the House Assassinations Committee in which he had stated that in 1962 Santos Trafficante had told him that President Kennedy would not be reelected in 1964, that he was "going to be hit." "From that day on," a relative claimed, "he believed he and his family were on a Mafia hit list."

In 1982 Associate Attorney General Rudolph Giuliani convinced President Ronald Reagan to devote $100 million toward an all-out attack on the mob. Soon Reagan was telling an audience in the Justice Department auditorium his ultimate aim was "to eliminate this confederation of professional criminals, this dark, evil, enemy within."

By January 1983 the Organized Crime Drug Enforcement Task Force, armed with $100 million and a new Justice Department ruling allowing for increased use of electronic surveillance, was in place, primed for its attack on the mob.

There followed a series of indictments of major Mafia bosses including Santos Trafficante, Jr., who up until 1983 had been seemingly immune from prosecution. After an intensive FBI investigation, Trafficante was indicted on federal racketeering charges. Frank Ragano defended Trafficante and obtained a mistrial in 1986 due to lack of sufficient evidence. During the trial Trafficante's health began to fail. He was suffering from heart disease and a number of related ailments.

It was approximately two weeks before his death in 1987 that Trafficante summoned Frank Ragano to his bedside and began unburdening himself of some of the regrets of a lifetime.

After confessing to some of the major mistakes he had made, Trafficante came to the Kennedy assassination. Trafficante had not brought up the subject with Ragano since November 1963 and Ragano had never questioned him about it. Now, in a hoarse, weakened voice, Trafficante looked at Ragano and startled him by saying "You know, Frank, Carlos screwed up. We should have killed Bobby, not Giovanni."

CHAPTER 6

★

The Plot to Kill
the President

Frank Ragano believed that Marcello was "the central planner of the assassination." However, he was never informed of the operational details of the assassination. When did Marcello actively begin planning the crime? Who were his closest accomplices? How was Lee Harvey Oswald recruited into the plot? How many shooters were there and who were they? Did Jack Ruby participate in the conspiracy to kill Kennedy, or was he only utilized in the plot to kill Oswald? Frank Ragano does not know. The last time he discussed the assassination with Hoffa and Marcello was in early 1964.

Although he remained an attorney of Santos Trafficante for twenty-seven years, the only times he discussed the assassination with him were over dinner the evening of November 22, 1963 and two weeks before his death in 1987.

What evidence is there for Ragano's belief that Marcello was "the central planner of the assassination"?

Let us consider when Carlos Marcello began to actively plan the assassination. Let us establish a chronology of the various stages of the conspiracy.

Stage one. September 1962. Marcello outlines his plan to kill President Kennedy in order to neutralize his brother, the attorney general. Witness: Edward Becker at the meeting in the farmhouse at Churchill Farms.

Stage two. February 1963. Frank Ragano delivers Hoffa's message to Marcello and Trafficante in New Orleans that he wants them to assassinate the President.

Stage three. April 24, 1963. The White House announces that President Kennedy will make a trip to Texas in November. On April 25, Lee Harvey Oswald arrives in New Orleans from Dallas and goes to stay with his uncle, "Dutz" Murret, an operative in the Marcello gambling network. Sometime in April: Ben Tregle, an associate of Carlos Marcello, expresses foreknowledge of the assassination: "There is a price on the President's head, and other members of the Kennedy family. Somebody will kill Kennedy when he comes down South." Sometime in late April: Lee Harvey Oswald is spotted in the restaurant at Carlos

Marcello's Town and Country Motel headquarters receiving money from a top Marcello lieutenant. From these events we can deduce that Marcello now knows that Kennedy will come "down South" in November and that he has told associates like Ben Tregle, of the contract on Kennedy's life. He is also aware of the existence in New Orleans of "Dutz" Murret's nephew, Lee Harvey Oswald, although he has not yet recruited him into the conspiracy to kill the President.

Stage four. May 27, 1963. The U.S. Supreme Court, in response to an appeal filed by Marcello's attorneys, declined to review the Marcello deportation action and upheld the earlier decision of the U.S. Circuit Court of Appeals. Marcello can now be deported as soon as a host country has been found by Attorney General Kennedy to accept him. He is also under two federal indictments brought against him by Attorney General Kennedy. The only thing now that can save Carlos Marcello from destruction is a change of presidential administration. Marcello's resolve to kill Kennedy when he "comes down South" hardens.

Stage five. June/July 1963. Lee Harvey Oswald goes to work as a part-time undercover agent and political demonstrator, for Guy Banister. He joins the Fair Play for Cuba Committee. He is seen in the port of New Orleans along the wharf where the USS *Wasp* is berthed, handing out pro-Castro leaflets to sailors. He meets David Ferrie in Banister's offices. Ferrie is meeting regularly with Carlos Marcello at the Town and Country Motel ostensibly to work on Marcello's federal case. But, more than likely, Marcello is discussing his plans to assassinate Kennedy with Ferrie, who he will soon make his master strategist in the conspiracy to kill the President. (Robert Morrow, a CIA contract employee in New Orleans from 1959 to 1964, who knew David Ferrie and Guy Banister, asserts in his book on the Kennedy assassination, *First-Hand Knowledge,* that "Dave Ferrie was the brains behind Marcello's operations. His organizational genius and ability to plan extraordinarily complex operations was unparalleled within the Mob.") By now Marcello is thoroughly aware of the presence of Oswald in New Orleans and may be discussing with his friend, Dave Ferrie, a way to frame Oswald for the impending presidential assassination. The ex-defector to the Soviet Union is the ideal "nut" for him to set up to take the blame for the assassination.

Stage Six. August 1963. Guy Banister, David Ferrie, and Carlos Marcello meet regularly. They discuss plans to assassinate President Kennedy when he comes to Texas in November. Jack Ruby is possibly recruited into the plot because of his connections with the Dallas Police. Banister supports Oswald's demonstrations on behalf of Castro. It will provide Oswald with a reputation as a pro-Castro "commie nut," which will divert attention away from Carlos Marcello when Oswald is arrested for assassinating the President. August 9: Oswald hands out Fair Play for Cuba Committee leaflets on Canal Street. Gets in a fight with anti-Castro Cuban exiles. He, and some of the Cuban exiles, are arrested and jailed. August 10: Oswald is bailed out by Emile Bruneau, an associate of Marcello's two top lieutenants, Nofio Pecora and

Joe Poretto. August 16: Incorrigible, Oswald hands out pro-Castro literature outside the International Trade Mart. His demonstration was filmed by television station WDSU. Oswald's credentials as a pro-Castro sympathizer are strengthened.

Stage Seven. September 1963. It was one year ago that Carlos Marcello, in the presence of Edward Becker, outlined his plan to assassinate President Kennedy. Now Marcello and Ferrie, with the assistance of Guy Banister, plan the murder in earnest. On September 12 the *New Orleans Times-Picayune* announces that President Kennedy will visit Dallas on November 21 or 22. David Ferrie, who has assumed control of Oswald, tells Oswald he will have to return to Dallas so he can demonstrate against Kennedy when he visits the city. But before that Oswald must make a trip to Mexico City in late September to further establish his credentials as a pro-Castro activist. Ferrie has by now conceived the idea of getting some people who resemble Oswald to impersonate him in Mexico City and Dallas with the aim of laying down a trail of incriminating information against Oswald that will be used to frame him for the assassination. Banister is assisting Ferrie in this effort under the supervision of Carlos Marcello. September 26: Oswald takes a Continental Trailways bus from Houston to Mexico City.

Before leaving for Mexico City Oswald sends his wife back to Dallas and tells her he would attempt to obtain a transit visa to visit Cuba from the Cuban Embassy in Mexico City. Once in Cuba he would try to obtain a visa from the Soviet Embassy in Havana that would enable him to return with her and their child to Russia. In reality it appears certain that Oswald was going to Mexico City for a different reason. From all indications he was going at the behest of Banister and Ferrie to bolster his credentials as a pro-Castro activist.

Credible evidence indicates that Oswald himself never visited the Cuban and Soviet embassies in Mexico City, for Banister and Ferrie had deployed an imposter to make those visits. The man representing himself as Lee Harvey Oswald made a conspicuous nuisance of himself at both embassies making sure consular and embassy personnel would remember him after the real Oswald was arrested for assassinating President Kennedy.

Stage eight. October 1963. The final planning of the assassination. On October 3 the real Oswald returned to Dallas. On October 5 the Dallas newspapers announce the President will visit Dallas on November 22. Jack Ruby is now active in the assassination plot. So are at least two Oswald impersonators. More than likely Marcello and Trafficante have recruited the marksmen who will fire on President Kennedy on November 22. On October 14 Oswald is notified of a job opening at the Texas School Book Depository in downtown Dallas. That same day he rents a room in a boarding house at 1026 North Beckley registering as O. H. Lee. On October 15 the Kennedy motorcade route is published in the Dallas papers. It calls for the motorcade to pass through Dealey Plaza via Main Street. The Texas School Book depository overlooks Dealey Plaza. Oswald is hired as an order filler in the depository the same day the route is announced. On

October 16 he goes to work in the depository. Marcello, Trafficante, Banister, and Ferrie are apprised of these developments. Oswald is in a position to be easily framed for the assassination. In all probability Marcello orders Ferrie and Banister to dispatch the marksmen to Dealey Plaza in a reconnaissance mission. They conclude that the best firing position is from behind the picket fence on the grassy knoll. They would also position shooters to the rear, in the Texas School Book Depository and the Dallas Records Building or the Dal-Tex Building, to catch Kennedy in a crossfire.

On October 31, 1963, an FBI listening device picks up a conversation between two of the Maggadino brothers of the Buffalo, New York, crime family.

> Peter Maggadino: President Kennedy he should drop dead.
> Stefano Maggadino: They should kill the whole family, the mother and the father too.

Again, J. Edgar Hoover does nothing about this tape. He does not inform either the Kennedy brothers or the Secret Service.

November 9, 1963. A Miami police informant, William Somerset tapes a conversation with wealthy ultraconservative Joseph Milteer, who is active in the Cuban exiles' cause to overthrow Castro. Milteer tells Somerset, President Kennedy is going to be assassinated.

> Somerset: I think Kennedy is coming here on the 18th, or something like that to make some kind of a speech . . .

Milteer: You can bet your bottom dollar he is
going to have a lot to say about the Cubans.

Somerset: Yeah. Well, he will have a thousand
bodyguards, don't worry about that.

Milteer: The more bodyguards he has, the easier it is to get him.

Somerset: Well, how the hell do you figure
would be the best way to get him?

Milteer: From an office building with a high-
powered rifle. . . . He knows he's a marked
man.

Somerset: They are really going to try and kill
him?

Milteer: Oh yeah, it is in the working . . . They
will pick somebody up within hours after-
wards . . . Just to throw the public off.

The Miami Police relay this to the FBI and the
Secret Service. No action is taken to warn the president. Since Milteer is active in the Miami Cuban exiles
community, he has probably heard about Marcello's
contract on Kennedy from certain Cubans. David
Ferrie's closest friend, Eladio del Valle, is a leader in
the Miami exiles' movement to overthrow Castro.

Over the weekend of November 9, 10, Marcello
and Ferrie hold strategy sessions in the farmhouse at
Churchill Farms. Oswald spends the weekend with
his family in the Dallas suburb of Irving where his
wife is living in an apartment belonging to her friend,
Ruth Paine.

On November 14 Secret Service Agent Winston
Lawson decides on the Kennedy motorcade route. It
will go through Dealey Plaza via Main Street as the
Dallas newspapers have already indicated.

Over the weekend of November 16, 17, Marcello and Ferrie hold a final strategy session at Churchill Farms. They study the site of the presidential ambush, Dealey Plaza. They decide on the location assignments of the marksmen chosen to assassinate the president. Oswald does not visit his family in Irving over the weekend of November 16, 17. His whereabouts that weekend is still unknown.

On November 18 the chief of the Secret Service in Dallas, Forrest Sorrels, makes a slight change in the motorcade route that provides for a turn off Main Street and onto Houston Street and then an abrupt dogleg turn onto Elm Street. This brings the presidential motorcade closer to the Texas School Book Depository and the grassy knoll and will force it to slow down as it makes the dogleg turn. The purpose of the turn is to gain better access to the Stemmons Freeway, which will take the President to the Trade Mart where he is scheduled to deliver an address. It is also designed to bring the presidential motorcade close to curbside onlookers, something Kennedy had specifically requested. The change is reported in the Dallas press the following day, November 19. Now the conspirators know the ambush of the President will be much easier to accomplish.

Meanwhile the Oswald impersonators are active in Dallas creating incidents that will be remembered after the assassination is blamed on Oswald. Jack Ruby is also active. Throughout October and November he has been making telephone calls to various mob associates throughout the country. On October 3 he telephones Russell Mathews, an associate of Santos Trafficante, and Joseph Campisi, a Dallas deputy of Carlos Marcello. A few days later,

Ruby is spotted in the New Orleans French Quarter at a striptease joint owned by Frank Caracci, another associate of Carlos Marcello, and the next day he is seen in Pete Marcello's Bourbon Street club, the Sho-Bar. Upon his return to Dallas, Ruby makes suspicious calls to an associate of West Coast gangster, Mickey Cohen, and several mob associates of Jimmy Hoffa, Sam Giancana, and Santos Trafficante. On October 30 he calls top Marcello lieutenant, Nofio Pecora.

It is likely that during the week preceding the assassination a member of the conspiracy goes to Ruth Paine's garage in Irving and absconds with Oswald's Mannlicher-Carcano rifle which is later planted on the sixth floor of the Book Depository to incriminate Oswald.

On the morning of November 20 two police officers on routine patrol entered Dealey Plaza, through which the presidential motorcade would pass on November 22, and noticed several men standing behind a wooden fence on the grassy knoll overlooking the plaza. The men appear to be engaged in mock target practice, aiming rifles over the fence in the direction of the plaza. The two police officers immediately make for the fence but by the time they get there the riflemen have disappeared, having departed in a car that had been parked nearby.

Evening of November 21. Jack Ruby dines on a steak at the Egyptian Lounge, a Dallas underworld restaurant, owned by Marcello associate Joe Campisi.

Early morning, November 22. Nine Secret Service agents, who will participate in the presidential motorcade later on, attend a raucous all-night drinking party at Pat Kirkwood's Cellar Door club in Fort Worth. Several of the sexy young women, who were plying the Secret Service agents with beer, wine, and hard liquor into the early hours of the morning, were strippers sent over from Jack Ruby's Dallas nightclub, the Carousel. Ruby is a friend of Pat Kirkwood. Later these Secret Service agents would exhibit unusually slow reactions, or responses, to the shooting at the presidential motorcade that broke out at 12:30 P.M.

CHAPTER 7

★

The Framing of
Lee Harvey Oswald

In September 1962, Carlos Marcello told Edward Becker and Carlos Roppolo that he would have to arrange the murder of President Kennedy in such a way that his own men would not be identified as the assassins. He would have to use, or manipulate, someone not connected to his organization into a position where he would immediately be blamed by the police for the crime. He had already thought of a way to set up a "nut" to take all the heat, "the way they do in Sicily."

How did Marcello and his men set up Lee Harvey Oswald to take the blame for assassinating President

Kennedy? When was Oswald recruited into the plot to kill the president?

As we know Oswald arrived in New Orleans on April 25, 1963, and went to live with his aunt and uncle, Lillian and Charles "Dutz" Murret, in the French Quarter. "Dutz" Murret, a minor operator in Marcello's gambling network, would give his nephew a part-time job as a "runner," or messenger boy, taking messages to bookmakers and betting customers. He would operate out of the Felix Oyster Bar on Iberville Street in the heart of the French Quarter not far from Pete Marcello's Sho-Bar.

It seems reasonable to assume that Carlos Marcello first learned of Oswald's presence in New Orleans in June, although there is evidence that he learned of him much earlier, if we are to believe in the Georgian informant's story of sighting Oswald in the Town and Country restaurant in late April.

Oswald was endowed with several credentials for being classified as a "nut." He was dishonorably discharged from the Marine Corps in September 1959 and defected to the Soviet Union in October 1959. After marrying a Soviet woman in 1960 and fathering a daughter in 1962, he fled the Soviet Union in June 1962 and returned to the United States to live with his brother Robert in Fort Worth.

It was probably in late June that Oswald went to work as a part-time agent and political demonstrator for Guy Banister Associates. It was at Banister's detective agency that Oswald renewed his acquaintance with David Ferrie whom he had first met as a cadet in the Louisiana Civil Air Patrol in 1954. Ferrie, as we know, was conferring regularly with

Carlos Marcello about Marcello's upcoming federal trial. It is therefore reasonable to assume that it was Ferrie who brought Oswald to the attention of Marcello. By the time of his arrest on August 9 for disturbing the peace it seems safe to say that Marcello and Ferrie had decided that Oswald was an ideal candidate to be the "nut" they would set up to take the blame for the assassination of President Kennedy.

In all likelihood Oswald was not recruited by Marcello, Banister, and Ferrie to participate in a conspiracy to assassinate the president. He probably was recruited to play a role in their anti-Castro activities. As we know, Guy Banister allowed Oswald to operate out of his offices when the ex-marine conducted his pro-Castro street demonstrations and allowed him to store his leaflets and placards in his offices as well.

It even might have been Banister who gave Oswald the job of demonstrating for Castro. For there is evidence that a deliberate attempt was made to assemble a pro-Castro résumé for Oswald, a résumé that would be used against him and against Castro, after his arrest for assassinating the President.

Which brings us to an important point. The Kennedy assassination appears to have been planned as an anti-Castro provocation, an act designed to be blamed on Castro to justify a punitive U.S. invasion of the island. Such an action would most clearly benefit the Mafia chieftains who had lost their gambling holdings in Havana because of Castro and the Cuban exiles desirous of returning to their homeland.

Oswald played his pro-Castro charade well in New Orleans in the summer of 1963. He joined the Fair

Play for Cuba Committee and founded a chapter in New Orleans consisting of one member, himself. After the Kennedy assassination a Fair Play for Cuba membership card would be found in his wallet. His arrest for disturbing the peace during one of his pro-Castro street demonstrations won him mention as a pro-Castro activist in the papers and an interview on radio station WSDU.

But Marcello, Banister, and Ferrie were not content to let Oswald's résumé reflect only his New Orleans activities. They had resolved to bolster it further so that when he would be arraigned for killing Kennedy there would not be the slightest doubt that he was a rabid pro-Castro "commie nut."

And so they packed him off to Mexico City to assist in playing, along with an imposter, what would be his grandest pro-Castro charade of all.

Ostensibly Oswald went to Mexico City in late September 1963 and visited the Cuban and Soviet embassies there in an effort to obtain a transit visa to enter Cuba and clear the way for an eventual return to the Soviet Union. While visiting the embassies, an individual representing himself as Oswald made a conspicuous nuisance of himself, loudly proclaiming his pro-Castro sympathies, and meeting with a Soviet official, who, it was later learned, was a KGB officer in charge of political assassinations in the Western Hemisphere. It wasn't until 1978 that it was learned beyond any doubt that the real Lee Harvey Oswald did not visit the Cuban and Soviet embassies in Mexico City, that it was an imposter who visited them, a man whose mission it appears was to help frame Oswald for the impending assassination of John F. Kennedy.

Who might Banister have recruited to impersonate Oswald in Mexico City? Banister did a great deal of investigative work for the CIA and it is thought that he might have recruited an ex-CIA or even an active CIA agent, who was bitterly opposed to Kennedy's Cuban policies, to impersonate Oswald. In 1978 the House Select Committee on Assassinations investigated this possibility and was unable to identify the imposter. CIA surveillance cameras spying on the Cuban and Soviet embassies had pictures of a man who represented himself as Oswald, but no one so far has been able to identify him.

From Mexico City Oswald traveled to Dallas where he rented a room in a boarding house and settled his family in an apartment belonging to Ruth Paine in the suburb of Irving. Throughout October at least one, perhaps two, Oswald look-alikes were active in Dallas impersonating Oswald in a variety of situations.

Living apart from his family, under an assumed name, Oswald was assured complete privacy. Now he could attend to his business unnoticed and unobserved. Apparently whatever business he conducted over the phone was not from a phone in the boarding house but from a public telephone in a garage nearby, for a garage attendant later testified he had often made change for Oswald so he could call long-distance.

The real Oswald had to work at the Texas School Book Depository Monday through Friday from 8:00 A.M. to 4:45 P.M. with only a forty-minute break for lunch, which, his fellow workers testified, he always ate in the depository's cafeteria.

Yet the morning of November 1, a weekday, a man

giving his name as Oswald, entered Morgan's Gun Shop in Fort Worth to purchase ammunition. He drew attention to himself by acting "rude and impertinent."

On November 4, the night manager of the central Dallas Western Union office observed "Oswald" picking up several money orders. Yet the real Oswald spent that evening with his wife and child in Irving.

Four days later, when the real Oswald was working at the Book Depository, a man named Oswald brought a rifle into the Irving Sports Shop and had three holes drilled in it to mount a telescopic sight. Oswald's rifle had only two holes, and they had been drilled before Oswald had purchased the weapon.

On November 8, another weekday, a man giving his name as "Harvey Oswald" went into Hutchison's Grocery Store in Irving to cash a check for $189. The real Oswald never cashed checks for such large amounts in stores and was not in Irving at the time.

The next day, when the real Oswald was in Irving, "Oswald" test drove a car at Downtown Lincoln-Mercury in Dallas and told the salesman, Albert Bogard, he would return in a couple of weeks (November 23) when he would have "a lot of money" to buy the car. The real Oswald was supposed not to have been able to drive.

On November 10, while again the real Oswald was in Irving, "Oswald" applied for a job as a parking attendant at Alright Parking Systems in Dallas. As he talked with the manager, Hubert Morrow, "Oswald" asked whether the Southland Hotel overlooking the parking lot provided a good view of downtown Dallas, which the manager took to mean the route the presidential motorcade would take on November 22.

Six days later, another weekday, "Oswald" was observed by several witnesses at the Sports Dome Rifle Range in Dallas firing a 6.5 mm Italian rifle with a four-power scope with remarkable accuracy. The witnesses had seen the same rifleman at the range once before firing the same rifle. This time "Oswald" called attention to himself by shooting at another rifleman's target. An altercation ensued, with "Oswald" acting particularly obnoxious. Witnesses later testified that this Oswald returned to the rifle range again, on the 20th and 21st, the two days preceding the assassination. Of course the real Oswald was working in the Book Depository both days.

The witnesses who observed "Oswald" participating in these suspicious activities were investigated by both the FBI and the Dallas Police and found to be credible. It therefore seems an inescapable conclusion that someone impersonating Oswald was methodically assembling a résumé for him in and around Dallas throughout October and November 1963, and may have been doing the same thing in Mexico City a few weeks earlier. The résumé would then be used to provide an incriminating profile of the suspected assassin of President Kennedy.

In view of the fact that no witnesses ever saw Oswald on the sixth floor of the Book Depository immediately before the assassination, but there were witnesses who saw him in the second floor lunchroom at 12:15 P.M. and at 12:32 P.M. (Kennedy was shot at 12:30 P.M.), it appears more than likely that the conspirators had not recruited Oswald to participate in a plot to assassinate the president, but had merely told him to be available for a possible pro-Castro demonstration when the presidential motorcade passed by the Book Depository, hoping he would be quickly identified as the nut who had killed the President.

CHAPTER 8

Ambush in Dallas

It was a bright, sunny morning in Dallas on November 22, 1963. The people were looking forward to President Kennedy's visit with keen anticipation. The city had a festive air about it.

At about 11:30 A.M. Julia Ann Mercer, a Dallas housewife, was driving west through Dealey Plaza on Elm Street, when she noticed an illegally parked green Ford pickup truck with Texas plates blocking her lane on the right. As she waited for traffic in the lane to her left to clear so she could drive past the truck, she saw "a white male who appeared to be in his late twenties or early thirties, wearing a gray jacket, brown pants, and a plaid shirt," take out what appeared to be a rifle case from the back of the truck, then carry the rifle case up the embankment to the right and disappear behind the bushes in what has come to be known as "the grassy knoll."

Mercer claimed the incident took place in full view of three Dallas police officers who stood nearby talking. After Jack Ruby shot Oswald on November 25, she told the office of the Dallas Sheriff that she thought the driver of the pickup truck was Jack Ruby.

Around noon, in blazing sunlight, Helen Forrest, who was standing on Elm Street, saw a man with a rifle in a window of the second floor of the Texas School Book Depository.

About fifteen minutes later Arnold Rowland was standing across from the Book Depository awaiting the arrival of the presidential motorcade when he noticed a man with a high-powered rifle standing a few feet back from the far southwest corner window of the sixth floor of the building. Later, when questioned about the southeast window from which Oswald allegedly fired, Rowland said he saw a black man lean out of that window minutes before the shooting.

At about the same time as Rowland's sighting, Carolyn Walther and Ruby Henderson noticed two men in the far southeast corner window of the sixth floor of the Book Depository. John Powell also saw two men on the sixth floor of the depository. He was looking across Dealey Plaza from his cell on the sixth floor of the Dallas County Jail.

At approximately 12:29 P.M. the presidential motorcade made a ninety-degree turn off Main Street onto Houston Street and headed for the intersection of

Elm Street where it made an abrupt dogleg turn to the left and proceeded slowly down Elm Street with the grassy knoll to its right and the Book Depository to the rear.

Suddenly a series of shots rang out. The first shot struck President Kennedy in the upper right back six inches below the neck line, and penetrated to a depth of no more than a little finger's length.

A second and a half later another shot was fired that struck Governor John Connally, who was seated in the limousine to the right of the President, in the upper back at the level of his left armpit, penetrated his rib cage, shattering one rib, then exited from his right front chest, pierced and shattered his right wrist, then entered inside his left thigh, where the bullet became embedded in tissue.

Two seconds passed, then, as the presidential limousine slowed to a crawl, a third shot struck the back of the President's head near the top of the skull and exited from the right side. The trajectory of the bullet suggested that it had been fired from the southeast corner window of the sixth floor of the Book Depository. For a fraction of a second the President's head was driven forward, then suddenly it lurched violently back as a fourth shot struck the President in the right temple and exploded out of the back of his head. The shot had come from behind the picket fence on the grassy knoll.

Several people were witnesses to this last shot. Jean Hill, who was standing across Elm Street from the grassy knoll, saw a gunman behind the picket fence. Malcolm Summers, a retired Dallas police officer, thought he heard a shot from the knoll and raced up the slope to find the shooter. Ed Hoffman saw a man behind the picket fence toss a rifle to a man who caught the rifle, quickly disassembled it and placed it in a brakeman's tool bag. Railroad tower supervisor Sam Holland, who was watching the grassy knoll area when the shooting broke out, saw a puff of smoke rise above the picket fence on the knoll. Railroad worker Lee Bowers, Jr. also saw "a flash of light or smoke or something" emanate from behind the picket fence.

One-and-a-half minutes after the shooting, Police Officer Marrion Baker and the head of the Texas School Book Depository, Roy Truly, entered the depository and encountered Lee Harvey Oswald calmly sipping a Coca-Cola on the second floor of the building. Later Marrion Baker testified that Oswald was not out of breath, that he appeared to be calm and collected. Roy Truly testified Oswald "didn't seem to be excited or overly afraid, or anything." On finishing his Coke, Oswald sauntered out the front door of the building, boarded a bus a few blocks away, then got off and took a cab to his boarding house.

Several minutes after the shooting, a man thought to be Lee Harvey Oswald, but now believed to have been a look-alike, and one of the shooters, was observed by a witness leaving the depository by the rear exit, hesitating a few minutes, then dashing down to the freeway, where he was observed convincingly by Deputy Sheriff Roger Craig climbing into a Nash Rambler station wagon, which promptly took off and disappeared.

Shortly thereafter, two suspects were arrested by the police in another edifice facing Dealey Plaza, the Dal-Tex Building. One of these, a young man wearing a black leather jacket and black gloves, was taken into custody by the Dallas County Sheriff's Office for questioning; no record of his name, capture, or release was made. The other individual arrested in the Dal-Tex Building told the police he was a Californian businessman by the name of Jim Braden. After a brief interrogation at the County Sheriff's Office, he was released. Seven years later a producer for CBS-TV affiliate, NNXT, in Los Angeles, Peter Noyes, discovered who Jim Braden really was. He was Eugene Hale Brading, a courier and liaison man for the mob with ties to Meyer Lansky and Carlos Marcello, who had a rap sheet showing thirty-five arrests with convictions for burglary, bookmaking, and embezzlement. Noyes also found out that Brading had spent the night in the Teamsters' owned Cabana Hotel, which was visited by Jack Ruby the evening of the assassination.

Five other arrests were made in and around Dealey Plaza minutes after the assassination: three men identified as "tramps," who were in an open boxcar parked on the railroad tracks behind the grassy knoll; another man in the Dal-Tex Building, and a thirty-one-year-old Dallas man who was kept in jail for over a week. All were released with no records of their testimony surviving.

What was the reason for neglecting all these potential suspects? The principal reason was that within fifteen minutes of the assassination, radio dispatchers at Dallas Police Headquarters had radioed a description of a man wanted for questioning about the shooting of the President: "an unknown white male, approximately 30, slender build, height 5 feet 10, weight 165 pounds." The description closely fitted Book

Depository employee Lee Harvey Oswald, but could have fitted countless other men too.

Lee Harvey Oswald had, in the meantime, returned to his room in the boarding house, changed his jacket, and picked up a pistol. While he was in his room his landlady, Earlene Roberts, heard an automobile horn sound twice. Looking out the window she noticed a police car parked outside the house with two uniformed officers in the front seats. After waiting a minute or so, the police car drove away. According to Mrs. Roberts, the man known to her as O.H. Lee left her house shortly after the police car departed and went to a bus stop.

Eight minutes later Dallas Police Officer J. D. Tippit, who was ordered to patrol the area Oswald was now in, was shot dead by someone, perhaps by Oswald, perhaps by someone else. About a half hour later, Oswald was seized in a neighborhood movie house, and taken into custody by the police on suspicion of having killed Officer Tippit and possibly also President Kennedy.

Before the police formally charged Oswald with anything, J. Edgar Hoover issued an internal FBI memorandum stating that the Dallas Police "very probably" had President Kennedy's killer in custody, an individual "in the category of a nut and the extremist pro-Castro crowd . . . an extreme radical of the left."

The two-month Marcello-Banister-Ferrie campaign to frame Lee Harvey Oswald for the assassination had worked like a charm.

Meanwhile, Carlos Marcello, on trial in a New Orleans courtroom, was acquitted of all charges that had been brought against him by Attorney General Kennedy. Word of President Kennedy's assassination had been announced in the courtroom shortly before the verdict was read.

Carlos Marcello declined to celebrate his court victory with friends, lawyers, and supporters after the trial. Instead he went straight from the federal courthouse to his office in the Town and Country Motel. If Marcello was involved in the conspiracy to assassinate the president, he was confronted with an urgent problem on the afternoon of November 22. As soon as he learned that Oswald had been taken into custody he would have been faced with the necessity of taking immediate action: a way would have to be found to prevent Oswald from opening his mouth, and the job would have to be done in the headquarters of the Dallas Police Department.

That predicament probably explains why David Ferrie embarked on a hurried trip to Texas soon after the assassination. Driving the 350 miles to Houston nonstop, through a tremendous Texas thunderstorm, he arrived at a hotel owned by Carlos Marcello, the Alamotel, around four in the morning. It was from the Alamotel, according to an FBI report, that Ferrie made a collect call to Carlos Marcello's headquarters in the Town and Country Motel in Dallas in the early afternoon of Saturday, November 23. Was he getting his instructions about the Oswald-in-custody problem?

Meanwhile, as Ferrie was hurtling toward Texas, two of his associates, Guy Banister and Jack Martin, a private investigator and friend of Ferrie's who worked for Banister, got into a fight that may possibly have been related to the Kennedy assassination.

According to Martin's testimony before the House Select Committee on Assassinations in 1978, he and Banister were having drinks in a local bar when they got into a furious argument. As the argument heated up the two went back to Banister's offices at 544 Camp Street to continue their discussion, and after some barbed remark by Banister, Martin shouted: "What are you going to do—kill me like you all did Kennedy?" Whereupon Banister drew his pistol and started beating Martin over the head with the butt, telling him to "watch himself and be careful." Finally Banister's secretary, Delphine Roberts, intervened and broke up the fight.

The next day, Saturday, November 23, with David Ferrie in Houston, Martin watched a television show on the Kennedy assassination during which three men discussed Oswald's New Orleans friends, mentioning David Ferrie as one of them. Suddenly Martin remembered that he knew Ferrie and Oswald were friends and became deeply suspicious of Ferrie, whom he had once overheard talking about assassinating President Kennedy.

The following day Martin phoned a friend of the assistant district attorney of New Orleans and told him he suspected Lee Harvey Oswald had conspired with David Ferrie to assassinate President Kennedy.

Soon, practically the entire New Orleans police force was searching for David Ferrie. Before long the FBI and the Secret Service joined the manhunt. But Ferrie was not to be found. Finally Carlos Marcello's attorney, G. Wray Gill, informed the District Attorney's Office that Ferrie had been in Texas over the weekend, but soon would return to New Orleans. Gill was then told to have Ferrie surrender to the district attorney upon his return, for he was wanted for questioning by the FBI and the Secret Service in connection with the assassination of President John F. Kennedy.

It must have been unsettling for Carlos Marcello to learn that his master strategist was wanted for questioning in regard to the assassination. As for Marcello's fellow conspirators, Santos Trafficante, Jr. and Jimmy Hoffa, they showed little concern over post-assassination developments.

The fact that Oswald had been taken into custody by the Dallas Police did not appear to trouble Santos Trafficante, Jr. We know that Frank Ragano found Trafficante jubilant the evening of the assassination, that he even went to the extent of proposing a toast to John F. Kennedy's death over dinner at Tampa's International Inn: "Our problems are over now," he told Ragano. "I hope Jimmy is happy now. We will build our hotels and casinos again. We will get back into Cuba now."

As for Jimmy Hoffa, he too was exulting over Kennedy's death. We know that he called Frank Ragano immediately after the assassination and exclaimed: "Have you heard the good news? They killed the sonofabitch. This means Bobby is out as Attorney General. Lyndon will get rid of him." Later, when Hoffa learned the Teamsters' leadership in Washington had lowered the flag over union headquarters to half mast, he flew into a rage and ordered the flag hoisted back up. He also chided his secretary for crying over the President's death. When a reporter asked him about the attorney general, Hoffa spat out: "Bobby Kennedy is just another lawyer now."

CHAPTER 9

☆

Jack Ruby and the Plot
to Kill Oswald

David Ferrie, in New Orleans, was in a state of panic the afternoon of November 22. After learning that Lee Harvey Oswald had been arrested and taken into custody by the Dallas Police, he went to Jesse Garner, Oswald's former landlady, inquiring whether she had come across the library card Oswald had used with his, Ferrie's, name on it, when he was living in one of her apartments. Mrs. Garner told investigators she had declined to speak with Ferrie and that he seemed terribly agitated. From Mrs. Garner's, Ferrie then went to Doris Eames, a former neighbor of Oswald's, and asked her about the library card bearing his name. She told him she knew nothing about it and observed that Ferrie was so nervous that evening he appeared nearly out of his mind.

For reasons that can only be guessed at, David Ferrie then made a long-distance call to a motel Carlos Marcello owned in Houston, the Alamotel, and made a reservation for himself and two companions for that night. He then placed a call to the owner and operator of the Winterland Skating Rink in Houston, inquiring about the rink's skating schedule. Next he picked up two friends in his Comet station wagon and took off for Houston, driving nonstop into the night for 350 miles through a blinding Texas thunderstorm, arriving at the motel around four in the morning.

After making a collect call to Carlos Marcello's Town and Country Motel, in the early afternoon of Saturday, November 23, Ferrie and his two companions went to the Winterland Skating Rink where they spent two hours. What did they do at the rink? Later, Ferrie told the FBI that he had made an appointment with the owner, Chuck Rolland, to discuss the problems of operating ice rinks because he was thinking of opening a rink in New Orleans. He then spent two hours skating and talking with Rolland about the costs of installing and operating his rink.

On investigating this story, the FBI found out from Rolland that Ferrie had never discussed with him the problems of operating ice-skating rinks and had not skated at all at his rink, but had spent his entire stay at Winterland making and receiving calls at a public telephone.

What are we to make of this scenario? Carlos Marcello's master strategist making and receiving calls at a skating rink in Houston while the man he had helped frame for assassinating President Kennedy was languishing in a Dallas jail, a suspect in the assassination.

Unfortunately, the known facts about what happened next are scarce. Investigators suspect that Ferrie was in Texas, at Carlos Marcello's behest, to make contact with Jack Ruby, or one of his associates, for the purpose of arranging for the silencing of Oswald at the Dallas Police Headquarters jail.

That brings us to Jack Ruby. What was he doing the afternoon of the assassination?

Immediately after the shooting of the president, Ruby drove to Parkland Memorial Hospital, arriving there a few minutes after Malcolm Kilduff, acting White House press secretary, announced to the world that President Kennedy was dead. Although Ruby later denied going to Parkland, Seth Kantor, White House correspondent for the Scripps-Howard newspaper chain, testified authoritatively that Ruby was at Parkland. He had known Ruby when he worked for the *Dallas Times-Herald,* and had exchanged greetings with Ruby at the hospital.

What was Jack Ruby doing at Parkland Hospital? If we assumed that Ruby was involved in a conspiracy to assassinate President Kennedy, his presence at Parkland at the moment of Kennedy's death must remain highly suspicious. Some investigators have speculated he was there to plant evidence against Oswald in the vicinity of the dying president, namely a bullet that had been fired from a Mannlicher-Carcano 6.5 mm caliber Italian-made rifle, allegedly owned by Oswald. Such a bullet, was, in fact found on a gurney in a corridor near the trauma room in which Kennedy died.

From Parkland, Ruby went to one of his night-clubs, the Carousel, where he was observed making and receiving calls throughout the afternoon. During the period corresponding to Carlos Marcello's getting down to business at his Town and Country office, and Ferrie's phone calls to the Alamotel and Winterland Skating Rink in Houston, visitors to the club noted that Ruby seemed to become progressively agitated by the calls he was receiving. Finally, after taking a last call he pocketed his revolver and went over to Dallas Police Headquarters, where Oswald was being detained on suspicion he had assassinated President Kennedy.

Ruby was on such good terms with the Dallas Police that he had no trouble gaining access to the headquarters. Around 7:00 P.M. Ruby, carrying a loaded snub-nosed revolver in his right trouser pocket, was observed on the third floor of Dallas Police Headquarters by several detectives he knew. Lee Harvey Oswald was being interrogated in Room 317 by Captain Will Fritz, chief of homicide of the Dallas Police. Local radio and TV reporter, Victor Robertson noticed Ruby attempting to enter Room 317 and being rebuffed by the guard outside the door.

By 11:30 P.M. Ruby was back on the third floor of police headquarters, still carrying his revolver, when Police Chief Jesse E. Curry entered the third-floor corridor and announced to the crowd assembled there that Oswald would be put on display in the assembly room in the basement for all to see.

Ruby then joined the large crowd of reporters, pho-tographers, and detectives surging toward the stair-way and soon found himself in the basement assembly room straining to see the prisoner through a forest of upraised cameras. Oswald's hands were manacled behind his back, his eyes blinded by a hundred flashbulbs going off at once, his ears deafened by all the reporters' questions being shouted at him. And yet Oswald was being held on the slenderest of evidence, without benefit of counsel. It was almost a lynching.

Soon Police Chief Curry announced the end of the "press conference" and had the prisoner removed from the room to protect him from the menacing crowd. After Oswald was escorted out of the room, District Attorney Henry M. Wade remained to answer reporters' questions and announce what had been learned about the identity and activities of Lee Harvey Oswald. At one point Wade told reporters that Oswald was a member of the pro-Castro Free Cuba Committee. Immediately Ruby corrected him, yelling out the right name, the Fair Play for Cuba Committee. How did Ruby know the correct name of the committee to which Oswald belonged and which counted only one member in its New Orleans chapter, Lee Harvey Oswald? And why did Ruby pack a gun on his two visits to police headquarters the afternoon of November 22? Was he stalking Oswald on someone's orders?

On Saturday, November 23, Police Chief Curry toyed with the idea of transferring Oswald to the county jail that day but decided not to because of the unusually heavy Saturday traffic. It would be best to transfer him Sunday morning when the traffic would be lighter. The exact time of the transfer would be decided upon in the morning.

Late that afternoon, while David Ferrie was making and receiving calls at a public phone in Houston's Winterland Skating Rink, Jack Ruby was observed by several witnesses in Dallas making calls on public phones from a variety of locations: a parking lot, a bar, a shoe-shine parlor, the corner of Browder and Commerce streets. That evening he spent several hours making and receiving calls at his Carousel Club, which was closed for the weekend out of respect for the dead President. Investigators have concluded that only one of Ruby's outgoing calls appeared suspicious, the 11:44 P.M. long-distance call he made to Dallas union official, Breck Wall, at a Galveston number an hour and a half after David Ferrie arrived in Galveston from Houston.

On Sunday morning, November 24, both the Dallas County Sheriff's Office and the FBI received nearly identical warnings from an anonymous caller that Lee Harvey Oswald would be killed during his transfer from police headquarters to the county jail. Consequently an elaborate transfer plan was decided upon by Police Chief Curry and Captain Fritz. It was decided to use an armored van accompanied by a police-car escort as a decoy during the transfer, while an unmarked car accompanied by an unmarked escort would actually transport Oswald from police headquarters to the county jail. Both the van and the unmarked car would be waiting on the ramp leading from the street to the headquarters basement. The detectives in the basement would form a protective human corridor leading from the elevator in which Oswald would come down from the third floor to the unmarked car on the ramp.

However, Jack Ruby now had his own plan, one that, it appears, was known to at least one member, perhaps two or three, of the Dallas Police, and to the man who had given him his final orders.

Ruby's roommate, George Senator, found Jack Ruby unusually edgy and uptight the morning of Sunday, November 24, as he awaited that all-important call from one of his police contacts informing him at what time Lee Harvey Oswald would be brought down to the basement for the transfer.

Meanwhile one of Ruby's closest police contacts, Officer W. J. "Blackie" Harrison, had gone to the Delux Diner for a coffee break. There he was notified by phone of the transfer plans and was told he would be needed to form security for Oswald at the time of the transfer. Not long after Harrison received the call, it is believed he phoned his friend Jack Ruby at Ruby's unlisted number and told him of the transfer plans.

George Senator later told investigators that after Ruby received a call at the apartment sometime around nine-thirty in the morning he began to pace nervously from room to room, mumbling to himself as a man laboring under an obsession. Ruby had known since the afternoon of November 22 what he had to do: Silence Lee Harvey Oswald forever. Now he knew where and when he had to do it.

Ruby had to quickly invent an excuse for carrying a gun and concoct a believable alibi.

His excuse for carrying a gun was that he was taking $2,000 in cash to his tax attorney to pay the federal excise taxes he owed, so he had to protect himself from possible robbery. And so he stuffed his pockets with nine $100 bills, thirty $10 bills, and forty $20 bills.

Ruby had laid the groundwork for his alibi the previous evening. Actually he had drawn one of his strippers, Karen Carlin, known as "Little Lynn," into the plot to kill Oswald without her knowing it. Saturday evening he told her to phone him Sunday morning and that he would telegraph her $25 from Western Union an hour later. The purpose of this was to establish an alibi to justify his shooting of Oswald as an impulsive act of revenge.

Telephone records indicate that Karen Carlin phoned Jack Ruby at 10:19 A.M. Sunday, November 24. Both she and Ruby later testified the call was a request for $25 she desperately needed for "rent and groceries." Ruby responded by telegraphing the money to Carlin from the Western Union office in downtown Dallas that was located a minute away from the entrance to the Dallas Police Headquarters basement. Ruby told the FBI that four minutes later he wandered into the basement of the Dallas Police Headquarters, after sending the telegram, "to find out what they were doing about Oswald," and shot Oswald impulsively when he saw the suspected assassin being led toward a police van.

At his appearance before the Warren Commission, Ruby used the Western Union receipt for the money sent to Karen Carlin as an alibi to support his claim that his shooting of Oswald was an unpremeditated act to avenge the assassination of President Kennedy.

After the killing of Oswald, three television crewmen told the FBI that they saw Jack Ruby lurking in the vicinity of Dallas Police Headquarters from around 10:00 A.M. on the morning of Sunday, November 24, indicating Ruby could not have taken the call from Karen Carlin at 10:19 A.M.

The FBI and the Warren Commission questioned Karen Carlin about Ruby and the murder of Lee Harvey Oswald. When she was interrogated by the

Warren Commission in 1964 Carlin told the commission that she suspected there was a conspiracy to kill Oswald and she feared she would be killed if she talked.

After the first trial of Jack Ruby, it was reported that Karen Carlin was shot to death in her room in a Houston hotel. From then assassination investigators official and unofficial, have assumed Karen Carlin was dead.

However, in October 1992, Karen Carlin came back from the dead. She contacted Gary Shaw, director of the JFK Assassination Information Center in Dallas, after almost thirty years living under an assumed identity, and told him she knew of a conspiracy to kill Lee Harvey Oswald, that Ruby told her to phone him Sunday morning and that an hour later he would telegraph her $25, just before shooting Oswald, to establish an alibi to justify his shooting of Oswald as an impulsive act of revenge.

And who was ultimately behind the conspiracy to kill Oswald? Karin Carlin mentioned two names to Gary Shaw, Carlos Marcello and Santos Trafficante, Jr.

In 1978 the House Select Committee on Assassinations heard testimony that Ruby was allowed to enter the basement of Dallas Police Headquarters the morning of November 24 by the officer in charge of basement security, Sergeant Patrick Dean, and that a police-car horn was sounded a minute before Oswald entered the basement, an apparent signal to Ruby. It was further established that Sergeant Dean was very close to Dallas Mafia boss, Joseph Civello, Carlos Marcello's deputy in Dallas.

Lee Harvey Oswald was rushed to Parkland

Memorial Hospital, where he was pronounced dead at 2:07 P.M. Dr. Charles Crenshaw, who had treated President Kennedy's wounds two days before, attended Oswald as he lay dying. In the trauma room he noted an unidentified man lurking in the shadows who was carrying a pistol. While he was treating Oswald's stomach wound, Dr. Crenshaw was summoned to the telephone. To his astonishment it was the new president, Lyndon Johnson. Johnson, who by then was anxious to quell any and all rumors of conspiracy, told Crenshaw he wanted a deathbed confession from Oswald, that there was a man in the room who was prepared to take the confession. When Crenshaw returned to Oswald's side he found that the suspected assassin was already dead. There would be no deathbed confession, he told the mysterious armed man.

Meanwhile Jack Ruby had been taken into custody by Dallas Police Officer Don Ray Archer. While Archer was detaining him, Ruby appeared to be extremely agitated and nervous, continually inquiring whether Oswald was dead or alive. It was not until another police officer, who, like many members of the Dallas Police force, knew Ruby, erupted into the detention area and told Ruby that Oswald was dead, that Ruby calmed down. "Jack, it looks like it's going to be the electric chair for you!" the officer exclaimed, "that fella Oswald is dead." At this, Don Ray Archer noticed that Ruby relaxed and even managed a wan smile. It seemed at the time that Ruby felt his own life depended on the success of his mission, that if Oswald had not died, he, Jack Ruby, would have been killed. This scenario, of course, is entirely consistent with that of the classic mob hit. According to the inexorable code of the Mafia, if you are ordered to kill someone and you fail, you yourself will killed.

Several weeks after Ruby shot Oswald, FBI agents interviewed Ruby's close associate, Paul Roland Jones, about Ruby's shooting of Oswald, and Jones told the agents he strongly doubted Ruby would have gotten emotionally upset over the assassination of the President and killed Oswald on the spur of the moment. Rather he believed Ruby would have shot him for money. Jones then went on to say that if Ruby "had been given orders by anyone to kill Oswald, Joe Civello would have known about it," informing the agents, as if they didn't know, that Civello was "the head of the syndicate in Dallas." In the FBI report of Jones' remarks, the interviewing agent neglected to add that Joseph Civello was also Carlos Marcello's deputy in Dallas.

Jack Ruby's murder of Oswald in Dallas Police Headquarters before seventy-seven armed police officers was a typical mob hit: the rubout of a key witness. Obviously the original assassination plan did not call for Ruby to kill Oswald while the suspected assassin was in the custody of the Dallas Police. Something had gone awry that had necessitated this desperate, and extremely risky, operation. The silencing of Lee Harvey Oswald by Jack Ruby was a flashing neon light that should have signaled to investigators the sources of the assassination.

Given Jack Ruby's readily discernible connections to the underworld—telephone records revealed he phoned more than twenty mobsters during the summer of 1963—it should have been apparent to the official investigators that this was the milieu from which the assassination of the President, and the murder of his suspected assassin, had come.

Clearly these crimes arose from the squalid, inter-connected Dallas–New Orleans underworld of book-ies, striptease joints, call-girl rings, slot-machine distributors, and drug dealers; it was the world of Pete Marcello's Sho-Bar and Jack Ruby's Carousel Club; Vincent Marcello's and Jack Ruby's slot-machine warehouses, Ben Tregle's bar and horse book, Joe Civello's heroin-smuggling operation, Carlos Marcello's Town and Country headquarters, and Joe Campisi's Egyptian Lounge.

The members of the Warren Commission had debated over and over again what was in it for Jack Ruby to go in and rub out Oswald. They could not dis-cern his motivation. They couldn't quite swallow Ruby's professed motivation: That he did it to spare Jacqueline Kennedy the agony of having to attend Oswald's trial. Since the commission concluded that Ruby was not connected to organized crime they were ignorant of the code by which a man like Ruby lived.

In the Mafia if you are ordered by a superior to kill someone, and you refuse to carry out the order, you pay for your refusal with your life.

CHAPTER 10

Aftermath in New Orleans

On the afternoon of Oswald's death, David Ferrie placed a call to his roommate in New Orleans, Layton Martens, and was shocked to learn from him that he was being accused of having been involved in the assassination of President Kennedy. The police, in fact, were conducting a massive manhunt for him. Carlos Marcello's attorney, and Ferrie's boss, G. Wray Gill, was advising that Ferrie return to New Orleans. Ferrie immediately headed back to Louisiana.

On the morning of November 25, the day after Ruby shot Oswald, the FBI and the Secret Service learned that Ferrie's library card had apparently been found on Oswald at the time of the accused assassin's arrest.

The information was contained in an FBI teletype from the New Orleans field office to Director J. Edgar Hoover and the special agent in charge of the FBI office in Dallas. Part of the teletype recounted an FBI interview with Ferrie's New Orleans roommate, Layton Martens, conducted on November 25 in Ferrie's apartment. During the interview Martens made reference to a visit to the apartment on the afternoon of November 24 by Carlos Marcello's attorney, G. Wray Gill.

> *Martens said that attorney G. Wray Gill visited Ferrie's residence and told Martens he was looking for Ferrie who was then not at home. Gill remarked to Martens that when Lee Harvey Oswald was arrested by the Dallas Police Oswald was carrying a library card with Ferrie's name on it. Gill instructed Martens to tell Ferrie to contact him and Gill would represent Ferrie as his attorney.*

The teletype raised a disturbing question. Who told Carlos Marcello's attorney that Ferrie's library card had been found on Oswald at the time of his arrest? In the Dallas Police Department's inventory of Oswald's personal effects no mention was made of Ferrie's library card. Yet there are some indications Ferrie's library card might well have been found on Oswald.

For on November 24 the Secret Service asked Oswald's wife, Marina, "Do you know a Mr. David

Farry [sic]?" Where did the Secret Service learn of the existence of David Ferrie, if not from Ferrie's library card found on Oswald?

That Ferrie's library card was found on Oswald was also implied when, after Ferrie returned to New Orleans and surrendered to the district attorney, an agent of the Secret Service asked him: "Did you loan your library card to Lee Harvey Oswald?"

The mystery of David Ferrie's library card was never solved because the FBI and the Secret Service did not want it solved. For by the time of David Ferrie's arrest on November 25, J. Edgar Hoover had proclaimed to all that Lee Harvey Oswald, acting alone, had killed the President. If the library card of an employee of Carlos Marcello's attorney had been found on Oswald at the time of his arrest, a clear signal would have been sent that Oswald probably did have confederates and powerful ones at that.

That Ferrie's library card was found on Oswald could have been the key to unlocking the conspiracy to assassinate the President. It could have led the investigators straight to the central planner of the assassination: Carlos Marcello. Furthermore, that the card was not included in the Dallas Police's inventory of Oswald's effects indicates that at least one Dallas police officer might have been linked to Carlos Marcello. For why would a Dallas police officer notify Carlos Marcello's attorney that Ferrie's card had been found on Oswald if it were not to put Marcello and Ferrie on guard?

Since Ferrie's library card was not turned over to the FBI, it is presumed that someone in the Dallas police force destroyed it. The question is immediately raised for what reason would a Dallas police officer destroy Ferrie's library card were it not considered evidence of an association between Ferrie and Oswald and, by extension, to Carlos Marcello?

As it turned out, the FBI was very circumspect in questioning Marcello's attorney, G. Wray Gill, on the matter. When the FBI questioned Gill about how he learned Ferrie's library card had been found on Oswald, Gill replied he could not recall who told him the "rumor." The FBI then let it go at that.

The FBI was correspondingly lax about David Ferrie's telephone records. When it requested the records from Gill, he turned over only the September and October 1963 records, claiming the crucial November ones were "unavailable." To this withholding of evidence, the FBI made no apparent objection.

Upon his arrest David Ferrie was subjected to intense questioning by the New Orleans Police, the FBI, and the Secret Service. They asked him about his relationship with Oswald, his trip to Texas immediately after the assassination, and about his relationship with Carlos Marcello. Then they checked out his answers, interviewing people who knew both Ferrie and Oswald, and interviewing the owner of the Winterland Skating Rink in Houston. The FBI's investigation of Ferrie lasted until December 18.

And what did the investigators find out? They located a former schoolmate and "best friend" of Oswald's, Edward Voebel, who told the interviewing agents that Oswald was never interested in communism and that he and Oswald "had been members of the Civil Air Patrol in New Orleans with Captain David Ferrie," and he believed Oswald "attended a party at the home of David Ferrie right after the members of the CAP received their stripes." The FBI investigation also determined that Ferrie had lied about his activities at the Winterland Skating Rink and extracted an admission from Ferrie that he indeed had a relationship with Carlos Marcello and had, in fact, conferred with the Mafia chieftain at Churchill Farms during the two weekends prior to the assassination of President Kennedy.

In other words, the FBI found out that a friend of the President's accused assassin had conferred with a sworn enemy of the Kennedy brothers before the assassination.

One would think that this would have been enough to warrant further investigation. But no, on December 18 J. Edgar Hoover ordered his agents in New Orleans to cease investigating David Ferrie.

Transcripts of Ferrie's interviews were immediately classified and buried in the National Archives. They would not be mentioned in the FBI's published investigation of the assassination, the *Summary Report,* nor would they be turned over to the Warren Commission. In 1976, one thirty-page FBI interview of Ferrie was found missing from the National Archives.

Persuasive evidence exists that talk of David Ferrie among reporters in Dallas was actively discouraged by the FBI. Word of Ferrie's arrest in New Orleans had traveled fast. By the middle of the week of November 25 all the newspaper and television reporters covering the assassination in Dallas were talking about Oswald's links to Ferrie and Ferrie's links to Carlos Marcello. CBS producer Peter Noyes recalls a conversation he had with a member of the NBC television team that had covered the murders of the President and Oswald, and a group of FBI agents. When the talk turned to a discussion of Oswald's possible links to Carlos Marcello, through David Ferrie, one of the FBI agents forcefully put an end to the discussion. Later the agent took Peter Noyes aside and told him that under no circumstances should he ever discuss what they had just been talking about with anyone again, "for the good of the country."

J. Edgar Hoover had been quick to enforce the cover-up. The gospel on the Kennedy assassination had been enunciated. Lee Harvey Oswald, the "lone, commie nut," had killed the President unaided by confederates. That was it. All talk of conspiracy was to be discouraged from now on "for the good of the country."

Meanwhile, back in New Orleans, David Ferrie, now in the clear, was free to reap his rewards. Not long after the FBI dropped its investigation of him, he became the owner of a lucrative gasoline-station franchise in an affluent New Orleans suburb. His sponsor was Carlos Marcello.

By mid-December, it was clear that the Oswald-Ferrie-Marcello connection threatened to be too unsettling to a government and a public that was growing accustomed to the Oswald-the-lone-gunman gospel proclaimed by J. Edgar Hoover within only three days of the assassination.

But, as it would turn out, David Ferrie's connection with Oswald and Marcello was not the only intimation of conspiracy J. Edgar Hoover had to contain. Allegations of conspiracy were arriving on his desk at an alarming rate and some of them had to do with Carlos Marcello.

On November 26 the allegation of the Georgian businessman, code-named SV T-1, who was convinced he saw Lee Harvey Oswald accept money from a man he believed was the owner of the Town and Country restaurant in New Orleans, reached Hoover's desk. The FBI director ordered an investigation of the allegation.

Accordingly, Special Agent Reed Jensen of the New Orleans field office, went to Carlos Marcello's headquarters the next day and interrogated Marcello's top lieutenant, Joseph Poretto, and one of Carlos' younger brothers, Anthony Marcello, in connection with SV T-1's allegation. After completing his interrogations Jensen reported back to Hoover as follows:

JOSEPH ALBERT PORETTO, owner, Town and Country Restaurant, 1225 Airline Highway, on interview was advised of the interviewing Agent's identity, that he was not required to submit to interview, that anything he might say could be used against him in a court of law and that he could first consult an attorney. No threats, rewards, promises or other inducements were made to PORETTO in connection with this interview and he voluntarily advised as follows:

On examination of a photograph of LEE HARVEY OSWALD New Orleans Police Department number 112723, Mr. PORETTO said he had never seen this individual in person before and was positive that he had never had any business dealings or association of any kind with this person.

According to Mr. PORETTO, since the assassination of President JOHN F. KENNEDY, he had seen numerous photos and TV shots of both LEE HARVEY OSWALD and JACK LEON RUBY since that time and had never seen or known of either person prior to this time. He said he had never heard of JACK RUBY even by reputation prior to his notoriety in the newspapers.

Mr. PORETTO stated he cannot recall having had any business dealing with anyone in about March or April 1963, or at any other time, who resembled OSWALD enough for a mistaken identity.

ANTHONY MARCELLO, Manager, Town and Country Motel, 1125 Airline Highway, New Orleans, Louisiana, on examining a photograph of LEE HARVEY OSWALD, New Orleans Police Department number 112723, advised that he had never seen this individual at the Town and Country Motel. He said that he had seen numerous photographs and TV shots of both LEE HARVEY OSWALD, suspected assassin of President JOHN F. KENNEDY, and of JACK LEON RUBY, suspected murderer of LEE HARVEY OSWALD and he was positive that he had never seen either of these individuals prior to their notoriety through the news media. Mr. MARCELLO made available registration records for the Town and Country Motel.

With these inconclusive, perfunctory interviews, Hoover shut down the FBI investigation of SV T-1's allegation that he saw someone resembling Oswald receive a payment from the owner of the Town and Country restaurant.

Then, on November 28, J. Edgar Hoover received the allegation of Eugene De Laparra that he was present when Marcello associate Ben Tregle told two friends: "There is a price on the President's head and other members of the Kennedy family. Somebody will kill Kennedy when he comes south."

Again Hoover ordered an investigation of the allegation and again it was carried out by Special Agent Reed Jensen. Jensen's report back to Hoover was as follows:

TREGLE stated that he recalls November 22, 1963, and all during that day he was around his place of business; and it is his recollection that NORMAN JOSEPH LEBLANC was either at the horse barns at Jefferson Downs Race Track or at 6115 Airline Highway that day. TREGLE said he has never known anyone frequenting TREGLE's Bar [now called the Lounnor Restaurant], called "the Professor."

According to TREGLE he believes in segregation and as a result has never agreed with President JOHN F. KENNEDY's Civil Rights Program; and in connection with this he feels that it is his prerogative to do so and express himself accordingly. He stated, however, that he can never recall at any time making any comments which could be construed as a threat on his part to kill the President of the United States or anyone else. He could not recall any incident in which he was looking at a rifle advertisement and then commenting that his rifle could be used to harm anyone; and further, he could not recall ever saying that the President of the United States would be shot if he made a visit to the Southern area of the country.

TREGLE stated that although he did not like President KENNEDY as a President he has never

*been associated with any organization of a political
nature that had a specific purpose "fighting" the
Kennedy administration's Civil Rights Program.*

*He stated he would never stoop to violence of
any kind against anyone and he has never been
associated with anyone to his knowledge who advo-
cates violence to promote their aims and purposes.
He said he considers himself a patriotic American
and he is appalled at anyone who would kill an
official of the United States Government, particularly the President of the country.*

Needless to say the response of Ben Tregle to
Reed Jensen's questioning had little to do with
Eugene De Laparra's allegation. De Laparra never
accused Ben Tregle of anything. He had merely
stated he had overheard Tregle mentioning that there
was a plan to kill President Kennedy when he came
down South. But Tregle's meaningless response was
duly relayed to J. Edgar Hoover who, in turn, apparently accepted it, putting an end to the investigation
of the De Laparra allegation.

By December 1, eight days after the assassination,
Carlos Marcello must have been fully aware that almost
everyone who had been arrested in connection with the
Kennedy assassination, and several people who had
been questioned by the FBI about the assassination,
were connected to his organization. He must have
known that a nephew of one of his bookmakers had
been arrested in Dallas and charged with murdering
President Kennedy, that an associate of his deputy in
Dallas had been arrested for murdering the President's

accused assassin, that his private investigator had been arrested in New Orleans for conspiring to assassinate the President, and both his brother, Anthony, and his lieutenant, Joe Poretto, had been questioned by the FBI in his headquarters as to whether they had seen the President's accused assassin in the Town and Country Motel, and that an associate of his brother, Vincent, Ben Tregle, had been questioned by the FBI about a plan to assassinate President Kennedy.

Was Carlos feeling nervous about all the attention his men were getting from the Feds? We do not know. We do know that there were others close to his organization who were questioned by the FBI in regard to the accused assassin's killer, Jack Ruby. One of these was Frank Caracci, a major gambler in the Marcello network, owner of striptease joints in the New Orleans French Quarter, and a close personal friend of Carlos. The FBI wanted to know from Caracci whether Jack Ruby had visited him in June. Caracci replied that Ruby did come by his place looking to hire strippers for his club in Dallas. Caracci told the inquiring agents that he advised Ruby to go to Pete Marcello's Sho-Bar and questioned either Pete Marcello or his night manager, Nick Graffagnini, about Jack Ruby.

By the sixth of December, Carlos Marcello knew that a total of at least eight persons associated with his underworld organization, were either arrested, or questioned by the Dallas Police and the FBI in regard to the assassination of President Kennedy. And yet he was being ignored by the police and the FBI. Was he in the clear? Did he get away with it?

If we are to believe Frank Ragano, Marcello did feel he had gotten away with it.

It was approximately two weeks after the assassination that Ragano went to New Orleans to see how Carlos was getting along. He had not seen the Mafia chieftain since that February meeting with Carlos and Santos Trafficante at the Royal Orleans Hotel when he had made Jimmy Hoffa's wishes about killing Kennedy known to the two mobsters. Now the assassination had taken place, the operation had been a tremendous success, and Ragano was eager to sense his friend Carlos' mood.

His mood, Ragano soon found out, was one of smugness, of self satisfaction. "Carlos looked like the cat who swallowed the canary," he told Jack Newfield in January 1992. His problems were now over. He need not fear being summarily deported anymore. The vast criminal empire had had labored all his life to build would not be destroyed.

But Ragano also sensed that Marcello was angry because Hoffa had not yet sent the three-million dollars he had promised him.

Looking Ragano straight in the eyes Carlos snarled: "Tell Jimmy he owes me and he owes me big!"

CHAPTER 11

Disinformation and Cover-up:

J. Edgar Hoover and

the FBI Investigation

> *It is a capital mistake to theorize before one has data.*
> *Insensibly one begins to twist facts to suit theories,*
> *instead of theories to suit facts.*
> —SHERLOCK HOLMES

J. Edgar Hoover made this capital mistake within hours of the assassination of President Kennedy. At 9:10 P.M. the evening of November 22, President Johnson phoned the FBI director at his office and told him the initial investigation of the President's murder would be his responsibility. Hoover had already assumed he would be given the task and had begun twisting the facts to suit his theory that the President had been killed by a lone gunman, "in the category of a nut and the extremist pro-Castro crowd," Lee Harvey Oswald. How satisfying it must have been for Hoover to have a communist suspect and not one associated with organized crime, which, as we know, Hoover, for many years declared did not exist.

Hoover was now confronted with the daunting task of twisting a multiplicity of facts to suit his theory and instituting a cover-up of certain facts that would disprove his theory. He would address this task by first launching a massive disinformation campaign designed to convince the American people as soon as possible that Lee Harvey Oswald, "an extreme radical of the left," had killed the President, unaided by confederates. Concurrently he would have to find a way of containing the many allegations of conspiracy that were pouring into his office, especially those suggesting that Carlos Marcello and his allies were behind the crime.

"But the truth will out," Sherlock Holmes had insisted. Inevitably bits and pieces of the evidentiary puzzle would be found and assembled by investigators that would reveal a murder plot far different from the scenario concocted by Hoover.

Hoover gave away his hand shortly after Oswald was murdered by Jack Ruby. Phoning President Johnson's White House aide, Walter Jenkins he said:

The thing I am concerned about, and so is [Deputy Attorney General Nicholas D.] Katzenbach is having something issued so we can convince the public that Oswald is the real assassin.

Spurred on by Hoover, Katzenbach then sent a memorandum to another Johnson aide, Bill Moyers, that revealed the FBI director's thoughts concerning the initial investigation of the assassination:

It is important that all of the facts surrounding

*President Kennedy's assassination be made public
in a way which will satisfy people in the United
States and abroad that all the facts have been told
and that a statement to this effect be made now.*

*1. The public must be satisfied that Oswald was
assassin; that he did not have confederates who are
still at large; that the evidence was such that he
would have been convicted at trial.*

*2. Speculation about Oswald's motivation ought
to be cut off, and we should have some basis for
rebutting thought that this was a Communist plot
or (as the Iron Curtain press is saying) a right-
wing conspiracy to blame it on the Communists.*

It is worth noting at this point that Hoover had
already taken steps to cut Attorney General Kennedy
and his aides out of his investigation of the assassination entirely. Two of Kennedy's most trusted aides in
the criminal division, Jack Miller and Robert
Peloquin, attempted to inject themselves into
Hoover's investigation of the President's murder and
were pointedly shunned by the FBI, on orders from
the director. Then Hoover deliberately withheld all
reports of his field agents on matters related to the
assassination from both Attorney General Kennedy
and Deputy Attorney General Katzenbach. Thus
Kennedy and Katzenbach never saw any of the FBI
reports of allegations from informants hinting that
Carlos Marcello and his allies might have been
involved in the assassination.

Years later, in an interview, Nicholas Katzenbach
told me that he thought Hoover's case against Oswald
was "a little fishy" at the time, that "it was too good to
be true."

So Hoover conducted his investigation of the assassination presuming Oswald was guilty from the start, which, of course, was contrary to a cardinal principle of U.S. jurisprudence, that of the presumption of innocence. Witnesses who were unsympathetic to Hoover's scenario were ignored. All those who believed they saw gunmen on other floors of the Texas School Book Depository than the sixth, or in other windows than the southeast corner one, were not listened to. Witnesses who believed they heard a shot from the grassy knoll, and there were many, were told to keep quiet. Evidence suggesting that Oswald had been framed, or that he might have had confederates, was suppressed.

One hundred twenty-six of the 266 known witnesses to the shooting were interviewed by the FBI and the Warren Commission about the direction of the shots. Thirty-eight expressed no opinion, 32 named the Texas School Book Depository, and 56 named the grassy knoll as the sources of the shots. Most of the sheriff's deputies watching the motorcade from the opposite side of Dealey Plaza testified the shots came from the triple underpass just beyond the grassy knoll. The Dallas police officers who witnessed the assassination were split: 4 said the grassy knoll, 4 said the Book Depository. Jean Hill, who was standing across the street from the grassy knoll, actually saw a gunman on the knoll. Malcolm Summers, a retired Dallas police officer, thought he heard a shot from the knoll and ran up to find the shooter. He encountered a suspicious individual who seemed to be concealing a rifle under his coat, challenged him, and was taken by surprise when the man flashed Secret Service credentials and told him to back off.

Later the Secret Service informed investigators that no Secret Service agents had been stationed in Dealey Plaza that day. Ed Hoffman also saw something suspicious going on in the area in back of the grassy knoll. From his vantage point behind the knoll he became aware of a flurry of movement on the north side of the picket fence. He saw a man running west along the north side of the fence wearing a dark suit, tie, and an overcoat. The man was carrying a rifle. As he reached a metal pipe railing at the west end of the fence, he tossed the rifle to a second man standing on the west side of the pipe near the railroad tracks that went south over the triple underpass. The second man caught the rifle, disassembled it, placed it in a railroad brakeman's tool bag, then walked north in the general direction of the railroad tower. Near that tower railroad supervisor Sam Holland was watching the grassy knoll area when the shooting broke out. He later testified that he saw a puff of smoke rise above the picket fence on the knoll.

Yet, while Hoover was assembling his case against Oswald-the-lone-gunman he was receiving reports and allegations suggesting conspiracy. One of them he saw fit to transmit to only one man, Secret Service Chief James J. Rowley.

On the morning of November 24, Hoover sent a five-page top secret memorandum, with a covering letter, to Rowley that clearly indicated he believed an impostor had been impersonating Oswald in Mexico City approximately two months before the assassination.

The memorandum was never brought to the attention of President Johnson or the Warren Commission and was withheld from the public until writer Mark Lane obtained an uncensored version of it from the

FBI, by means of a Freedom of Information Act lawsuit, in 1978:

The Central Intelligence Agency advised that on October 1, 1963, an extremely sensitive source had reported that an individual identified himself as Lee Oswald, who contacted the Soviet Embassy in Mexico City inquiring as to any messages. Special Agents of this Bureau, who have conversed with Oswald in Dallas, Texas, have observed photographs and have listened to a recording of his voice. These Special Agents are of the opinion that the above-referred-to individual was not Lee Harvey Oswald.

That an impersonator claiming to be Oswald had visited the Soviet Embassy in Mexico City clearly suggested that someone was deliberately attempting to fabricate an image of Oswald that would be used to frame him for the impending assassination of the President.

Perception of this possibility, which clearly suggested the existence of a conspiracy to assassinate Kennedy that the FBI should have detected in advance, must have been deeply disturbing to J. Edgar Hoover.

But that was not all. On Monday, November 25, the day of the President's funeral, Hoover received an allegation from Mexico City that a man (code-named "D") had shown up at the American Embassy and had told embassy personnel that he had been in the Cuban consulate on September 18 and saw "Cubans pay Oswald a sum of money and talk about Oswald's assassinating someone."

Later on that day Hoover received a telephone call from the New Orleans FBI field office informing him of the arrest of David Ferrie, an alleged friend of Oswald's, on suspicion of having conspired with Oswald to assassinate President Kennedy.

Then, on Tuesday, November 26, the day following Kennedy's funeral, President Johnson and CIA Director John McCone were informed that the U.S. Ambassador to Mexico was convinced that the Cuban government was involved in the assassination.

By the time he received this news, President Johnson had become extremely fearful that circumstantial evidence linking Castro to the assassination would become known to the general public. As we know, Oswald had already been identified by Hoover as a lone gunman "in the category of a nut and the extremist pro-Castro crowd." Johnson and his closest advisers knew they could not control the public's demand for revenge against the Cuban dictator in the event they strongly suspected his involvement in Kennedy's murder. And Johnson knew that a conflict with Cuba could entail a conflict with Cuba's chief ally, the Soviet Union.

Johnson is said to have exclaimed that if rumors of a possible Oswald-Cuban-KGB plot spread they could "lead us into a war that would cost 40 million lives." Accordingly, he telephoned Hoover and told him to put a stop to the rumors and discourage all talk of conspiracy. The Dallas Police were then notified of the President's wishes.

Today, after thirty years, the spirit behind J. Edgar Hoover's response to the assassination of President Kennedy has finally come into full focus. Hoover had no interest whatsoever in uncovering the truth behind the assassination or in bringing the guilty to justice; he was only interested in protecting his reputation and that of the FBI. Hoover, therefore, conducted an investigation that ignored, or suppressed, all evidence suggesting that others, besides Oswald, might have been involved in the assassination.

As Hoover went about conducting his investigation, designed to pin the blame for the assassination wholly on the lone, nut, gunman, Lee Harvey Oswald, who could no longer defend himself since he too had been murdered, what was he actually learning about the crime?

First of all, he already knew that Carlos Marcello had taken out a contract on Kennedy's life in the fall of 1962 and that Santos Trafficante had expressed knowledge of the contract to José Alémán several weeks later. Furthermore, he was aware that a friend of both Marcello and Trafficante, Jimmy Hoffa, had divulged a plan to kill the Kennedy brothers to Edward Partin in the summer of 1962.

Hoover also knew the allegation of FBI informant, Eugene De Laparra, that a Marcello associate, Ben Tregle, had expressed foreknowledge of the impending assassination seven months before it occurred. In addition, he had learned from another FBI informant, Gene Sumner of Darien, Georgia, that someone closely resembling Oswald had been observed accepting some money from a Marcello lieutenant at Marcello's New Orleans headquarters in the Town and Country Motel.

Then, on December 27, two days after Jack Ruby killed Oswald, Hoover received an allegation from an FBI informant in Oakland, one Bobby Gene Moore, who had once worked for Jack Ruby, that Ruby had "gangster connections" in Dallas, that he was close to Mafia boss, Joe Civello.

Hoover knew only too well who Joe Civello was. He knew that Civello had attended the Apalachin, New York crime conclave in 1957 as Carlos Marcello's representative and that he was Marcello's deputy in Dallas. Hoover knew that the two men who had been arrested for assassinating Kennedy, Oswald and Ferrie, were connected to Marcello. Now he knew Jack Ruby was also connected to Marcello.

During the last days of November and the first week of December, Hoover and his agents were working frantically to complete their initial investigation of the assassination, what would, by December 9, become the five-volume FBI *Summary Report*. In this massive pile of paper, Hoover would depict Oswald as a lone, communist gunman, without confederates of any stripe, who fired all the shots that wounded Kennedy and Governor John Connally from the sixth-floor southeast window of the Texas School Book Depository, using an Italian rifle he had ordered by mail. And he would depict Oswald's killer, Jack Ruby, as a patriotic nightclub owner, with no connections to organized crime, who acted on impulse, to spare Mrs. Kennedy the agony of having to attend an eventual trial of Oswald. To buttress his contentions, Hoover ignored all witnesses who testified they heard shots being fired from the grassy knoll and all witnesses who saw armed men in windows of the Texas School Book Depository other than in the sixth-floor southeast corner window. It goes without saying that the testimony of Julia Ann Mercer that she saw a white male take a rifle case out from the back of a pickup truck on Elm Street and carry it up the slope to the grassy knoll the morning of the assassination was not included in the *Summary Report*.

During the same period Hoover's agents in New

Orleans were conducting an intensive investigation of David Ferrie that revealed Oswald had seen a great deal of Ferrie during the summer of 1963 and that Ferrie was also seeing a great deal of Carlos Marcello during the same period.

Meanwhile President Johnson had formed the Warren Commission to investigate the assassination, and on December 6 the Warren Commission held its first executive session.

While Hoover was busy pinning the blame for the assassination on Oswald, acting alone, he was also having his agents in New Orleans reinvestigate David Ferrie, ordering them to reinterview Ferrie on December 5 and 13.

And what did those agents find out? More evidence that Ferrie had lied about the purpose of his post-assassination all-night drive to Texas through a blinding thunderstorm and more evidence that he had lied in denying his friendship with Oswald. By December 13, four days after Hoover had submitted his five volume *Summary Report* on the assassination to President Johnson and the Warren Commission, concluding that Oswald had killed the President, acting alone, Hoover knew that Oswald had a close personal relationship with David Ferrie who, in turn, had a close relationship with Carlos Marcello, a man who had revealed his plans to assassinate the President as early as September 1962. Furthermore, he now knew that Oswald had been brought up by Charles "Dutz" Murret, who was an associate of Carlos Marcello, and that Jack Ruby was closely connected to an associate of Carlos Marcello.

Yet just when all the threads of an apparent conspiracy were coming together, what does J. Edgar

Hoover do? He instructs his agents in Dallas to shut down their investigation of Ferrie on December 16.

The FBI's secret investigation of David Ferrie's links to Oswald and Marcello fill some one-hundred pages and yet none of the information on those pages is included in the *Summary Report,* and none of it apparently reached the Warren Commission.

Furthermore, Hoover chose to withhold from his *Summary Report* and from the Warren Commission, Edward Partin's allegation that he witnessed Jimmy Hoffa outline a plan to kill the Kennedy brothers and that during the two years and two months and ten days of the Kennedy administration, the CIA, in alliance with the Mafia, made at least eight attempts, probably more, to assassinate the president of a neighboring state, Fidel Castro.

The FBI's *Summary Report* of December 9, 1963, and its *Supplemental Report* of January 13, 1964, were masterpieces of disinformation and suppression of vital evidence. They were J. Edgar Hoover's greatest achievement as a twister of facts to suit theories. For a while they satisfied the public. But, as Sherlock Holmes admonished, "the truth will out." Within three years of their promulgation Hoover's theories would begin to crumble as writers such as Sylvia Meagher, Mark Lane, Richard Popkin, Harold Weisberg, Edward Epstein, and Josiah Thompson successfully challenged them.

As might be expected, these writers enraged Hoover. But it was not until Hoover was made aware in 1967 of an unpublished manuscript by Pulitzer-prize-winning journalist, Ed Reid, that alleged Carlos Marcello had outlined a plan to assassinate President Kennedy at a meeting with Edward Becker at his

Churchill Farms estate in September 1962, that Hoover attempted to censor such writers. In a June 5, 1967 memorandum from the Los Angeles FBI office to Director Hoover, it was stated that Agent George Bland had contacted author Ed Reid on May 26, on behalf of the bureau, "to discredit Becker to Reid in order that the Carlos Marcello incident would be deleted from the book by Reid."

Ed Reid would not give in to FBI pressure and therefore let Ed Becker's allegation of a Marcello plan to assassinate President Kennedy stand in his book.

The question inevitably arises: If J. Edgar Hoover was aware of Hoffa's and Marcello's plans to kill Kennedy and Trafficante's apparent foreknowledge of those plans, why didn't he notify the Secret Service and the Kennedy brothers of them and all the other threats against the President uttered by mobsters throughout 1962 and 1963?

Hoover was obliged by federal law to notify the Secret Service of all threats made against public officials that came to his attention as director of the FBI.

One is tempted to conclude that Hoover did not tell the Secret Service about the plots because he wanted them to succeed. Hoover detested the Kennedy brothers and was fearful they would retire him from the FBI in 1964 when Kennedy would presumably be reelected President. On the other hand, Hoover had long enjoyed a close relationship with Lyndon Johnson, his neighbor in Washington for many years. In all probability if Kennedy were killed and Johnson succeeded to the presidency, Johnson would keep him on as FBI director, which is precisely what happened.

On May 8, 1964, President Lyndon Johnson issued an executive order waiving the mandatory retirement age provision for the position of director of the FBI and in so doing renewed Hoover's term of office indefinitely.

If, as it appears to be the case, J. Edgar Hoover knew of the existence of a conspiracy to assassinate President Kennedy, and did nothing to prevent it from succeeding, he, in the eyes of the law, must be regarded as an accessory to the crime. An accessory before the fact and after the fact since in addition to allowing the presidential murder to take place he also attempted to cover it up and prevent the identities of the conspirators from becoming known.

It took twenty years from his death for J. Edgar Hoover's legacy to the American people to finally come into focus. That legacy was allowing organized crime to grow and flourish into a force powerful enough to assassinate a president of the United States and get away with it.

CHAPTER 12

President Johnson,
J. Edgar Hoover, and
the Warren Commission

Lyndon Johnson, the man who had
the most to gain from the assassination of President
Kennedy, was understandably anxious to quell all
rumors of conspiracy in the wake of the murder in
Dallas. He was especially fearful of the consequences
of rumors linking the suspected assassin, Lee Harvey
Oswald, to Castro's Cuba and to the Soviet Union for
he felt they could lead to war if they were not emphatically suppressed. He was also acutely sensitive to
suspicions that he himself might have been involved
in the crime. For these reasons he took immediate
steps to discourage all talk of conspiracy. He told his

good friend, J. Edgar Hoover, to quench the flames of conspiracy wherever they erupted. Pinning the blame for the assassination on Oswald, the lone "commie nut," was politically acceptable to Johnson. On the morning of Saturday, November 23, he took the trouble of phoning the chief of homicide of the Dallas Police, Will Fritz, who was questioning Oswald, to order him to discourage all rumors of conspiracy. So concerned was he with this issue that he even phoned the Parkland Memorial Hospital physician, Charles Crenshaw, as he was attending the dying Oswald, asking him to obtain a deathbed confession from the stricken suspected assassin. Unfortunately it was too late. Oswald went to his death in silence.

It was primarily to quell rumors of conspiracy that President Johnson on November 29, 1963, issued an executive order establishing The President's Commission to investigate the assassination of President Kennedy, the wounding of Governor John Connally, and the murder of Police Officer J. D. Tippit, popularly known as the Warren Commission after its chairman, Chief Justice Earl Warren.

The seven men Johnson picked to serve on the commission represented a spectrum of the American establishment that Johnson felt would not be inclined to uncover any sinister conspiracies capable of unsettling the collective American psyche. Each of them represented an area of the national life he might be counted on to defend against any accusations that someone associated with that area might have been involved in the assassination. Chief Justice Earl Warren, who had agreed to serve as chairman of the commission with extreme reluctance, was the highest-ranking government official on the commission and as such could be expected to protect the reputation of the government he served. He therefore would be unlikely to countenance discussion of such potentially reputation damaging government initiatives as the CIA-Mafia plots to assassinate Fidel Castro in the deliberations of the commission. Former director of the CIA, Allen Dulles, who had been fired by President Kennedy for his role in the Bay of Pigs disaster, could be expected to look after the interests of the agency he had served for eight years. (Years later, it was discovered that he regularly briefed CIA chief of counterintelligence, James Jesus Augelton, on the commission's secret deliberations.) Likewise, Congressman Gerald R. Ford, a close friend of J. Edgar Hoover, might be expected to make sure that any allegation linking Oswald or Ruby, or any other suspect in the assassination, to the FBI would be quickly disposed of (Later, it was revealed that Ford was regularly briefing the FBI's liaison with the White House, Cartha de Loach, on the commission's secret deliberations. "He was our man, our informant, on the Warren Commission," wrote J. Edgar Hoover's deputy director at the time of the assassination, William Sullivan, in his memoirs.)

Commission members Richard Russell, a Georgia Democrat, and John Sherman Cooper, a Kentucky Republican, as arch conservatives not prone to conspirational thinking, might be counted on to protect the interests of the South against suspicions of the possible involvement of southern white segregationists in the assassination. As it turned out, however, Senator Russell would be the one member of the commission who refused to accept the commission's verdict of no conspiracy and the sole member who asked Chairman Warren to list him as a dissenter in the commission's final report.

Former international banker and high commissioner for Germany, John J. McCloy, the incarnation of the "sound," statesman-businessman, could be counted on to look after the interests of the military-industrial complex. And Congressman Hale Boggs, Democrat from Louisiana, could be relied on to defend the reputation of Lee Harvey Oswald's home state, and see to it that his principal financial backer, and behind-the-scenes power in the state government, Carlos Marcello, would not be mentioned in the commission's deliberations, which, as it turned out he never was. Boggs, however, was, with Senator Russell, a dissenter on the commission. Years later a former aide to the Louisiana congressman recalled: "Hale always returned to one thing: Hoover lied his eyes out to the Commission—on Oswald, on Ruby, on their friends, the bullets, the guns, you name it . . ."

J. Edgar Hoover was against the formation of the Warren Commission and told President Johnson he was, to no avail. As soon as Johnson appointed the seven commissioners Hoover perceived the commission as an adversary to *his* investigation and proceeded to do all that was in his power to subvert it. Since the Warren Commission had no investigative arm of its own, it had to rely perforce on Hoover's FBI for all evidence and information on the case. Realizing the power this situation gave him, Hoover adopted a strategy vis-à-vis the Warren Commission of manipulation and the selective withholding of evidence.

How did Hoover manipulate the Warren Commission?

The Warren Commission was faced with the impossible task of determining who was behind the assassination of President Kennedy and the murders of Officer Tippit and Lee Harvey Oswald and at the same time satisfying Lyndon Johnson's wish that the commission lay to rest all allegations of conspiracy.

J. Edgar Hoover was faced with the challenge of convincing the commission that Lee Harvey Oswald, acting alone, killed President Kennedy and Officer Tippit, and that Jack Ruby, in turn, killed Oswald out of patriotic indignation, also acting alone. Above all he had to make sure that the Marcello contract on Kennedy's life and Lee Harvey Oswald's and Jack Ruby's ties to Marcello never saw the light of day.

As it would turn out, Hoover met those formidable challenges with consummate skill.

On November 26, the day after Ruby shot Oswald, Hoover told assistant FBI director, Alan Belmont, that the FBI *Summary Report* he was preparing on the assassination "is to settle the dust, insofar as Oswald and his activities are concerned, both from the standpoint he is the man who assassinated the President, and relative to Oswald himself and his activities and background."

Meanwhile allegations of possible conspiracy were pouring into the FBI field offices from all over the nation and were ending up at headquarters on J. Edgar Hoover's desk.

One of these was a long teletype from the New Orleans FBI office about the interrogation of David Ferrie who had been arrested the day before on suspicions that he had conspired with Oswald to murder President Kennedy. The teletype told of the arrest of Ferrie after his mysterious two-day post-assassination trip through Texas, and the testimony of Jack Martin, which alleged that Ferrie had taught Oswald how to fire a rifle with telescopic sight and had once overheard him discussing with Oswald the necessity of assassinating President Kennedy. It went on to tell of Ferrie's association with the violently anti-Castro Cuban Revolutionary Council and of his employment by Carlos Marcello's lawyer, G. Wray Gill.

The next day Hoover received a report of an allegation made to the FBI office in Oakland that linked Jack Ruby to an associate of Carlos Marcello's. The report of Wednesday, November 27, told of an interview with Bobby Gene Moore in which he reported to an FBI agent that Jack Ruby had "gangster connections" in Dallas, including Joseph Civello, Marcello's deputy in that city.

Then, on the following day, November 28, there arrived on Hoover's desk the allegation of FBI informant Eugene De Laparra that he had overheard Vincent Marcello's associate, Ben Tregle, saying "There is a price on the President's head, and other members of the Kennedy family. Someone will kill Kennedy when he comes down South."

What had been Hoover's response to these allegations? He ignored them in favor of leaking news to the press of the FBI's forthcoming *Summary Report* on the assassination, indicating Oswald was the lone unaided assassin.

The press dutifully reported the leak:

> *An exhaustive FBI report nearly ready for the White House will indicate that Lee Harvey Oswald was the lone and unaided assassin of President Kennedy, government sources say.*

The manipulation of the Warren Commission, and the press, had begun.

Hoover was fortunate to have at least one member of the commission as anxious as he was to pin the blame for the assassination on Lee Harvey Oswald, acting alone, and that was former CIA Director Allen Dulles. There would be no need to manipulate Dulles, for, of all the commissioners, he had potentially the most to lose from a finding of conspiracy.

At the first executive session of the commission, held on December 6, Dulles gave each one of his fellow commissioners a copy of a book about U.S. political assassinations, which claimed that all presidential murders had been the work of lone, alienated madmen. This suggests that Dulles was attempting to predispose the commissioners against a finding of conspiracy possibly because he was fearful that during the course of the investigation of the Kennedy murder, the elaborate conspiracy to murder Fidel Castro that he, Dulles, had been so involved in, might come to light.

For, as we know, Dulles had been one of the major conspirators behind the CIA-sponsored plot to assassinate the president of Cuba that included four CIA officers besides himself, and at least three, possibly four, Mafia leaders, including Santos Trafficante and Carlos Marcello.

Allen Dulles was aware that if persuasive evidence were presented to the commission suggesting that Oswald or Ruby, or both, might have been used by the Mafia or the CIA, a comprehensive investigation of the Kennedy murder might uncover the plots to assassinate the Cuban president. Accordingly Dulles never told his fellow commissioners about the CIA-Mafia conspiracy against Castro and did everything possible to promote the lone-assassin solution to the Kennedy murder case.

It did not take long for J. Edgar Hoover to foist that solution on the Warren Commission.

The Commission had held its first executive session on December 6. By December 9 the FBI's five-volume *Summary Report* of its investigation of the assassination had been printed and copies had been sent to the members of the Warren Commission. On that same day Hoover made his first major move toward manipulating the commission's investigation of the assassination. He had Deputy Attorney General Katzenbach send a message to commission chairman, Earl Warren, recommending that the commission immediately issue a public statement that the FBI report clearly showed Oswald was the sole assassin and that he was unaided by confederates.

That the FBI *Summary Report* did clearly indicate Oswald was the sole assassin was true. But, unknown to anyone, save Hoover and some of his agents in New Orleans, an FBI investigation of David Ferrie was unfolding in Texas and New Orleans at the very moment the *Summary Report* was being disseminated that threatened to produce convincing evidence to contradict the conclusions of the report.

FBI reports on that highly secret investigation, which, it will be recalled, lasted until December 18, did not strengthen the notion that Lee Harvey Oswald, acting alone, killed Kennedy. Rather they *strengthened suspicions that David Ferrie might have been involved with Oswald, and Carlos Marcello, in a conspiracy to assassinate the president.*

J. Edgar Hoover had included in his *Summary Report* only documents that pointed toward Oswald as the sole assassin of the President unaided by confederates. Thanks to his selective withholding of documents, the members of the commission never learned that a friend of Lee Harvey Oswald's, the openly anti-Kennedy David Ferrie, met with a man who had repeatedly threatened to kill Kennedy, Mafia boss Carlos Marcello, at Marcello's Louisiana estate on the two weekends immediately preceding the assassination. Needless to say, Ferrie and Marcello were never called to testify before the commission.

Because Hoover withheld from the commission Edward Partin's allegation about Jimmy Hoffa's threat to kill both Kennedy brothers, and José Alémán's testimony to the FBI that Santos Trafficante had told him President Kennedy was "going to be hit," the commission did not call Jimmy Hoffa, Edward Partin, José Alémán, and Santos Trafficante to testify before it either.

Hoover was also remiss in not informing the Warren Commission that Lee Harvey Oswald's uncle and surrogate father, Charles Murret, was a bookmaker and gambler affiliated with one of Carlos Marcello's major associates.

Assistant counsel for the Warren Commission, Burt Griffin, now a federal judge, told the House Select Comittee on Assassinations in 1978 that the commission had been aware of Jack Ruby's underworld connections, but since it had no evidence that Oswald had any contacts with the underworld, it discounted the possibility that organized crime could have been behind the assassination.

Today Judge Griffin is bitter about the way the Warren Commission conducted its investigation of Jack Ruby. Griffin, a young attorney not long out of law school, had been specifically assigned the investigation of Jack Ruby. He had felt in 1964 that Ruby might have been the key to unlocking an underworld conspiracy to assassinate the President, but he had been severely restricted by lack of time, staff, and information. "There's no way we're going to do this job in the period of time we're talking about," he told the commission general counsel, J. Lee Rankin. But Rankin, under intense pressure from Johnson, was unwilling to extend the term of the investigation. "At this stage we are supposed to be closing doors, not opening them," he told another staff counsel, Wesley Liebeler, who had raised other issues that threatened to prolong the investigation.

Griffin recalls today that he felt extremely frustrated by the almost total lack of cooperation he experienced on the part of the two government agencies the Warren Commission was most dependent on for reliable evidentiary data, the FBI and the CIA. Since we now know that J. Edgar Hoover withheld vital FBI documents from the Warren Commission linking Ruby to members of organized crime, Griffin simply did not have the information that would have led him to suspect a Mafia conspiracy in the assassination. According to Griffin, the CIA's lack of cooperation was even worse. Griffin had sent the CIA a memorandum outlining what he knew about Ruby's underworld contacts and requesting further information on such contacts from the CIA. His request drew no response from the agency (which, it was later learned by the House Assassination Committee in 1979, had an abundance of information on Ruby's mob connections in its files).

But what irritates Judge Griffin more than anything else today is that when it came time to interrogate Jack Ruby in depth, he, the foremost expert on Ruby on the commission, was excluded by the commission from participating in the interrogation, which, in the end, was held in June 1964 by commission chairman, Earl Warren, and commission member, Gerald Ford. (During Warren's questioning of Ruby, Ruby told Warren he could not answer any questions in the Dallas jail, but if he were taken to Washington he would open up. Warren refused to take him to Washington.)

What, in the end, happened to the FBI field office reports of allegations suggesting conspirational activity on the part of the Marcello organization once they reached the Warren Commission, if they ever did?

The answer seems to be they were buried under an avalanche of crank allegations, "nut stuff," as one Warren Commission staff member called them. More than likely they were not taken seriously because Hoover failed to elucidate their sinister significance to the commission. Thus when the FBI report of Eugene De Laparra's allegation that an associate of Vincent Marcello, Ben Tregle, expressed foreknowledge of the impending assassination reached the Warren Commission no explanation of who Vincent Marcello and Ben Tregle were was provided by Hoover. And so it was disregarded as yet another example of the "nut stuff" that came pouring into FBI headquarters in avalanche proportions.

As the Warren Commission's tedious deliberations ground on, Hoover's efforts to control and manipulate the commission became apparent to several Commission members as the following exchange between Dulles, Rankin, and Boggs attests:

> Dulles: Why would it be in their [the FBI's] interest to say he [Oswald] is clearly the only guilty one?
>
> Rankin: They would like us to fold up and quit.
>
> Boggs: This closes the case, you see. Don't you see?
>
> Rankin: They found the man. There is nothing more to do. The commission supports their conclusions, and we can go home and that is the end of it.
>
> Boggs: I don't even like to see this being taken down.
>
> Dulles: Yes. I think this record ought to be destroyed.

Another section of the same Warren Commission transcript reveals that General Counsel Rankin was deeply suspicious of the way the FBI had been conducting the investigation of Kennedy's murder. As a former solicitor general, Rankin had long experience dealing with Hoover and the FBI, and this was the first time he had found Hoover's organization coming so quickly to a firm "evaluation" of a case, without running out all leads.

> Rankin: There is this factor too that . . . is somewhat of an issue in this case, and I suppose you are all aware of it. That is that the FBI is very explicit that Oswald is the assassin, or was the assassin, and they are very explicit that there was no conspiracy, and they are also saying they are continuing their investigation. Now in my experience of almost nine years, in the first place it is hard to get

them to say when you think you have got a case tight enough to convict somebody, that this is the person who committed the crime. In my experience with the FBI they don't do that. They claim that they don't evaluate [come to conclusions] and it is my uniform experience that they don't do that. Secondly, they have not run out all kinds of leads in Mexico or in Russia and so forth which they could probably—It is not our business, it is the very . . .

Dulles: What is that?

Rankin: They haven't run out all the leads on the information and they could probably say . . . that isn't our business.

Dulles: Yes.

Rankin: But they are concluding that there can't be a conspiracy without those being run out. Now that is not from my experience with the FBI.

Dulles: It is not. You are quite right. I have seen a great many reports.

Rankin's suspicions were well founded. There were indeed "all kinds of leads in Mexico and Russia" and also in Miami and New Orleans that Hoover had been supposed to "run out" and had not, while still insisting categorically there had been no conspiracy.

An analysis of what Hoover chose not to report to the Warren Commission, or chose not to elucidate for the commission, reveals that what he was trying to conceal was the possibility that members of organized crime might have been involved in the assassination, and specifically that the Marcello organization might have played a leading role in plotting and carrying out the crime. For almost all of Hoover's withholding of information and failures to elucidate information that might have cast light on the existence of a conspiracy had to do with organized crime.

One has to conclude that Hoover knew far more about the circumstances surrounding the President's murder than he let on. One does not deliberately withhold, or suppress information in a criminal investigation if one considers that information innocuous.

It is my opinion that J. Edgar Hoover knew, or at least suspected, that Carlos Marcello and his criminal organization might have played a significant role in both the assassination of the President and the murder of the President's suspected assassin, and that Hoover deliberately concealed evidence of the possibility from the Warren Commission out of a combination of fear and egotism. Fear that the FBI's failure to detect an assassination conspiracy involving Marcello would result in his and the FBI's disgrace. Egotism in that he was willing to cast aside his suspicions, and in so doing renounce the pursuit of truth and justice in the case, in favor of incriminating a man whose apparent credentials as a "commie" vindicated his insistence that communism, not organized crime, was America's number-one enemy.

In its final report the Warren Commission concluded that Lee Harvey Oswald, acting alone, had assassinated President Kennedy and that Jack Ruby, acting alone, had killed Oswald.

The commission left behind an enormous quantity of documents. Most of them were deposited in the National Archives. Others were incorporated in twenty-six volumes accompanying the commission's final report, which became known as the *Warren Report*. In 1980, two Kennedy assassination researchers, Sylvia Meagher and Gary Owens, compiled a ninety-four-page index to the *Warren Report* and its twenty-six volumes of hearings and exhibits. Nowhere in that index can the names Jimmy Hoffa, Santos Trafficante, and Carlos Marcello be found. J. Edgar Hoover had seen to that.

CHAPTER 13

The Kennedys: Unwitting Accessories After the Fact

> *George De Mohrenschildt: Janet, you were Jack Kennedy's mother-in-law and I am a complete stranger. I would spend my own money and lots of my time to find out who were the real assassins or the conspirators. Don't you want any further investigaiton? You have infinite resources.*
>
> *Janet Auchincloss: Jack is dead and nothing will bring him back.*

The apparently passive reaction of the Kennedy family and its in-laws to the murder of John F. Kennedy has been one of the more elusive mysteries of the Kennedy assassination case. The response of Jacqueline Kennedy's mother, Janet Auchincloss, to George de Mohrenschildt's question was typical. De Mohrenschildt, the Russian émigré nobleman who had been a friend of both Lee Harvey Oswald and Jackie's family, the Bouviers, recorded his post-assassination conversation with Janet

Auchincloss in his unpublished manuscript on his relationship with Oswald entitled *I am a Patsy! I am a Patsy!* Like her mother, Jacqueline Kennedy also remained opposed to further investigation of the assassination stating publicly: "What good will it do? Nothing can bring Jack back."

Robert Kennedy admitted he never read a line of the *Warren Report* but publicly declared he accepted the conclusion of the Warren Commission that Oswald, acting alone, was solely responsible for killing his brother.

Edward M. Kennedy, like his brother Robert, admitted he never read the *Warren Report*, but nevertheless accepted the Warren Commission's findings as the final solution to the crime.

On the eve of the 1975 investigation of alleged assassination plots against foreign leaders by the Senate Intelligence Committee and of the response of the U.S. intelligence agencies to the assassination of President Kennedy, Eunice Kennedy Shriver, speaking on behalf of the Kennedy family, declared that the family saw no reason to reopen the investigation of President Kennedy's assassination.

What are we to make of this? For thirty years the Kennedy family has remained publicly indifferent to the question of who was responsible for the murder of their most prominent family member, the thirty-fifth president of the United States.

As we shall see the family has been repeatedly guilty of obstruction of justice in the assassination case and has even, albeit unwittingly, acted as accessories after the fact to the crime.

Now, finally, on the thirtieth anniversary of the assassination, the reasons behind the Kennedy family's seeming indifference to the resolution of the assassination case are coming into focus.

First, it is now known that Robert Kennedy privately suspected that one or both of his two principal targets in his war against organized crime—Jimmy Hoffa and Carlos Marcello—may have been involved in the murder of his brother. His suspicions are hinted at by certain post-assassination comments of his about the crime.

Robert Kennedy and William Hundley, head of the Organized Crime and Racketeering division of the Justice Department, had been presiding over a conference on organized crime at the Justice Department the day of John Kennedy's assassination, and had been looking forward that morning to receiving word from New Orleans of a favorable verdict in the Justice Department's case against Carlos Marcello. If the verdict came in on time, Kennedy wanted to announce it at the afternoon session. It would give the conference a lift. But instead of receiving word of Marcello's conviction, Kennedy received word of his brother's murder in Dallas in the midst of a lunch break at his McLean, Virginia estate. Calling off the afternoon session at the Justice Department, Kennedy got into a discussion of the assassination with his press secretary, Edwin Guthman. According to Guthman, Kennedy said:

> *I thought they might get one of us . . . but Jack, after what he'd been through never worried about it . . . I thought it would be me.*

It seems obvious that by "they" Kennedy was referring to certain leaders of organized crime. At his morning conference he and Walter Sheridan and William Hundley had been addressing U.S. attorneys from all over the country on the prosecutions of Jimmy Hoffa in Nashville and Carlos Marcello in New Orleans.

Two weeks later, while Kennedy was having dinner with historian Arthur Schlesinger in Washington, the two discussed Lee Harvey Oswald briefly. Kennedy remarked that there seemed little doubt Oswald was guilty but there was still doubt if he had acted alone or was part of a larger plot, "whether organized by Castro or gangsters."

Three years later, during the Garrison investigation, Robert Kennedy asked his former chief of the "get Hoffa squad" at the Justice Department, Walter Sheridan, who was covering Garrison's investigation for NBC, if he would look into the matter of whether Carlos Marcello might have been involved. Sheridan, aware that allegations of Marcello involvement were swirling around New Orleans at the time, conducted an informal investigation and concluded guardedly that Marcello might well have been involved. When he voiced his suspicions to Kennedy, Kennedy told him not to continue, that he "didn't want to know" anything further. Obviously if his brother had been killed as a result of a conspiracy involving Marcello, he, Robert Kennedy, as the persecutor of Marcello, bore a degree of blame for his brother's murder.

Since Frank Ragano first made his allegation on January 14, 1992 that Hoffa, Trafficante, and Marcello plotted and carried out the assassination of President Kennedy, several former associates of Robert Kennedy have come forward and voiced their suspicions as to who was behind the assassination, and

Senator John F. Kennedy questioning a witness at a Senate rackets committee hearing. (1959)

Photo credit: Hank Walker, *Life* magazine, © Time Inc.

Carlos Marcello (left), his brother, Vincent Marcello, and Los Angeles gangster, Mickey Cohen, at a Senate rackets committee hearing. (1959)

Photo credit: AP/Wide World Photos

Jimmy Hoffa and Robert Kennedy face off during a recess at a Senate rackets committee hearing. (1959)

Photo credit: UPI/Bettmann

Photo credit: Reprinted with permission from *The Tampa Tribune*

Jimmy Hoffa with his attorney, Frank Ragano. (August 1962)

★

FBI Director J. Edgar Hoover with President Kennedy, October 31, 1962. Hoover appears to have the upper hand.

Lee Harvey Oswald handing out *Fair Play for Cuba* pamphlets in New Orleans, summer of 1963. The pro-Castro operation was subsequently demonstrated to have been a charade.

✮

Guy Banister, associate of Carlos Marcello and David Ferrie, for whom Oswald worked part-time in the summer of 1963. He is believed to have plotted the murder of President Kennedy with Marcello and Ferrie.

David Ferrie, anti-Kennedy friend of Oswald, and anti-Castro activist. He worked as an investigator for Guy Banister and Carlos Marcello in the summer of 1963 and was arrested in New Orleans, on November 25th, as a suspect in the assassination in November 1963.

Edward Becker, private investigator and Las Vegas businessman, who was present when Carlos Marcello outlined a plan to murder President Kennedy in September 1962. In 1978 he testified before the House Select Committee on Assassinations.

Jack Ruby, Dallas striptease nightclub owner and low level gangster in the Marcello organization, who killed Oswald in Dallas Police Headquarters on Sunday, November 24, 1963. He is pictured at his 1965 murder trial.

President Lyndon B. Johnson congratulates J. Edgar Hoover upon waiving Hoover's mandatory retirement in 1964. Hoover remained director of the FBI until his death in 1972.

Carlos Marcello at the height of his power in 1968.

Santos Trafficante, Florida Mafia boss and friend of Carlos Marcello, with his attorney, Frank Ragano, October 3, 1970.

Edward Grady Partin, Louisiana Teamsters official who witnessed Jimmy Hoffa outlining a plan to murder John and Robert Kennedy in the summer of 1962. He testified before the House Select Committee on Assassinations in 1978.

Photo credit: UPI/Bettmann

Photo credit: AP/WideWorld Photos

José Aléman, a witness to Santos Trafficante expressing foreknowledge of the Kennedy assassination in Miami, October 1963. He testified before the House Select Committee on Assassinations in 1978.

★

Frank Ragano, former attorney for Jimmy Hoffa and Santos Trafficante and friend of Carlos Marcello, as he is today. In 1987 he heard a deathbed confession of Trafficante's about the assassination of President Kennedy.

Five of the thirteen Mafia leaders arrested at the La Stella restaurant in Forest Hills, New York on September 22, 1966, return with their attorneys for lunch. Frank Ragano is at the head of the table; to his right are Santos Trafficante and Carlos Marcello.

who Robert Kennedy suspected was behind the crime.

Frank Mankiewicz, Robert Kennedy's former press secretary, believes Ragano's allegation is the most "plausible explanation of the assassination." He, too, recalls that Robert Kennedy was deeply suspicious of Marcello's possible involvement.

Adam Walinsky, another former aide to Robert Kennedy, agrees. Walinsky told Jack Newfield of the *New York Post* that he was convinced Ragano's scenario is the most plausible one.

Finally Richard Goodwin, a former aide to John, Robert, and Edward Kennedy, told Newfield that Frank Ragano's allegation is far and away the most convincing explanation of the assassination and one which, if he were alive today, Robert Kennedy would have certainly subscribed to.

Yet, despite these suspicions, Robert Kennedy knew that if Hoffa or Marcello was involved, even though he was still attorney general he could do nothing about investigating their possible complicity, much less initiate legal proceedings against them. This realization must have given Kennedy such a debilitating sense of frustration and futility that he had no choice but to swallow his suspicions and issue a pro-forma endorsement of the Warren Commission's findings, even though he suspected they were invalid.

To understand why Robert Kennedy felt he was powerless to do anything about investigating the possibility of Hoffa's or Marcello's involvement in his brother's murder, we must consider the extent to which Robert Kennedy and his family were compromised in relation to organized crime and how, as a result, Robert Kennedy had become a virtual hostage to his enemies, including, above all J. Edgar Hoover.

What did Hoover and the Mafia know about the Kennedys that would render Robert Kennedy a virtual hostage to them?

The list is long and complicated. We shall consider what Hoover knew that certain Mafia leaders and Mafia-controlled labor union leaders knew also. Hoover knew that Joseph P. Kennedy had done considerable business with Frank Costello during the prohibition era. He knew that Joseph P. Kennedy had solicited a contribution from Sam Giancana to his son Jack's campaign to win the West Virginia primary, and that when Robert Kennedy later turned the heat on Sam Giancana, the Chicago Mafia boss let it be known that he felt he had been double-crossed. Hoover was fully aware that the Kennedy brothers knew of the CIA-Mafia plots to assassinate the president of Cuba and did nothing to stop them. He knew of John F. Kennedy's innumerable affairs with women of dubious reputation, both before and during his marriage to Jacqueline Bouvier, the two most imprudent of which were with Sam Giancana's girlfriend Judith Campbell and the actress Marilyn Monroe. Recently Hoover had received persuasive reports from Scotland Yard that the President had been involved with one of the call girls from the ring that had brought down Great Britain's Minister of Defense, John Profumo. And he had evidence in his files also of the attorney general's brief fling with Miss Monroe and of the tapes Jimmy Hoffa's wireman, Bernard Spindell, had secretly recorded of their encounters.

Considering what Hoover knew about Robert

Kennedy and his family, could Robert have *not* accepted the FBI director's solution to the murder of his brother? Could he as attorney general, have disputed publicly the conclusions of his subordinate, J. Edgar Hoover, without risking the gravest personal and political consequences? Nicholas Katzenbach told me that when Robert Kennedy resumed his duties as attorney general in late January 1964 he seemed to disassociate himself from the investigation of the assassination and even told Katzenbach that he *preferred that there be no investigation at all.* Katzenbach also told me that Hoover never sent any of the FBI teletypes and reports on the assassination case either to him, Katzenbach, or to Robert Kennedy. This, of course, meant that the two highest officials of the Justice Department never received any of the conspiracy allegations involving associates of the Marcellos or the reports linking Jack Ruby to organized crime. Nor did they receive transcripts of any of the taped conversations the FBI had made of various Mafia bosses threatening the lives of the Kennedy brothers in 1962 and 1963.

Several conversations of members of organized crime about the Kennedy brothers, which the FBI had picked up through wiretaps and concealed listening devices, revealed the extent of their hatred and resentment of the President and the attorney general.

On February 9, 1962, Angelo Bruno, boss of the leading organized crime family of Philadelphia, was overheard talking with one of his capiregime, Willie Weisburg.

Weisburg: See what Kennedy done. With

Kennedy a guy should take a knife, like one of them other guys, and stab and kill the fucker, where he is now. Somebody should kill the fucker. I mean it. This is true. Honest to God. It's about time to go. But I tell you something. I hope I get a week's notice. I'll kill. Right in the fuckin' in the White House. Somebody's got to get rid of this fucker.

Angelo Bruno agreed with Weisburg but advised him to be cautious, telling him that sometimes the man following the man who has been eliminated turns out to be worse.

On May 2, 1962, the FBI overheard Michelino Clemente, a capo-regime in the Genovese family, express sentiments similar to Weisburg's:

Clemente: Bob Kennedy won't stop today until he puts us all in jail all over the country. Until the commission meets and puts its foot down, things will be at a standstill. When we meet, we all got to shake hands, and sit down and talk, and, if there is any trouble with a particular regime, it's got to be kept secret, and only the heads are to know about it, otherwise some broad finds out, and finally the newspapers.

At around the same time, the FBI overheard an unidentified Genovese family member saying:

> I want the President indicted, because I
> know he was whacking all those broads.
> Sinatra brought them out. I'd like to hit
> Kennedy. I would gladly go to the peniten-
> tiary for the rest of my life, believe me.

On October 31, 1963, the FBI picked up a conversation between two of the Maggadino brothers of
Buffalo:

> Peter Maggadino: President Kennedy he should
> drop dead.
> Stefano Maggadino: They should kill the whole
> family, the mother and father, too.

Seen with the advantage of thirty years of research
into the investigations of the Kennedy assassination,
it seems outrageous that Hoover never informed
Robert Kennedy of the FBI's wiretaps of Mafia leaders threatening him and his brother and of the several allegations that had been made to the FBI within
a week of the assassination hinting at the possible
involvement of the Marcello organization in the
President's murder.

It is now clear that Robert Kennedy's passive
response to his brother's assassination and his
acquiescent acceptance of the findings of the FBI's
and Warren Commission's investigations of the
crime were due in part to the fact that Hoover withheld so much information from him suggesting the
possibility that organized crime was behind the
assassination and his own fear of what might come
out about his slain brother and himself if a thor-

ough investigation of a possible conspiracy were undertaken.

What could come out during a trial of Carlos Marcello and his coconspirators for plotting and carrying out the assassination of President Kennedy that could possibly be damaging to the Kennedy reputation?

The existence of the CIA-Mafia plots to assassinate Fidel Castro, for one. How would the American people have reacted to the revelation that the administration of its slain president had attempted to assassinate the president of a neighboring state?

The Kennedy brothers' respective relationships with Judith Campbell and Marilyn Monroe for another.

We now know that the leadership of the underworld in 1963 was well aware that John Kennedy had been having affairs with Sam Giancana's girlfriend and Marilyn Monroe and that Robert Kennedy had also carried on an affair with Monroe.

On August 20, 1962, sixteen days after Marilyn Monroe's mysterious death, an FBI-listening device picked up a conversation between three well-known Mafia figures that made reference to Robert Kennedy's affair with the celebrated Hollywood actress:

> They will go for every name—unless the
> brother—it's big enough to cause a scandal
> against them. Would you like to see a headline
> about Marilyn Monroe to come out? And him?
> How would he like it? Don't you know? . . . He
> has been in there plenty of times. It's been a hard
> affair—and this [deleted name of a friend of

*Marilyn's] said she used to be in all the time with
him—do you think it's a secret?*

J. Edgar Hoover saw the transcript of this tape. Did
he show it to Attorney General Kennedy? If he did
Kennedy would have known he could never oppose
Hoover's hasty solution to the murder of his brother.
He had to swallow it and hold his tongue.

I am convinced that not long after the assassination
Robert Kennedy met with Jacqueline Kennedy and
told her what the official policy of the Kennedy family
must be in regard to the assassination. He told her
there probably was a plot to kill the president and if
the plot were fully investigated it could severely damage his and Jack's reputations.

Robert no doubt told the same thing to his brother,
Ted, and sisters, Eunice, Pat, and Jean.

There is no other plausible explanation of why the
Kennedys did not strenuously push for a thorough
investigation, choosing instead to passively accept
Hoover's hasty, flawed solution to the crime.

Jacqueline Kennedy's argument against investigating a possible conspiracy was so specious it had to be
concocted to conceal something. "Why bother to
investigate further? Nothing can bring Jack back."

If one applied that concept to every homicide there
could be no such thing as justice. Don't bother to investigate the murder of Mafia boss, Sam Giancana, because
nothing can bring him back.

It is interesting to note that Eunice Kennedy
Shriver stated publicly that the Kennedy family did
not wish any further investigation of President
Kennedy's murder on the eve of the Senate
Intelligence Committee's investigation of the intelli-

gence agencies and alleged assassination plots against foreign leaders. It was that 1975 Senate investigation that turned up, quite by accident, John F. Kennedy's mysterious affair with Judith Campbell, the girlfriend of CIA-Mafia conspirator against Castro, Sam Giancana.

It was during the late seventies that every conceivable damaging revelation came out about the Kennedy brothers, yet the Kennedy family still opposed the 1976–79 House Select Committee on Assassinations' reinvestigation of the Kennedy murder. What more could they be hiding?

As it turned out, the new investigation discovered more information damaging to the Kennedy image. It found out that Jacqueline and Robert had been, from a strictly legal standpoint, unwitting accessories after the fact in the President's murder.

First, the Assassinations Committee determined that it was principally Jacqueline Kennedy and the so-called "Irish Mafia" trio of Dave Powers, Kenny O'Donnell, and Larry O'Brien who were responsible for removing Kennedy's body from Parkland Hospital to *Air Force One* and then to Bethesda Naval Hospital outside Washington. The move was illegal and resulted in the President receiving a wholly inadequate autopsy, a calamity that has stirred innumerable controversies over the past thirty years.

Furthermore, the Assassinations Committee determined that Jacqueline and Robert exerted undue influence on the autopsy surgeons at Bethesda Naval Hospital preventing the President from receiving a complete autopsy and even interfering with standard autopsy procedures regarding the tracking, or dissection of gunshot wounds.

Finally the committee determined that Robert Kennedy had actually caused crucial physical specimen evidence to disappear from the custody of the National Archives, namely slides of the President's wound-edge tissues and his formaldehyde preserved brain.

William Manchester chronicled the events surrounding the illegal removal of Kennedy's body from Parkland Hospital in his 1967 book *Death of a President.*

According to state law when a homicide occurs on Texas soil, an autopsy must be performed on the victim in Texas before the body is permitted to leave the state. The official appointed to uphold that law in Dallas was Earl Rose, M.D., the Dallas County Medical Examiner, with an office in Parkland Hospital. Dr. Rose insisted that Kennedy's body remain in Dallas until a thorough autopsy was performed and he would sign a release permitting the body to be transported out of state.

Jacqueline Kennedy was becoming impatient to return to Washington. Sitting in a corridor outside of Trauma Room One, after Kennedy had been declared dead, she turned to Dallas Police Sergeant Robert Dugger, who had been assigned to guard her, and asked: "Sergeant, why can't I get my husband back to Washington?"

The sergeant did not respond. Dr. Earl Rose had appeared on the scene and had let it be known that the President's body would remain in Dallas until the autopsy had been completed. That was the law.

"There has been a homicide here. They won't be able to leave until there has been an autopsy," Dr. Rose said sternly.

But, the President's men had other ideas. Representing the wishes of Mrs. Kennedy that they return with the body to Washington, were presidential aides Dave Powers, Ken O'Donnell, and Larry O'Brien, the President's personal physician, Dr. George Burkley, a navy admiral, the President's Air Force aide, Brigadier General Godfrey McHugh, and the special agent in charge of the White House detail of the Secret Service, Roy Kellerman.

"We are taking the body back to Washington," Kellerman told Dr. Rose.

"You're not taking the body anywhere. There's a law here. We're going to enforce it," barked Dr. Rose.

Dr. Rose then phoned the Dallas Sheriff's Office and the homicide bureau of the Dallas Police. They both agreed an autopsy was mandatory. It had to be performed in Texas. Under the law they had little choice.

Dr. Burkley pleaded with Dr. Rose saying that Mrs. Kennedy wished to return with the body to Washington.

"Mrs. Kennedy can go," said Dr. Rose, "the remains stay. Procedures must be followed. A certificate has to be filed before any body can be shipped out of state."

"It's the President of the United States," Dr. Burkley pleaded.

"That doesn't matter," said Dr. Rose. "You can't lose the chain of evidence."

A furious argument then ensued between Dr. Rose and the Kennedy party. Rose summoned a Justice of the Peace to his side. It was his duty to order an autopsy in a homicide case. Ken O'Donnell then assumed leadership of the Kennedy group. "We're leaving," he said. "Get the hell over. We're getting out of here. We don't give a damn what these laws say. We're not staying here three hours or three minutes. Dave, we're leaving now." Then, turning to Kellerman, who was standing near the coffin, he ordered him to "wheel it out."

The Kennedy phalanx then bullied past Dr. Rose, climbed into an ambulance, and headed across the tarmac for *Air Force One.*

Once on the plane, the question of where the president's body would be taken arose. Would it be Walter Reed Army Hospital or the Bethesda Naval Hospital?

"Of course the President was in the navy," observed Dr. Burkley.

"Of course," said Jacqueline Kennedy, "Bethesda."

The decision to have the autopsy performed at Bethesda was a fateful one. Jacqueline Kennedy had no way of knowing that there would not be a single, practicing, forensic pathologist present in the autopsy room, and the naval doctor who would be in charge of the autopsy, Commander James J. Humes, director of laboratories at the U.S. Naval Medical School, had never performed an autopsy on a gunshot victim.

The autopsy of President Kennedy was so botched it left a permanent legacy of doubt about the nature of the President's wounds. That doubt was to spawn dozens of conspiracy theories.

Complicating the procedure was the presence of Robert Kennedy and Jacqueline Kennedy in a tower suite on the seventeenth floor of the hospital transmitting orders and instructions to the autopsy surgeons through an intercom phone. FBI agents Francis

O'Neill and James Sibert had been assigned to cover the autopsy for the bureau. They took copious notes on the procedure and later gave testimony on the autopsy before the House Select Committee on Assassinations. Francis O'Neill testified that "Mrs. Kennedy had given permission for a partial autopsy and that Dr. Burkley, the President's physician, reiterated her remarks in the autopsy room." And James Sibert testified that he "had the impression the Kennedy family was somehow transmitting step-by-step clearances to the pathologists."

Contrasting descriptions of the President's wounds soon emerged. The Dallas doctors, who had wanted to conduct the autopsy, claimed the wound in the President's throat, which they had further enlarged to perform a tracheotomy, was a wound of entry, but the Bethesda doctors, at first not detecting the wound at all because of the tracheotomy incision, eventually determined it to be a wound of exit. However, the Bethesda doctors failed to dissect the wound's track through the back and neck, and, in fact, were unable to manually probe the back wound to a depth of more than five inches.

It is now widely believed that either Robert, or Jacqueline Kennedy, or both told the autopsy surgeons through presidential physician, Admiral George Burkley, not to track the neck wound, for reasons that remain unclear.

Whatever the reasons, it was a crucial decision. Agents Sibert and O'Neill wrote in their report that the wound in the President's back "was probed by Dr. Humes with the finger, at which time it was determined that the trajectory of the missile entering at this point had entered at a downward position of 45 to

60 degrees. Further probing determined that the distance traveled by this missile was a short distance inasmuch as the end of the opening could be felt with the finger."

Secret Service agent, Roy Kellerman, testified to the Warren Commission that there was consternation over the absence of a bullet that might be responsible for the hole in the president's right shoulder. Kellerman was standing next to one of the three autopsy surgeons, Colonel Pierre Finck, who was probing the back wound with an instrument. "I said, 'Colonel, where did it go?' He said: 'There are no lanes for an outlet of this entry in this man's shoulder.'"

Years later assassination-researcher David Lifton interviewed a former Navy laboratory technician at Bethesda, James Jenkins, who had assisted at the President's autopsy. Jenkins was at Commander James Humes' side when the autopsy surgeon probed Kennedy's back wound with his little finger. Jenkins told Lifton that Humes "could probe to the bottom of it with his little finger which would mean it was very shallow." Later on in the autopsy, Jenkins watched a doctor open up the chest cavity and begin probing the back wound again with his finger. "I remember looking inside the chest cavity," Jenkins told Lifton, "and I could see the probe . . . through the pleura . . . You could actually see where it was making an indentation . . . where it was pushing the skin up . . . There was no entry into the chest cavity . . . No way that [bullet] could have exited in the front because it was low in the chest cavity." This also implied that the bullet could not have traveled through the President's body as it penetrated no further than his shoulder.

Jenkins contradicted one of the Warren Commission's most sacred dogmas, that a single bullet fired from the Texas School Book Depository in a downward trajectory struck the President in the back below his neck, passed through the body, somehow exited from his throat, above the shirt and the necktie, at a higher point than where it had entered, then somehow veered off to the right striking Governor Connally in the back causing multiple wounds also in his arm and thigh: The "magic-bullet" theory. This amazing, gravity-defying bullet was the linchpin of the Warren Commission's conclusion that there was no conspiracy in the case. But if President Kennedy and Governor Connally had been hit by separate bullets—as Governor Connally has always maintained—there had to have been two shooters from the rear, for it would have been impossible for one lone gunman to have gotten off two shots in such a short space of time with a nonautomatic weapon such as the bolt-action, one shot-at-a-time rifle that was recovered at the scene of the crime. All this confusion could have been avoided if the autopsy surgeons had not been prevented from tracking the bullet's path from the back to the throat.

Further complicating the question of the back wound is the matter of where the bullet that caused the wound ended up. The Warren Commission theorized that the bullet that had caused so much damage to two men was the one that was recovered by an orderly from a stretcher in the Parkland Hospital corridor believed to have been, but not proved to have been, Governor Connally's stretcher. The bullet matched Oswald's rifle but was undamaged and contained no residue of flesh or blood.

Contrasting with this pristine bullet was a damaged bullet Agents O'Neill and Sibert had received from Commander Humes during the autopsy, which was turned over to Captain J. H. Stover, Jr., commanding officer of the U.S. Naval Medical School of the Naval Medical Center at Bethesda. That bullet has disappeared. No record of it exists outside of the O'Neill and Sibert FBI report.

Was the pristine bullet found on the Parkland Hospital stretcher a plant? And if so, who planted it? And where is the bullet Dr. Humes handed to Agents Sibert and O'Neill that, in turn, they handed to Captain Stover? If it disappeared, who made it disappear and why?

These questions have fueled conspiracy theorists for thirty years, especially those researchers obsessed with pinning the blame for the President's murder on the federal government, or the military-industrial complex, or a combination of both.

In the end, the confusion has arisen from the Kennedys' insistence on removing the body of the President from Parkland Hospital and then interfering with the autopsy at Bethesda Naval Hospital. From a strictly legal standpoint the Kennedys' actions at Parkland and Bethesda hospitals amounted to tampering with the evidence in a homicide case, making them unwitting accessories after the fact in the crime.

However, interfering with the disposition of the body and with the autopsy on the body was minor compared to what Robert Kennedy did with the most crucial evidence in the case.

In 1979 the House Select Committee on Assassinations concluded, after an exhaustive investigation, that, for reasons that are still unclear, Robert

Kennedy had suppressed key evidence in his brother's murder case. The evidence in question consisted of certain autopsy-related materials that had been confiscated by Robert Kennedy in 1965 and had later been either destroyed by him, or "otherwise rendered inaccessible."

These autopsy materials consisted of black-and-white and color negatives and prints of autopsy photographs, X rays, bone fragments found in Dallas after the assassination, 119 microscopic slides of sections of certain tissues, including many specimens of John F. Kennedy's wound-edge tissues, and the president's formaldehyde-preserved brain.

Immediately after the autopsy the photographs, X rays, and physical specimens were transferred from the Bethesda Naval Hospital to the custody of the Secret Service White House detail in the Executive Office Building, adjacent to the White House, where they were stored in a locked Secret Service file cabinet under the control of President Kennedy's former White House physician, Admiral George C. Burkley, who, in a sense, represented the rightful owner of the materials—the U.S. Navy.

The physical-specimen evidence, especially the wound-edge tissue slides, was the key to determining the origin and trajectory of the gunshots that wounded the President and Governor Connally, and the identification of the weapons and ammunition used in the shooting.

Yet there, in that Secret Service file cabinet this crucial evidence remained, either forgotten or deliberately ignored, until over a year after the Warren Commission had issued its final report.

On April 22, 1965, Senator Robert F. Kennedy instructed Dr. Burkley to transfer personally to another location what he referred to in his letter to Burkley as "the material of President Kennedy of which you have knowledge," without specifically mentioning what was to be transferred included the autopsy physical-specimen materials. The transfer of the materials was to be made from the custody of the Secret Service to the care of Evelyn Lincoln, former personal secretary to President Kennedy, for "safekeeping" at the National Archives, where Mrs. Lincoln had been maintaining a temporary office.

What could have caused Robert Kennedy to suddenly and surreptitiously order Dr. Burkley to remove the autopsy evidence from the custody of the Secret Service on April 22, 1965? It appears it must have been Kennedy's awareness, as a member of the Congress, that Congress was then considering the enactment of a law providing for the acquisition by the U.S. government of certain items of evidence in the assassination of President Kennedy, held by the Kennedy family, within a year of its enactment, scheduled for the fall of 1965. This gave Kennedy little time to lose.

Upon receiving various containers of autopsy materials from Dr. Burkley, Mrs. Lincoln stored them in a small footlocker, in a secure closet in her office. And there they remained until approximately a month later, when Robert Kennedy telephoned her to inform her he was sending his personal secretary, Angela Novello, to remove the footlocker from her office. Mrs. Lincoln later testified that Miss Novello did, in fact, remove the footlocker and its two keys from her office in the presence of an official of the National Archives. She was not sure where Miss Novello then stored it, but got the impression that Miss Novello took it to a courtesy storage space in the National Archives that had been made available to Robert Kennedy.

Subsequently the U.S. government took formal possession from the Kennedy family of certain items of evidence pertaining to the assassination of President Kennedy, including the autopsy physical-specimen materials.

On October 31, a number of high officials of the General Services Administration (GSA) and the National Archives gathered at the National Archives to formally receive the autopsy materials from the representative of the Kennedy estate and to conduct an inventory of those materials. Angela Novello, representing the Kennedys, then gave William Brewster, a GSA official representing the government, the key to the footlocker and quickly departed. Brewster then opened the footlocker. Accompanying the autopsy materials were a carbon copy of Robert Kennedy's letter to Dr. Burkley of April 22, 1965 and the original letter from Dr. Burkley to Evelyn Lincoln of April 26, 1965, which itemized all the materials transferred at that time, including the physical specimens. William Brewster and the other officials then removed all the materials from the footlocker and inspected them, checking each item off against the inventory, and were astonished to discover that many of the items were missing.

Most of the black-and-white and color photographs and X rays of the autopsy listed in the inventory were present, but all the physical specimens had vanished. Photographs of the interior cavity of the President's chest were missing, as were most of those taken of the brain during a supplemental examination conducted after the official autopsy. These, of course, were the sites of Kennedy's gunshot wounds. Also

missing were three plastic boxes containing microscopic slides of tissue sections, and "one stainless
steel container, 7 x 8 inches in diameter, containing
gross material," the gross material being the president's bullet-riddled brain.

The government officials were appalled, well aware
that the autopsy physical specimens constituted the
most crucial evidence in the assassination case. Who
had removed them from the footlocker and why?

The dean of Kennedy assassination researchers,
Harold Weisberg, suspected the FBI stole the specimen materials from the footlocker, simply by picking
the lock. Other researchers suspect the Secret
Service absconded with them. But when the House
Select Committee on Assassinations investigated the
highly suspicious disappearance of these autopsy
materials in 1978 it concluded, after an exhaustive
effort, that "circumstantial evidence tends to show
that Robert Kennedy either destroyed these materials
or otherwise rendered them inaccessible."

What happened to the wound-edge tissue slides
and the brain?

Some have speculated that if Robert Kennedy
absconded with them he might have done so to avoid
their being put on public display at the National
Archives or some public institution such as the
Smithsonian. However, in the Kennedy executors'
deed of gift to the National Archives, it was specifically stipulated that "none of the materials shall be
placed on public display." And as the author of a 1985
book on the assassination, Henry Hurt, pointed out, it
would be much more likely that a future hypothetical
displayer, out to cause a sensation, would want to display some of the ghastly photographs of the

President's blasted head—the photographs that Chief Justice Warren admitted kept him from sleeping for three consecutive nights—rather than microscopic slides of tissues and preserved brain matter that would appear indistinguishable from those of any other deceased person.

The House Assassinations Committee also speculated that perhaps Robert Kennedy had buried the tissue slides and the brain when President Kennedy's body was reinterred in 1967. An investigation of this possibility revealed nothing was added to the President's coffin upon reinterment.

Strangely, the National Archives apparently did not notify Robert Kennedy of the missing autopsy materials. They simply let him get away with the destruction, or confiscation, of vital evidence pertaining to the assassination of his brother.

What are we to make of it all? To me the reasons behind Robert Kennedy's actions are inescapable. The Kennedys, fearful of what a thorough investigation of the assassination might uncover, felt comfortable with the solution the FBI and the Warren Commission arrived at, even though they did not necessarily believe it. Jack Kennedy's image was not tarnished by Oswald, the lone assassin charged with the crime. Therefore confiscate the evidence that would conclusively prove that more than one gunman fired at President Kennedy and Governor Connally, for the discovery of that evidence could lead to a new investigation that could conceivably uncover things damaging to the Kennedy image.

Even though J. Edgar Hoover did not share FBI intelligence about the assassination with him, I think Robert Kennedy had a pretty good idea where the assassination came from. As we have seen from certain remarks he made to some of his aides—Guthman, Schlesinger, Sheridan, Mankiewicz—he suspected it came from organized crime. Specifically, he thought his two top priority targets in his war against organized crime, Carlos Marcello and Jimmy Hoffa, might have been behind it. And knowing that Santos Trafficante was close to both Marcello and Hoffa, he probably suspected that Trafficante was also in on the plot.

In a hypothetical future investigation of the assassination focusing on the subjects of Frank Ragano's allegation, Hoffa, Trafficante, and Marcello, what could conceivably come out that would not be flattering to the Kennedy image?

First of all, it would come to light that the action that provoked Marcello's thirst for revenge, Robert Kennedy's "kidnap deportation," was illegal. Second, it would inevitably come to light that Santos Trafficante was a conspirator in the Kennedy administration's secret effort to murder Fidel Castro and that the President was carrying on an affair with the girlfriend of one of Trafficante's coconspirators, Sam Giancana. Third, Jimmy Hoffa would let it be known during the course of such an investigation that his wireman, Bernard Spindell, had made secret recordings of the Kennedy brothers' frolicking with Marilyn Monroe.

To avoid the calamity of such revelations Robert Kennedy got his hands on the last remaining chunk of hard evidence that could prove, beyond reasonable doubt, that President Kennedy's assassination was the result of a conspiracy, and made sure it would never see the light of day.

* * *

Returning to the weeks immediately following the assassination, we can understand the extent of Robert Kennedy's demoralization. As J. Edgar Hoover's hostage, and as a victim of his own, and his slain brother's indiscretions, he was powerless to do anything about bringing his brother's killers to justice.

Upon resuming his duties as attorney general toward the end of January 1964, Robert Kennedy found himself totally isolated and bereft of all power. Hoover, who would not even return his calls, stopped reporting to him in favor of reporting directly to the White House. The FBI ceased sending an official car to pick him up during his travels around the country. Years later, Hoover boasted that he did not speak once to Robert Kennedy during his last six months as attorney general.

With his control of the FBI irretrievably lost, and his relationship with the new president strained and unproductive, Robert Kennedy had been effectively neutralized. Before long his war on the Mafia would run out of steam, and he himself would lose interest in pursuing the Mafia bosses he once had vowed to destroy.

I spoke to William Hundley, chief of Robert Kennedy's Organized Crime and Racketeering division at the Justice Department, and with Ron Goldfarb, an attorney in the division under Hundley, about the fate of Kennedy's crusade against organized crime. It came to an abrupt halt at 12:31 P.M., Central Standard Time, November 22, 1963, in Dallas, they both told me. On Tuesday, November 26, the day after the President's funeral, there was silence in the Organized Crime and Racketeering division. "Everyone knew it was all over," Ron Goldfarb told me, "everyone knew the Mafia had won."

CHAPTER 14

The Garrison Investigation: Protecting Marcello

In 1967, around the time when District Attorney Jim Garrison was launching his reinvestigation of the assassination of President Kennedy, Frank Ragano met Carlos Marcello and Santos Trafficante in New Orleans.

Ragano was curious to learn Marcello's reaction to the Garrison investigation.

"Who is this fellow Jim Garrison?" Ragano asked the diminutive mobster.

"He's my man," replied Marcello.

"And his investigation of the assassination of Kennedy?"

"It ain't goin no where. Nothin' to worry about."

Frank Ragano's exchange with Marcello corroborates what many Kennedy assassination investigators had long suspected. Big Jim Garrison, "the jolly green giant," the crusading prosecutor who had the temerity to reopen the Kennedy assassination case, was in Marcello's pocket.

It was known that Garrison kept Marcello happy by publicly insisting for some time that organized crime did not exist in New Orleans and by consistently ignoring Marcello's vast and blatantly open gambling network, which embraced all of the Gulf Coast from east Texas to Mobile, Alabama. And Marcello had contented Garrison by doing him such favors as having his Las Vegas associate, Mario Marino, provide him with free hotel accommodations and substantial casino credits whenever the ebullient New Orleans district attorney sought weekend amusement in Nevada. Marcello had further contented Garrison by arranging for him to buy an expensive home in an affluent New Orleans suburb at a cut-rate price from one of Marcello's major business associates, Frank Occhipinti, the builder of Marcello's Town & Country Motel.

Curiously, Jim Garrison decided to launch his reinvestigation of the Kennedy assassination at a time when serious allegations were being made that organized crime was involved in the murder.

The first of these allegations was made by Mafia-fixer Johnny Rosselli in February 1967. It was then that Rosselli came forward and told Chief Justice Earl Warren, through his attorney, that he had been involved with the CIA in a number of attempts to assassinate Fidel Castro and that Castro's agents in association with CIA-Mafia conspirator Santos Trafficante had retaliated by killing John Kennedy. Two days later J. Edgar Hoover informed the chief of the U.S. Secret Service, James J. Rowley, that the FBI was "not conducting any investigation" of Rosselli's allegation.

The next day the *New Orleans States-Item* disclosed that Orleans Parish district attorney, Jim Garrison, was reopening the investigation of President Kennedy's assassination and that one of his chief suspects was David W. Ferrie, "a former investigator for Carlos Marcello and a friend of Lee Harvey Oswald's."

The day after the article in the *States-Item* Garrison confirmed he was reopening the investigation of the assassination and announced that he was placing one of his chief suspects, David Ferrie, in protective custody.

Ferrie was then put up in a New Orleans hotel and assigned a bodyguard. Shortly thereafter Garrison announced to the press that he planned to indict David Ferrie for participating in a conspiracy with the CIA to assassinate President Kennedy. Then, for reasons that remain unclear, on February 21 Ferrie was released from protective custody and allowed to return to his apartment. That Garrison linked David Ferrie with the CIA in a conspiracy to assassinate Kennedy was perplexing to many for it was well known that Ferrie's principal connection was not to the CIA but to Carlos Marcello.

Garrison himself knew that Ferrie had been, and continued to be, closely associated with Carlos Marcello. He knew, for example, that just before the Kennedy assassination the normally impecunious

Ferrie had deposited $7,093.02 in his bank account, and that not long after the assassination someone had bought him a lucrative gasoline-station franchise in a New Orleans suburb. If Garrison knew this—and he stated that he did in his book Heritage of Stone— he must have known that Ferrie's only source of income immediately preceding the assassination had been his work as an investigator for Carlos Marcello's attorney, G. Wray Gill, and that it had been Marcello who had bought the gas-station franchise for Ferrie after the assassination. Furthermore, since he claimed he had conducted such a thorough investigation of Ferrie, Garrison must also have known that not long after the assassination Marcello had secured a steady job for Ferrie with an air cargo service firm controlled by one of his associates, Jacob Nastasi, a job Ferrie continued to hold at least through the end of 1966. Yet Ferrie's connections to Marcello were apparently not worth considering when it came to Garrison's suspicions about Ferrie's role in the Kennedy assassination.

But what did Marcello think about Garrison's pointing a finger at David Ferrie? We can only specu- late that if Marcello had been involved with Ferrie in a plot to assassinate President Kennedy, he would have been very disturbed over the prospect of Ferrie being cross-examined in a courtroom.

David Ferrie was found dead in his apartment in the early morning hours of February 22, 1967, an apparent suicide. The death was suspicious. Investigators, including Aaron Kohn, suspect he was killed by agents of Carlos Marcello, who was understandably fearful of what the desperate Ferrie might tell law enforcement authorities after he was formally indicted.

News of Ferrie's death traveled fast. When it reached FBI informant Eugene De Laparra, it prompted him to make another allegation to the FBI, a new, and expanded, version of the one he had made on November 27, 1963, about Marcello associate Ben Tregle's apparent foreknowledge of the assassination. In this revised version De Laparra revealed that it was Carlos Marcello's brother, Tony, who had told Tregle about the impending assassination, saying, within earshot of De Laparra: "The word is out to get the Kennedy family. The President will be shot when he comes South."

Then, on March 28, 1967, another FBI informant, Gordon Novel, startled J. Edgar Hoover by reporting to him that Garrison planned "to indict Carlos Marcello in the Kennedy assassination conspiracy."

Shortly thereafter, on April 11, Hoover received a strange AIRTEL from the special agent in charge of the Tampa FBI office describing a conversation between Marcello and Trafficante:

> While driving through New Orleans in Marcello's car, Marcello was driving and Trafficante was seated in the front seat and he [Ragano] was in the back, when a radio broadcast related events concerning District Attorney Garrison's escapades revolving around the assassination of President Kennedy. Santos turned and remarked to Marcello, "Carlos, the next thing you know they will be blaming the President's assassination on us."

It was around this time that the FBI learned about Edward Becker's allegation to Ed Reid that he had been present when Marcello outlined a plan to kill

President Kennedy. Word of this allegation traveled fast and soon reached Jim Garrison's ears along with Rosselli's allegation about Santos Trafficante being involved in a conspiracy to assassinate Kennedy.

We can also assume it reached Marcello's ears. Therefore, it can be said that the underworld and its political powers and supporters knew early in 1967 that Edward Becker had pointed a finger at Carlos Marcello and Johnny Rosselli had pointed a finger at Marcello's friend, Santos Trafficante, as possible conspirators in a plot to kill President Kennedy.

Then, who comes along at this time but New Orleans District Attorney Jim Garrison, an admitted acquaintance of Marcello, suggesting not an organized crime conspiracy but one involving principally the CIA. How was it that Garrison decided to launch an investigation of the Kennedy assassination that would implicate the CIA precisely when serious allegations were being made that organized crime was behind the murder?

There is strong evidence that Jim Garrison was persuaded to reopen the case by two Louisiana politicians close to Carlos Marcello, Congressman Hale Boggs and Senator Russell Long. According to former Justice Department official, Walter Sheridan, Long induced Garrison to believe either the CIA or the Cuban government might have had a hand in the assassination by telling Garrison of certain privileged information he claimed he had acquired as a senator from confidential sources linking Oswald to both pro-Castro Cubans and the agency.

Was Russell Long insinuating possible CIA involvement in the Kennedy assassination into District Attorney Garrison's ear to divert attention away from his principal financial backer, Carlos Marcello? Marcello had a long association with the Long family. Russell's father, Huey Long, had helped the young Marcello get started in the slot-machine business, in partnership with Frank Costello, in Louisiana. And Marcello had reciprocated by becoming the principal financial backer of Russell Long's senatorial campaigns.

Did Senator Russell Long manipulate Jim Garrison into conducting an investigation of the Kennedy assassination that would attempt to implicate the CIA and the military-industrial complex in the crime and so divert attention away from Carlos Marcello?

Frank Ragano thinks that is precisely what happened. Ragano is convinced that for all his bluster Garrison's investigation of the Kennedy murder, which ended up by pinning the blame for the assassination on the hapless New Orleans businessman, Clay Shaw, who, it was alleged, had tenuous connections to the CIA, was a hoax designed principally to protect Carlos Marcello.

To substantiate this conclusion Ragano cites a remark Garrison made to him during his visit to the New Orleans DA in the spring of 1967. Asking Garrison what he thought of Carlos Marcello, Garrison replied, "he's good people."

The nature of Jim Garrison's investigation of the assassination and his prosecution of Clay Shaw seems to bear out Ragano's contention. Garrison's case turned into a dishonest circus utterly lacking in integrity. Reduced to inducing testimony by means of bribery, truth serum, and hypnosis, Garrison's prosecution of Clay Shaw turned out to be a monumental fraud. It took the jury less than an hour to find Shaw not guilty. His reputation nevertheless irretrievably tarnished, Shaw died a few years later a ruined man.

Perhaps the most disgraceful aspect of Garrison's investigation of the Kennedy murder was the New Orleans district attorney's acquiescence to a plot by Marcello and Hoffa to induce Garrison to involve Edward G. Partin, the witness who had sent Hoffa to jail, in the Kennedy assassination.

Jimmy Hoffa had been convicted of conspiracy and jury tampering and on March 7, 1967 was sent to the federal penitentiary at Lewisburg to serve a sentence of thirteen years.

Shortly thereafter the "spring Hoffa" movement was launched by Hoffa's principal allies in the Teamsters and organized crime to overturn Hoffa's conviction and obtain his release from prison. Hoffa's allies knew they had to find a way to either threaten or bribe the government's chief prosecution witness, Edward G. Partin, head of Teamsters Union Local 5 in Baton Rouge, Louisiana, into changing his damning testimony against Hoffa. If threats and bribes did not work they would have to find a way to publicly discredit him.

As it would turn out the attempt of Hoffa's forces to intimidate Partin came to no avail. Partin, a tough, courageous man, knew too much about Hoffa to be intimidated by threats. Among other things, Partin knew that Hoffa had seriously contemplated killing Robert Kennedy in the summer of 1962. As we know, he knew this firsthand, because Hoffa had once expounded his murder plans directly to him at the Teamsters' headquarters in Washington. How would Hoffa and his allies like that to be made public?

But perhaps Partin could be bought. The father of two young children and separated from his wife, Partin was known not to be very well off financially. If he could be bought, what was his price?

Walter Sheridan, former head of Robert Kennedy's "get Hoffa squad," remained close to the intrigue surrounding the effort to liberate Hoffa from jail, and, having been assigned by NBC to cover the Garrison investigation in New Orleans, was also close to the action itself. According to Sheridan, the man the "spring Hoffa" forces selected to find out whether Edward Partin could be bought was one of Carlos Marcello's chief advisors and fixers, the swindler, D'Alton Smith, whose sisters were married to Marcello's top associates Joseph Poretto and Nofio Pecora.

In his book, *The Fall and Rise of Jimmy Hoffa*, Walter Sheridan wrote that, among Smith's accomplishments on behalf of Marcello, Smith got Russell Long elected Senate whip by traveling to Washington with a suitcase full of Marcello cash before the Senate vote and distributing it to seven undecided senators disposed to swing their votes to Long.

Edward Partin testified that D'Alton Smith, acting for Carlos Marcello, offered him $25,000 a year for ten years to repudiate his trial testimony against Hoffa, then, after Partin refused, offered him a flat one million dollars. Partin told Smith to go to hell.

Finally Hoffa's allies hit upon a way to try and destroy Partin's reputation and credibility. It was in Jim Garrison's circus-like investigation of the Kennedy assassination that they found what they thought would be the perfect vehicle. How would Partin look if Garrison could get the public to believe

Partin had been involved in a plot to assassinate President Kennedy? Accordingly in late June 1967 Carlos Marcello's forces, led by D'Alton Smith, induced District Attorney Garrison to come up with the preposterous claim that Partin had consorted with Oswald and Ruby in New Orleans in the summer of 1963 for the purpose of planning the assassination of President Kennedy. The sensational news was reported over radio station WJBO in Baton Rouge on June 23, 1967. The attempt by Garrison, in alliance with Marcello, to publicly discredit Partin had begun.

But by then Garrison's prosecution of Clay Shaw had become so discredited by the press and law-enforcement authorities throughout the nation that Garrison himself lost all credibility and therefore found himself in no position to cast doubt upon Edward Partin, least of all to cast suspicions upon him for having conspired to assassinate President Kennedy.

In June 1992, I was a guest on a live, syndicated television special produced by George Paige Associates in Los Angeles entitled "The Kennedy Assassinations—Coincidence or Conspiracy?" which was principally concerned with the allegation of Frank Ragano that Hoffa, Trafficante, and Marcello had conspired to assassinate President Kennedy.

Other guests on the show were Frank Ragano, Dan Moldea, author of *The Hoffa Wars*, Philip Melanson, author of books on Lee Harvey Oswald and the Robert Kennedy assassination case, James Spada, author of *Peter Lawford—The Man Who Kept the*

Secrets, and Victor Marchetti, author of *The CIA and the Cult of Intelligence.* When at the end of the two-hour show the guests were asked by the host what the ultimate purpose of the Garrison investigation was, the vote was unanimous: to protect Carlos Marcello from being named a suspect in the Kennedy assassination.

CHAPTER 15

The House Select Committee

on Assassinations

In 1976 the U.S. House of Representatives, responding to a tidal wave of pressure from private citizens, established the Select Committee on Assassinations to reinvestigate the assassinations of John F. Kennedy and Martin Luther King, Jr.

It was essentially the reaction of the public to the shocking revelations of the Church Committee (Senate Intelligence Committee) in 1975 and the first public showing of the Zapruder film, that prompted Congress to reinvestigate the assassination of President Kennedy. The Church Committee had discovered the Kennedy administration's top secret CIA-

Mafia plots to assassinate Fidel Castro and the unsettling fact that both the FBI and the CIA had withheld evidence from the Warren Commission.

After a year of inconclusive wrangling, during which the first House Select Assassinations Committee chairman resigned and the first chief counsel was fired, the Assassinations Committee finally got down to business in April 1977 under the leadership of its new chairman, Congressman Louis Stokes, Democrat from Ohio, and its new chief counsel, Cornell law professor, G. Robert Blakey, a former Justice Department attorney under Robert F. Kennedy.

The committee then labored a year and a half to arrive at the conclusion that President Kennedy had probably been killed as a result of a conspiracy and that Jimmy Hoffa, Santos Trafficante, and Carlos Marcello were the most likely suspects to have participated in such a conspiracy.

In other words the Assassinations Committee corroborated, *ante factum*, in 1979 the allegation Frank Ragano was to make in 1992.

Considerable credit must go to staff counsel Robert Tannenbaum, who had been independently investigating certain conspiracy allegations that had been ignored by Hoover's FBI and the Warren Commission, for turning the Assassinations Committee's attention toward organized crime. For it was in April 1977 that Tannenbaum recommended to the committee that it investigate possible ties between Carlos Marcello and the assassination of John F. Kennedy. It was the first time since the events of November 22, 1963, that Marcello had been mentioned by any official investigative body as a possible suspect.

Robert Tannenbaum thought he was on to something. On March 12, 1977, before the Assassinations, Committee had acquired a new chief counsel, Tannenbaum had interviewed Cuban exiles' leader José Alémán about his September 1962 allegation, and Alémán confirmed that Trafficante had personally told him that President Kennedy was "going to be hit." Alémán went on to tell Tannenbaum that Trafficante "had made it quite clear to him implicitly that he was not guessing about the impending assassination; rather he gave the impression that he knew Kennedy was going to be killed." Alémán further stated that "Trafficante had given him the distinct impression that Hoffa was to be principally involved in planning the presidential murder."

Since Tannenbaum was aware of the close ties among Carlos Marcello, Trafficante, and Hoffa it seemed logical that what Trafficante was expressing to Alémán was foreknowledge of a plot to assassinate Kennedy possibly planned by Hoffa and Marcello.

These first tentative steps taken by the Assassinations Committee were in stark contrast to the initial phases of the FBI's and the Warren Commission's investigations thirteen years before. The Assassinations Committee immediately set out to determine whether there had been a conspiracy to assassinate President Kennedy whereas the FBI and the Warren Commission had set out to quell all rumors of conspiracy in favor of pinning the blame for the President's murder on Lee Harvey Oswald acting alone.

However, despite the fact that the Assassinations

Committee was disposed to find a conspiracy in the Kennedy case, we shall see there was, on the part of a good many members of the committee, a hidden bias toward accepting certain conclusions of the Warren Commission. This tendency was particularly evident in the committee's unwillingness to seriously consider the notion that Oswald had been framed and its willingness to ratify certain conclusions of the Warren Commission in regard to the forensic evidence, particularly the infamous "single-bullet" theory.

The challenge the House Assassinations Committee and its chief counsel, G. Robert Blakey, confronted was gigantic in scope and weighty in its possible historical significance. Since the assassination in Dallas, some fifteen years before, compelling conspiracy allegations had been made suggesting the complicity of Fidel Castro or his loyalists, the anti-Castro Cuban exiles, the government of the Soviet Union, the Central Intelligence Agency, the Federal Bureau of Investigation, the Secret Service, and "the national syndicate of organized crime." It was the committee's task to investigate and evaluate all these possibilities and report its findings to the nation and the world.

As it turned out, the committee was not confronted with any evidence whatsoever suggesting the CIA, as an agency of the U.S. government, might have been involved in a conspiracy to assassinate President Kennedy, but it was confronted by evidence persuasively suggesting that rogue elements of the CIA, acting either on their own or in concert with members of organized crime, might have been involved.

We have already considered this evidence. It concerned reliable reports that someone representing himself as Lee Harvey Oswald had visited the Cuban and Soviet embassies in Mexico City on several occasions during the period from September 27 to October 2, 1963, who, in reality, was not Oswald, but an impostor. This individual had made such a spectacle of himself that his presence at the two embassies would not soon be forgotten. Especially disturbing had been a CIA report of October 10 that a man purporting to be Oswald visited the Soviet Embassy in Mexico City on October 1 and spoke with Vice-Consul Valery Vladimirovitch Kostikov. Kostikov, it was later learned, doubled as a KGB officer in charge for Western Hemisphere terrorist activities, including assassination. Equally disturbing was a CIA report that the individual representing himself as Oswald had actually made an offer to officials of the Cuban Embassy to kill President Kennedy.

The implications of all this were only too clear: it appeared that a conspirator had deliberately attempted to inspire terror in U.S. government officials over the national security implications of an Oswald-Kostikov meeting, and an Oswald offer to Cuban officials to kill President Kennedy, by laying a false trail of evidence against Oswald to induce a future official cover-up of the impending assassination.

"Such a conspirator," wrote Kennedy assassination researcher Paul L. Hoch, "would not be a maniac, or 'social outcast,' but a sophisticated planner who was counting on the CIA's surveillance of the Soviet

Embassy in Mexico City to detect his contact with KGB officer Kostikov. . . . Such an individual would almost certainly have had to be associated with the global intelligence milieu, an insider privy to special knowledge of CIA procedures."

Was someone "associated with the . . . intelligence milieu" a conspirator in the alleged Hoffa-Trafficante-Marcello plot to kill Kennedy? We do not know for sure but the Mexico City evidence seems to point toward one. However, it is entirely possible that Guy Banister and David Ferrie possessed the sophistication to deploy such an individual. Whatever the case, the discovery of a conspirator with ties to maverick elements of the CIA was perfectly consonant with a Mafia conspiracy to assassinate the President. Had not the CIA recently entered into a conspiracy to assassinate Fidel Castro in alliance with the Mafia? We know that both Carlos Marcello and Santos Trafficante were active in the CIA-Mafia plots to kill Castro. Could they not have had someone who had been associated with the CIA-Mafia plot to kill Castro aid them in a possible plot to assassinate President Kennedy?

As for suspicions of possible FBI involvement in the assassination, there had been a persistent rumor that Oswald had been an FBI informant during the months preceding the assassination and might have passed on information about an assassination plot, which the FBI did nothing about, by either design or neglect. The Assassinations Committee investigated this allegation and concluded it had no substance. Regrettably the committee did not bother to investigate whether Hoover's FBI had foreknowledge of Carlos Marcello's plans to assassinate Kennedy and Trafficante's awareness of those plans. In the end the committee declared the FBI played no role in a conspiracy to assassinate the president. However, the committee did conclude that the FBI had failed "to investigate adequately the possibility of a conspiracy to assassinate President Kennedy."

The Assassinations Committee also concluded that neither the Soviet Union nor the government of Cuba was involved in a conspiracy to assassinate the President, despite a good deal of persuasive, but insufficiently evaluated, circumstantial evidence suggesting that Castro's Cuba might have been involved. It also went on to exonerate the Cuban exiles, "as a group" from complicity but did not preclude that individual Cuban exiles, acting on their own, could have been involved.

As for the possible complicity of the Secret Service in the assassination, the committee concluded there was none but it did declare that "the Secret Service was deficient in the performance of its duties," adding that "Secret Service agents in the motorcade were inadequately prepared to protect the President from a sniper."

The Assassinations Committee did not, however, acquit military intelligence of possible involvement in the assassination because the committee learned late in its investigation that the Department of Defense had destroyed its entire file on Oswald in 1973 and had never sent the file to the Warren Commission.

In the end, it was in the area of the possible involvement of organized crime in the assassination that the committee developed its most well-founded suspicions.

To evaluate the possibility that organized crime was involved, the committee examined FBI surveillance of members of the Mafia's national regulatory body, the commission, and failed to turn up so much as a hint of discussion of a plot to kill President Kennedy. As a result the Assassinations Committee concluded that "the national syndicate of organized crime, as a group" was not involved in a conspiracy to assassinate the president.

However, the committee concluded that there were three individuals associated with organized crime who circumstantial evidence suggested might have participated in a unilateral plan to assassinate the President, a plan unknown to, and therefore unapproved by, the national commission. These were Jimmy Hoffa, Santos Trafficante, and Carlos Marcello, all three of whom, the committee noted, were under siege from the U.S. government at the time of the assassination.

In assessing the role of Jimmy Hoffa in a possible plot to assassinate President Kennedy, the committee noted that "as opposed to Marcello and Trafficante, Hoffa was not a major leader of organized crime. Thus his ability to guarantee that his associates would be killed if they turned government informant may have been somewhat less assured. . . . Indeed," the Assassinations Committee noted, "much of the evidence against Hoffa was supplied by a federal government informant, Edward Grady Partin," implying that since Teamsters official Partin had survived despite his collaboration with the Justice Department, Hoffa was not capable of covering up an assassination plot. "It may be strongly doubted, therefore, that Hoffa would have risked anything so dangerous as to plot against the President."

When Santos Trafficante was called to testify before the Assassinations Committee in public session on September 28, 1978, he admitted, in his immunized testimony, that he had conspired with the CIA to kill Castro but "denied any fore-knowledge of, or of participation in, the President's murder."

Frank Ragano told me in 1992 that Trafficante's performance before the Assassinations Committee was a masterpiece of deception. According to Ragano, Trafficante's alleged participation in the CIA-Mafia plots to kill Castro was a sham. "He was stringing the CIA along," Ragano said, "he didn't do anything about Castro, just gave the CIA a lot of big stories." On the other hand Ragano was convinced his client did actively plot with Hoffa and Marcello the assassination of President Kennedy.

FBI wiretaps on Trafficante's phones in 1963, recorded his desperation over Robert Kennedy's crackdown on his criminal empire, revealed that Trafficante had sufficient motive to rid himself of the Kennedy brothers. Still, the Assassinations Committee concluded that it was "unlikely that Trafficante plotted to kill the President." After all, there seemed to be no evidence suggesting that Trafficante had personally plotted the President's murder, only evidence that he had foreknowledge of such a plot.

Carlos Marcello appeared as a witness before the House Select Committee on Assassinations in

Washington on January 11, 1978, in a secret executive session, to answer questions relating to the assassination of President John F. Kennedy. His sworn testimony was given under a grant of immunity.

The veteran Senate committee witness who had successfully stood up to Senators Estes Kefauver, John McClellan, John F. Kennedy, and Attorney General Robert F. Kennedy, now faced committee Chief Counsel G. Robert Blakey, who would author the RICO statute that would one day help send Marcello to jail.

Blakey: Mr. Marcello, have you ever been
    involved in organized crime?
Marcello: No, I don't know nuttin' about dat.
Blakey: Did you threaten the life of President
    Kennedy at a September 1962 meeting at
    Churchill Farms?
Marcello: Positively not. I never said anything
    like dat. The way the paper puts it and the
    books put it in dere it makes it look like
    you had some kind of secret meetings
    because I have heard the book about what
    you are telling me.

Marcello then told Blakey that his huge swampland property was full of duck blinds and was used only for hunting and fishing.

David Ferrie had already exposed this lie when he was arrested three days after the assassination and questioned by the FBI about his meetings with Marcello during October and November 1963. It will be recalled that he told the FBI then that he had met with Marcello in his farmhouse at Churchill Farms to discuss legal strategy in connection with Carlos' upcoming conspiracy and perjury trial in federal court.*

When questioned about his relationship with David Ferrie, Marcello admitted Ferrie had worked for his attorney, G. Wray Gill, in helping him prepare his defense against the charges the Justice Department had brought against him, but denied that Ferrie was a friend. When asked about the $7,093 that suddenly turned up in the normally impecunious Ferrie's bank account after the assassination, Marcello admitted he had paid the money to Ferrie for his paralegal services.

According to Robert Blakey, Marcello, for the most part, remained unruffled during his questioning, but he lost his cool when the name of Robert Kennedy came up.

> Blakey: Mr. Marcello, did you ever hear about
>   Robert Kennedy's intention to step up the
>   Justice Department's investigation of the
>   leaders of organized crime before becom-
>   ing attorney general?
> Marcello: Yeah, but I didn't pay any attention
>   to it at dat time.
> Blakey: When did you begin to pay attention to
>   it?

---

*And this lie would again be exposed by a federal undercover agent, who told me in 1986 that he had met with Marcello in the farmhouse at Churchill Farms to discuss important business. The agent noted that when he was there the farmhouse contained a long room furnished with a conference table, with chairs for eight people.

Marcello: When he got to be attorney general
... He was goin' to get organized crime an
all that stuff. But the only time I really
knowed about it was when they arrested
me and threw me outa de country.

Blakey: Did you express outrage to Edward
Becker over your deportation?

Marcello: (growing red in the face and raising
his voice) I didn't need to tell no one about
dat ... Everybody in de United States
knowed I was kidnapped, dat what dey
done was illegal. I didn't have to discuss it
with nobody. I told de whole world it was
unfair. Anybody who talked to me said it
was unfair!

Blakey told me that although this exchange was
inconclusive, and, in a sense, futile, the fact that
Marcello completely lost his composure when he,
Blakey, brought up the subject of Robert Kennedy
indicated the extent of the Mafia boss's indignation
over Kennedy's 1961 "kidnap-deportation" of him.
Now seventeen years later Marcello was still furious
over what Robert Kennedy did to him. Beyond doubt
Carlos Marcello had a compelling motive for assassinating President Kennedy. He knew it would strip his
nasty little brother of his power.

For reasons that have never been satisfactorily
explained Blakey never asked Marcello whether he
knew Lee Harvey Oswald, or Oswald's uncle, "Dutz"
Murret, who was active in Marcello's gambling operations and did not consider the possibility that Oswald
had been set-up to take the blame for the assassination.

During the decade and a half since the assassination a substantial body of opinion had developed that suggested Oswald did not kill anyone on November 22, 1963, that he had been deliberately and cunningly framed for the crime.

We have already reviewed the evidence suggesting that during the months preceding the assassination someone impersonating Oswald, the so-called Oswald double (or the second Oswald, or the Oswald imposter), had deliberately laid a trail of incriminating evidence, that would lead the official investigators to conclude the real Oswald shot the President at the behest of Fidel Castro, or the Cuban government, perhaps with the connivance of the Soviet Union.

In addition, compelling evidence had been developed over the years that Oswald could not have possibly killed Kennedy.

Consider the following time frame. Oswald was alleged to have fired on the President from a sixth-floor window of the Texas School Book Depository at 12:30 P.M. and yet a depository worker testified that he was eating his lunch on the sixth floor at 12:15 P.M. and saw no one else on the floor. Another witness, Carolyn Arnold, who was secretary to the vice president of the depository, testified that she spotted Oswald in the second-floor lunchroom, eating alone, at 12:15 P.M. As we know, after that sighting, the next person to spot Oswald was a motorcycle policeman, who, accompanied by the superintendent of the depository, had encountered Oswald in the second-floor lunchroom calmly drinking a Coca-Cola only a minute and a half after the shooting broke out. Later the police officer testified that Oswald was not out of breath, that he appeared calm and collected. And the Book Depository superintendent testified Oswald "didn't look excited or overly afraid, or anything."

When the Warren Commission concluded that Oswald had fired on the President at 12:30 P.M. it did not have the benefit of Carolyn Arnold's precise testimony because the FBI had misrepresented it by arbitrarily changing the time of her sighting from 12:15 to 12:35. But when the Assassinations Committee considered the problem in 1978, it had Carolyn Arnold's accurate testimony and still went along with the Warren Commission's conclusions. This led many to believe the committee's chief counsel was predisposed to accept the Warren Commission's conclusions on the issue from the start.*

This is not to say that Robert Blakey usually tended to ratify the Warren Commission's conclusions. Often he vigorously opposed those conclusions. On the still controversial matter of the precise location of the President's four wounds Blakey's Forensic Pathology Panel refuted the Warren Commission's conclusion that the President had been shot first in the right posterior base of the neck. Instead the Forensic Pathology Panel concluded the shot had entered the upper-right part of Kennedy's back, slightly below the shoulder blade, a full six inches below where the commission had located the wound (in order to accommodate the lone gunman "magic-bullet" explanation of the crime). Blakey also went along with the Forensic Pathology Panel's refu-

---

*Privately, however, Robert Blakey told me that he would not exclude the possibility that Oswald had been framed. Clearly the public Blakey and the private Blakey were not always of the same mind.

tation of the Warren Commission's placement of the
President's head wound. The panel, relying on X rays
and autopsy photographs the Warren Commission
had probably not seen, placed the wound no fewer
than four inches higher on the right posterior part of
the skull than where the Warren Commission had
placed it.

However, even though the Forensic Pathology
Panel moved the president's back wound down six
inches, and determined the trajectory of the bullet
through the president's body was virtually horizontal,
even slanting slightly upward, the Assassinations
Committee nevertheless ratified the Warren
Commission's controversial "magic-bullet" theory
that posited one bullet fired from the southeastern-
most sixth-floor window of the Book Depository
entering Kennedy's "neck" (in reality, his back), exiting from his throat (though the path of the bullet was
never dissected at autopsy), then traveling on to
make an abrupt right turn in midair, entering
Governor John Connally's back, exiting his chest,
traveling through his right wrist, shattering his
radius bone, before finally lodging in his left leg.
Later while the governor rested on a stretcher, the
Warren Commission asserted this extraordinary bullet must have fallen out. For it was found by a hospital orderly on a gurney in miraculously pristine
condition.

Critics were quick to point out that by locating the
wound in the back, below the shoulder blade, a full
six inches lower than where the Warren Commission
had located it, and by determining its trajectory was
slightly upward, the Forensic Pathology Panel made
it virtually impossible for a bullet fired at a 45- to 60-

degree angle from above to have exited from the President's throat above the collar line then veered upward and to the right to strike Governor Connally in the back near his right armpit.

Dr. Cyril Wecht, chief pathologist of Pittsburgh's Central Medical Center, the lone dissenting member of the Forensic Pathology Panel, pointed out, in his vigorous critique of the "magic-bullet" theory, that, among other things, a bullet doesn't just fall out of a wound unless it makes a big gaping hole of entry. In Governor Connally's case the bullet went deep into the leg where it became lodged in tissue so tightly it never could have just fallen out.

But it was Governor Connally himself who contradicted the "magic-bullet" theory most convincingly. He testified before the Warren Commission and the House Select Committee on Assassinations that he was not struck by the same bullet that struck Kennedy but by a bullet from a second shot. If this were true there were two gunmen shooting from the rear, one who hit Kennedy and another who hit Connally.

The Forensic Pathology Panel of the Assassinations Committee proved to be also incapable of going against the Warren Commission's conclusion that a bullet fired from Oswald's Mannlicher-Carcano rifle caused the fatal wound to the President's head. X rays of the wound indicated that the missile exploded the President's head, disintegrating into scores of tiny bullet fragments and depositing them in the brain and surrounding tissues.

Since the type of ammunition used in a Mannlicher-Carcano rifle is infrangible, the exploding bullet that caused the fatal wound in the President's head could not have come from a low-velocity Carcano rifle, but could only have come from a high-velocity automatic rifle whose bullets were designed to explode on contact, which was exactly what the bullet that struck Kennedy in the back of the head did.

In the end, Dr. Wecht observed that so far as the Assassinations Committee's treatment of the forensic evidence was concerned, "the investigation of the Committee was not an objective fact-finding mission conducted by an impartial staff, . . . but an attempt to make persuasive the Warren Commission's essential conclusions regarding the assassin's shots and the wounds they inflicted on the President and the Governor."

However, when it came to the question of possible conspiracy in the assassination, Robert Blakey came to differ radically from the Warren Commission. Whereas the Warren Commission, under the spell of J. Edgar Hoover, bent over backward to dogmatically assert that the President had been killed by a lone, emotionally disturbed, "commie" gunman, acting without confederates, Blakey became convinced early in his investigation that Kennedy had been assassinated as a result of a conspiracy.

The most important factors that contributed to the Assassinations Committee's ultimate finding of "probable conspiracy" were an acoustical analysis of a police tape recording that seemed to indicate that four shots in all were fired, one of which came from the grassy knoll, the many ear- and eyewitnesses whose testimony that at least one shot came from the knoll had been ignored by the Warren Commission but now appeared both plausible and convincing to the Assassinations Committee; unimpeachable evidence that the FBI and the CIA had deceived the Warren Commission on a number of important issues and had occasionally withheld vital information from it; the committee's extensive investigation of Jack Ruby's many ties to organized crime, especially his many connections to close associates of Jimmy Hoffa and Carlos Marcello; and the discovery of many secretly taped conversations between leaders of organized crime, obtained by FBI undercover agents before and immediately after the assassination, expressing their hatred of the Kennedy brothers, their rage over Robert Kennedy's campaign against them, and of their desire that both brothers be killed.

The possibility that Carlos Marcello might have played a significant role in the assassination of the President was given considerable credence by the Assassinations Committee. Reading between the lines of the committee's guardedly worded final report it is clear that the committee suspected Marcello's complicity above all others. For, as the final report, stated:

> *In its investigation of Marcello the Committee identified the presence of one critical evidentiary element that was lacking with the other organized crime figures examined by the Committee: credible associations relating both Lee Harvey Oswald and Jack Ruby to figures having a relationship, albeit tenuous, with Marcello's crime family or organization.*

Although the Warren Commission never received *any* evidence linking Oswald to organized crime, thanks, as we know, to the deliberate suppression of such evidence by FBI Director Hoover, the Assassinations Committee discovered that Oswald's uncle and surrogate father, "Dutz" Murret, was a bookmaker in the Marcello gambling network who had functioned as a collector for top Marcello deputy Sam Saia. The committee further established that Oswald's mother, Marguerite Oswald, cultivated friendships with two Marcello associates, Sam Termine and Clem Sehrt. It was discovered as well that as a result of the Oswald-Murret family ties with Marcello associates, Oswald was bailed out of jail in the summer of 1963 by Emile Bruneau, a close associate of high-ranking Marcello aide, Nofio Pecora, and a friend, as well, of the head of Marcello's racing wire service, Joe Poretto. And we have already discussed Oswald's relationship with Marcello associate David Ferrie.

What the Assassinations Committee did not discover was that Oswald actually worked for the Marcello organization as a runner, or messenger, in its gambling network in the months prior to the assassination, and during the course of this employment had met such important associates of the Marcellos as Joe Poretto and Ben Tregle. Nor did the Assassinations Committee appear to be aware that Dean Andrews, the New Orleans attorney Oswald had consulted several times during the summer of 1963, who had informed the Warren Commission that Oswald told him he was being paid for demonstrating on behalf of Castro, and who claimed someone had phoned him the day after the assassination to ask him to represent Oswald as his defense attorney against the charges the Dallas Police had brought against him, was one of Carlos Marcello's attorneys.

And what did the Assassinations Committee discover about Jack Ruby's connections to the Marcello crime family?

The committee established that Jack Ruby was a friend and business associate of Joseph Civello, Carlos Marcello's deputy in Dallas and the boss of Dallas's relatively small Mafia family, a reality that J. Edgar Hoover tried to keep from the attention of the Warren Commission. Furthermore, it established that Ruby was on very cordial terms with Joseph Campisi, who, the committee found out, was considered to be the number two man in the Dallas Mafia hierarchy and a man on such friendly terms with the Marcello brothers that he sent the family 260 pounds of home-made sausage every Christmas.

Campisi told the committee that he knew all of the Marcello brothers and used to go often to New Orleans to play golf and go to the track with Vincent, Anthony, and Sammy. It was Vincent who first introduced Campisi to Carlos and Joe Civello, and Carlos had taken Campisi several times to his fishing camp at Grand Isle, where Campisi would cook spaghetti for Carlos and all the brothers and their friends.

Joe Campisi, as we know, owned and operated a notorious mob hangout in Dallas, the Egyptian Lounge. In an interview with Campisi, the Assassinations Committee obtained an admission from him that Jack Ruby had dined with him at the lounge the evening before Kennedy was assassinated. Campisi also admitted that he had visited Ruby in the Dallas County Jail eight days after the assassination.

It is one of the traditional practices of the Mafia to visit a member of the brotherhood who has been jailed for a crime in which the brotherhood was involved soon after he first enters his cell. One of the purposes of such a visit is to remind the jailed colleague that he is to keep his mouth shut or else something unpleasant might happen to him or to a member of his family. This is usually done in subtle ways, such as inquiring after the health of the imprisoned man's sister.

Joe Campisi was Ruby's first visitor after his imprisonment for murdering the President's alleged assassin. Campisi brought his wife along with him—an unusual move, for mafiosi almost never include their wives in meetings at which urgent business matters are to be discussed, however obliquely. Former Chief Counsel Blakey speculates today that Campisi brought his wife along so as not to arouse suspicion by the police. When questioned by the Assassinations Committee as to what Ruby said during their meeting, Campisi did not recall much but did remember vividly what had already become Ruby's stock answer to the question of why he killed Oswald: to spare Jacqueline Kennedy and her children the pain of an eventual trial of Lee Harvey Oswald. (Later, a handwritten note of Ruby to one of his attorneys was discovered in which Ruby admitted he was lying, that a former attorney of his, Tom Howard, a friend of Joe Campisi's, told him to use the Jacqueline Kennedy story as an alibi.)

In the end the Assassinations Committee had little choice but to regard the Ruby-Campisi relationship and the Campisi-Marcello relationship as yet another set of associations strengthening the committee's

growing suspicion of the Marcello crime family's
involvement in a conspiracy to assassinate President
Kennedy, or execute the President's alleged assassin,
or both.

Frank Ragano has alleged that Jimmy Hoffa conspired with Carlos Marcello and Santos Trafficante in
a plot to assassinate President Kennedy. What did the
Assassinations Committee find out about the
Marcello-Hoffa relationship?

That the relationship between Carlos Marcello and
Jimmy Hoffa was particularly strong was evidenced
after the assassination when it was Carlos Marcello,
more than any other man, who came to Hoffa's aid as
the Teamsters boss confronted imprisonment during
the years 1965 to 1967. For at Hoffa's darkest hour it
was to Marcello and his close associate, Irving
Davidson, that the besieged Teamsters boss and the
national syndicate of organized crime turned to coor-
dinate a national campaign to "save Hoffa" from
imprisonment. FBI intelligence discovered that the
mob had placed one million dollars at Marcello's disposal to be used to bribe prosecution witness Edward
Partin and make payoffs, when necessary, to judges,
prosecutors, and state officials who were in a position
to help thwart Hoffa's imprisonment. In taking on this
large and risky responsibility was Marcello paying
back Hoffa for whatever services Hoffa had rendered
to him in the Kennedy assassination?

Possibly prominent among those services could
have been simply providing Marcello with useful intelligence (for instance, on the Kennedy brothers' extra-
marital affairs), which might have encouraged Carlos

to believe he could get away with murdering John Kennedy. Hoffa, as we know, was privy to the Kennedy brothers' reckless sexual adventures. Knowledge of them could have served to convince Marcello that Attorney General Robert Kennedy would never want to conduct a thorough investigation of his brother's murder for fear Jack's sexual dalliances with the likes of Marilyn Monroe and Judy Campbell might come to light during the course of the investigation.

In the end, the Assassinations Committee came to the guarded opinion that perhaps Carlos Marcello *had* been involved in the assassination. For, in its concluding statements on Marcello, the committee's final report remarked:

> *Any evaluation of Marcello's possible role in the assassination must take into consideration his unique stature within La Cosa Nostra. The FBI determined in the 1960's that because of Marcello's position as head of the New Orleans crime family (the oldest in the United States), the Louisiana crime leader had been endowed with special powers and privileges not accorded to any other La Cosa Nostra members. As the leader of the First Family of the Mafia in America, according to FBI information, Marcello had been the recipient of the extraordinary privilege of conducting syndicate operations without having to seek the approval of the national crime commission.*

Then, with this statement as a preamble, the committee issued its final statement on the possibility of Marcello's complicity:

> *On the other hand, the evidence that he had
> the motive and the evidence of links through asso-
> ciates to both Oswald and Ruby, coupled with the
> failure of the 1963–64 investigation to explore
> adequately possible conspirational activity in the
> assassination, precluded a judgement by the
> Committee that Marcello and his associates were
> not involved.*

What was Carlos Marcello's reaction to the House
Select Committee on Assassinations' publicly
declared suspicion that he or his "crime family or
organization" might have played a major role in the
assassination of President Kennedy?

There is evidence that he was quite disturbed, for,
in the summer of 1979, when those findings were
finally published by the government printing office,
he assigned the matter to his most brilliant and
trusted attorney, Harvard-trained Jack Wasserman,
for investigation. Wasserman immediately set about
obtaining the available FBI files on the Kennedy
assassination, which included the extensive files on
David Ferrie and some documents on the allegations
of Eugene De Laparra and Gene Sumner as well as
the Edward Becker story of Marcello's threat to kill
Kennedy.

These files, amounting to over 220,000 pages of
documents, had been released through a lengthy and
costly Freedom of Information Act lawsuit brought
against the Justice Department by Harold Weisberg,
noted Kennedy assassination researcher and author
of several books relating to the assassination. Now
the FBI was putting them at the disposal of Carlos
Marcello's attorney.

Did Carlos expect there would be an investigation of his possible complicity in the assassination by the Justice Department—an investigation that might have led to the convening of a grand jury and the returning of an eventual indictment for conspiracy to murder the president of the United States?

If he did, Carlos could have done no better than to put his defense in Jack Wasserman's hands. If Wasserman could successfully defend him against the Immigration and Naturalization Service for over thirty years, in what had been the longest and costliest deportation case in U.S. history, he could surely give the U.S. district attorney in New Orleans, who would prosecute any assassination conspiracy case against Marcello, the battle of his life.

But Jack Wasserman never got to defend his client against the charge that he had conspired to murder President Kennedy, for shortly after Wasserman began preparing for the anticipated case, he died suddenly of a heart attack.

However, as it turned out, the Justice Department was not preparing to prosecute Carlos Marcello for conspiring to murder Kennedy when Wasserman died in 1979. The Justice Department was not in the least bit interested in pursuing any of the leads the Assassinations Committee had developed in its two-year investigation. Rather it was conducting a sting operation against Marcello that the government hoped would send the Louisiana Mafia boss to prison for the rest of his life.

CHAPTER 16

The Fates of Hoffa,
Trafficante, and Marcello

The government's plan to finally nail Carlos Marcello, after decades of frustrated attempts, was part of a national undercover operation against corruption in labor and business called BRILAB (so-called after bribery and labor). The FBI had hired a Los Angeles-based insurance operator and convicted swindler, Joseph Hauser, to lure Marcello into a fraudulent scheme to bribe key Louisiana public officials to award important union, state, and municipal insurance contracts to a fictitious insurance brokerage the FBI had set up called Fidelity Financial Consultants. Aiding Joe Hauser in the sting would be two FBI undercover agents, Michael Wacks and Larry Montague.

Joseph Hauser had already met Carlos Marcello through a mutual acquaintance, veteran Washington lobbyist, I. Irving Davidson, and had done enough business with him to enjoy the mobster's trust.

Davidson, a friend of Marcello's since 1959, was a specialist in "putting people together" who counted among his friends such apparently disparate bedfellows as Rafael Trujillo, J. Edgar Hoover, Jimmy Hoffa, Clint Murchison, Bobby Baker, and Santos Trafficante. When Marcello was summarily deported to Guatemala by Bobby Kennedy in 1961 and Jimmy Hoffa disappeared off the face of the earth in 1975, the first person Washington syndicated-columnist Jack Anderson phoned to get the inside stories was Irv Davidson. He was a registered lobbyist for the Teamsters, the Somozas of Nicaragua, the Duvaliers of Haiti, the Trujillos of the Dominican Republic, the Murchisons of Dallas, and Coca-Cola. He lobbied in behalf of the CIA on Capitol Hill and represented Fidel Castro's interests in the United States after the Cuban revolution. According to Edward Partin, Davidson witnessed a secret meeting in late 1960 between Hoffa and Marcello during which a "$500,000 cash payment to the Nixon campaign was made."

The FBI, well aware of how closely associated Marcello and Davidson were, instructed Joe Hauser to pursue Davidson undercover as well. To further surveil Davidson the FBI secured authorization from the attorney general to tap the lobbyist's phones.

Meanwhile, under the direction of FBI Special Agent Harold Hughes, FBI agents and technicians in

New Orleans succeeded in installing a listening device in Marcello's office in the Town and Country Motel and placing interceptions on all Marcello's phones. The stage was now set for what was to become the most extensive, and successful, government sting operation against a Mafia leader up to that time.

It was at the time the sting was getting underway that Davidson's friend, Jack Anderson, wrote an entire syndicated column on Carlos Marcello, identifying him as "the most powerful mobster in the nation" and the House Assassinations Committee's "chief suspect in the John F. Kennedy assassination plot."

FBI undercover agent Larry Montague remembers hearing about the column but did not discuss it with Marcello at the time, even though he was meeting with him practically every day. "I didn't want to throw Marcello off," he told me eight years later. "I didn't want to make him suspicious by raising such an issue as the Kennedy assassination with him at the time. I considered it but came to the conclusion that I could possibly blow up the whole operation if I brought it up with him . . . also from a legal standpoint I was supposed to confine my conversations with Carlos strictly to the operation at hand. We got the title threes [authorizations to eavesdrop] only for that."

Besides, as Montague pointed out, he didn't think Carlos would say anything about the assassination conspiracy because he had noticed a sign on the inside door of Marcello's suite of offices at the Town and Country Motel that hinted at Marcello's attitude toward talking about his crimes. It read:

THREE CAN KEEP
A SECRET
IF TWO ARE DEAD

Joe Hauser was not so circumspect. The House Select Committee on Assassinations' findings and suspicions were constantly in the New Orleans papers in the spring and summer of 1979, and Hauser occasionally mentioned them to Marcello during their innumerable conversations in the restaurants of Metairie and New Orleans.

What Hauser told me he received from Carlos was a casual admission that both Lee Harvey Oswald and his uncle, "Dutz" Murret, had worked in his downtown bookmaking network and that during the summer of 1963 Oswald worked as a part-time "runner" for Sam Saia and Murret out of one of Saia's bookmaking establishments, the Felix Oyster House, a restaurant Saia owned on Iberville Street in the French Quarter, just around the corner from Pete Marcello's Sho-Bar.

Hauser reconstructs Marcello's remarks on his organization's relationship with Oswald, which he did not record because they were made in informal conversation, when his wire wasn't turned on, as follows:

> Oswald? I used to know his fuckin' family. His uncle he work for me. Dat kid work for me too. He worked for Sam outa his place downtown, you know, Felix or somethin' like dat. The feds came up to the motel once askin' about him, but my people didn't tell 'em nuttin'. Like we never heard of the guy, y'know.

Hauser claims he also elicited from Carlos's brother Joe a hint that the Marcellos might have been involved in the Kennedy assassination. One day Hauser brought up the subject of the Kennedys as he was reading, in Joe's presence, in the *New Orleans Times-Picayune* an account of Teddy Kennedy's 1979 announcement of his candidacy for the Democratic presidential nomination. Looking up from the paper, Hauser said something like: "Well, the Kennedys are at it again, Joe. Now it's Teddy. Boy his brothers sure gave ole Carlos a rough time back when they deported him." To this Joe Marcello had remarked: "Don't worry, we took care of 'em, didn't we?"*

Agents Wacks and Montague also recall Marcello indulging in a long monologue about his "kidnapping by Bobby Kennedy" in 1961. In the summer of 1979 they were driving from Lafayette to New Orleans in Marcello's car when Carlos saw fit to suddenly hold forth for at least a half hour on his ordeals in Guatemala, El Salvador, and Honduras. Montague told me that Carlos got red in the face and broke out in a sweat as he recounted his sufferings in the jungles of Honduras.

The FBI sting operation against Marcello and Davidson went exceedingly well. Carlos fell easily into the trap set by Hauser, Wacks, and Montague and in the process the three FBI agents and the ceiling bug in Marcello's office recorded 1200 reels of tape of Marcello's unguarded conversations.

At the first of his two BRILAB trials Marcello's defense team argued forcefully that the jury not be

---

*FBI Agent Mike Wacks told me eight years later that he remembers Hauser telling him what Joe Marcello had said.

allowed to hear any taped conversations between Marcello and the undercover agents about the Kennedy family or the assassination of President John F. Kennedy on the grounds that such references would be "overwhelmingly prejudicial."

In the end Judge Sear went along with the defense on this motion and decided that the tapes about Kennedy would not be played in court but that the jury would hear all tapes pertaining specifically to the BRILAB operation.

This meant that the overwhelming majority of the taped conversations would not be played in court and therefore would remain beyond Freedom of Information Act access. In the end, Marcello was convicted, but Davidson was acquitted.

In 1987, after stiff opposition from the Justice Department to a Freedom of Information Act request for the tapes to which I was, by law, entitled—those admitted into evidence at the two BRILAB trials—I sued the department for release of those tapes. In the process I learned that among the tapes not admitted into evidence at the trials were four containing conversations between Carlos Marcello, the undercover agents, and others, about the John F. Kennedy assassination and the House Select Committee on Assassinations' investigation. According to an inventory sent by the Justice Department to my attorney, Judge Sear had put these tapes under judicial seal during the 1981 pretrial hearings, thus placing their release forever beyond the provisions of the Freedom of Information Act.

As of May 1993 the precise content of these tapes has not been made public, and neither former Chairman Stokes nor former Chief Counsel Blakey of the House Assassinations Committee has listened to them or read transcripts of their contents. Blakey told me in a July 1988 interview that he was informed of the tapes' approximate content over the phone by an FBI official after the BRILAB operation went overt in 1980. He found only one of the reported conversations—a nonconversation as it turned out—suspicious.

As roughly described to Blakey, that conversation had been recorded by the ceiling bug in Carlos's Town and Country office. An unidentified individual had come into Carlos's office one day in the spring of 1979, when the New Orleans papers were reporting the results of the Assassinations Committee's investigation, and, after some preliminary banter, had asked Carlos how he would respond to the committee's suspicions of him. Carlos immediately told the man to shut up, that they would go outside and talk. Noises were heard of Carlos pushing his chair away from his desk and two men walking out of the room.

Curiously, while I was given a rough idea of what was on the tapes by several officials who had been associated with the BRILAB operation and trials, I was not told anything about the particular tape that had been described to Blakey.

As it turned out, Carlos Marcello was convicted of conspiracy and mail and wire fraud, in violation of the RICO statute, in the first of his two trials and was convicted of conspiracy to bribe a federal judge in the second. For these two convictions the seventy-two-year-old Marcello was given a cumulative sentence of seventeen years in federal prison. Irving Davidson was acquitted of all charges against him.

Carlos was first sent to the Medical Center for Federal Prisoners at Springfield, Missouri, where he spent about a year, then was incarcerated in the maximum security level-three federal penitentiary at Texarkana, Texas, near the Texas-Arkansas state line. For reasons that have never been explained by the Bureau of Prisons he was transferred to the level-two correctional institution at Seagoville, Texas on February 19, 1986, and then, after only four months at Seagoville, he was transferred again, on June 2, 1986, to the serene beauty of the minimum security level-one Federal Correctional Institution at Fort Worth. There he could even meet with visitors around a picnic table on a neatly trimmed lawn, well out of earshot from any government bug. But again for reasons the Bureau of Prisons has refused to disclose, Carlos's stay at the country-club style facility at Fort Worth was abruptly terminated on May 21, 1987, and in the dead of night Marcello was taken from his cell by federal marshals and driven under heavily armed escort back to the level-three federal prison at Texarkana. Had his life been threatened? We do not know.

The twenty-fifth anniversary of the assassination of President Kennedy was marked throughout November 1988 by many radio and television shows and a plethora of books and articles on the assassination. Books and magazines mentioning his name in connection with the assassination were delivered to Marcello's cell. Journalists tried and failed to interview him about them. Then, not long after the new year rolled around Carlos suffered a series of minor strokes that left him severely impaired. By the time the sixth-floor exhibit on the assassination opened in the Texas School Book Depository in Dallas, Marcello had become so disoriented he was no longer aware he was in prison believing instead that he was living in a hotel. Finally, as his health and state of mind continued to deteriorate the Bureau of Prisons transferred him from Texarkana to the Medical Center for Federal Prisoners at Rochester, Minnesota (near the Mayo Clinic), for an indeterminate stay.

Then, on July 23, 1989, not long after Marcello's removal to Rochester, a surprising judicial decision was handed down by the fifth U.S. circuit court that threw out Marcello's 1981 New Orleans BRILAB conviction, enabling the ailing old Mafia chieftain to be released from prison on October 6, 1989. He returned to his home and family in Metairie, Louisiana on that date, a helpless and mentally confused old man of eighty-one, who was finally beyond questioning or confessing whether he was involved in a plot to assassinate President Kennedy.

Carlos Marcello lingered on another three and a half years, suffering a progressive loss of memory it is thought from Alzheimer's disease, until his death on March 2, 1993 at eighty-three. According to sources close to his large family, Carlos simply went to bed one evening and never woke up, a death denied most Mafia bosses.

His Associated Press obituary stated: "Marcello's name was often mentioned in connection with the assassination of President John F. Kennedy, but he was never charged . . . Earlier this year the PBS program *Frontline* interviewed an associate of Tampa crime boss Santos Trafficante who said he "thought Marcello had 'messed up' when he had Kennedy killed."

The death of Marcello has benefited my lawsuit against the Justice Department to have the Marcello tapes released. The judge in the case has scheduled final oral arguments for May 18, 1993, but it is anyone's guess when he will order the tapes released.

A motion for an order to release the four Marcello tapes on the Kennedy assassination has also been made by me in the light of the new provisions governing disclosure of Kennedy assassination records set forth in the President John F. Kennedy Records Collection Act of 1992, signed by President George W. Bush shortly before he left office, providing for the release of all documents relevant to the Kennedy assassination case.

My motion was accompanied by a declaration of G. Robert Blakey as follows:

> *When I was Chief Counsel of the HSCA, we investigated the possible role of Carlos Marcello in a plot to assassinate President Kennedy. In conversations with law enforcement officials who had access to the BRILAB tapes, I was informed that they contained materials relevant to the investigation of Carlos Marcello's possible involvement in the assassination of President Kennedy. Frank Ragano, who served as attorney for both Teamsters' leader Jimmy Hoffa and organized crime boss Santos Trafficante, recently stated that Trafficante had made a deathbed confession to him that he and Carlos Marcello assassinated Kennedy.*
>
> *It is my view that the records sought by John Davis in this case should be considered Kennedy assassination records subject to disclosure under terms of the JFK Records Act. These records are all relevant to determine character, possible motivation, relationships and associations.*

So much for the fate of Carlos Marcello who, it is widely believed took some possibly very big secrets to his grave.

As for alleged conspirator Jimmy Hoffa, it will be recalled that on March 7, 1967, he surrendered to U.S. marshalls in Washington, D.C., and was transported to the Lewisburg Federal Penitentiary in Pennsylvania to serve a term of thirteen years.

When, on March 16, 1968, a year after Hoffa's incarceration Robert Kennedy announced he would run for the Democratic nomination for the presidency, a shudder ran through the underworld that soon gave rise to fresh new plots on the senator's life.

In May 1968 as Robert Kennedy's campaign shifted into high gear, an inmate informant in the Lewisburg prison told the FBI that he had heard Jimmy Hoffa and New York Mafia boss, Carmine Galante, an ally of Carlos Marcello's, discussing a "mob contract to kill Kennedy."

Then, around June 1, the FBI received word from an informant that "a wealthy southern California rancher who had ties to the Minutemen and detested Robert Kennedy because of his support of agricultural workers organizer Cesar Chavez, reportedly pledged $2,000 toward a $500,000 to $750,000 Mafia contract to kill the senator in the event it appeared he could receive the Democratic nomination for President." It is not known whether J. Edgar Hoover, who had not spoken to Robert Kennedy in four and a half years, brought the matter to the attention of Kennedy.

As we know, Robert Kennedy was murdered on June 6, 1968, in Los Angeles and Richard Nixon won the presidential election over Hubert Humphrey.

No sooner did Richard Nixon take office as president than a powerful "spring Hoffa" movement was launched, spearheaded by Carlos Marcello, to bring pressure to bear on President Richard Nixon to pardon the Teamsters boss.

Marcello was in a good position to persuade Nixon to pardon Jimmy Hoffa because one of his own men had an office in the Nixon White House. He was California mob attorney Murray Chotiner, a special assistant to the president. Chotiner was very close to Marcello's chief fixer D'Alton Smith, whose two sisters were married to two of Carlos' top henchmen, Nofio Pecora and Joseph Poretto. It will be recalled that D'Alton Smith had induced New Orleans District Attorney Jim Garrison to announce that the man who sent Hoffa to jail, Edward Grady Partin, consorted with Oswald and Ruby in the summer of 1963 for the purpose of planning the assassination of President Kennedy as a means of discrediting the government's chief witness against Hoffa.

By December 1971 Murray Chotiner had everything arranged for Richard Nixon to commute Hoffa's thirteen-year sentence to five, via an executive pardon. Hoffa then received a grant of executive clemency from President Nixon on December 23, 1971, on condition he not engage in labor union management of any kind. Thus was Robert Kennedy's campaign to put the Teamsters chief behind bars for at least a decade was undone by his own assassination.

Despite the condition Nixon imposed on Hoffa's release from prison, Hoffa immediately began campaigning for his old job as Teamsters boss issuing a challenge to the man who had taken his place, Frank Fitzsimmons. Fitzsimmons did not take the challenge quietly. He began consulting with his mob sponsors Anthony "Tony Pro" Provenzano and Anthony J. Giacalone. On July 30, 1975, Hoffa went to an early afternoon appointment with, he thought, Provenzano and Giacalone, at the Machus Red Fox Restaurant outside Detroit. Hoffa was never heard of again.

Although no charges were ever brought over Jimmy Hoffa's disappearance, the FBI believes Hoffa's foster son, Charles "Chuckie" O'Brien, without knowing what was to happen, picked up Hoffa late at the Machus Red Fox and drove him to a house where three of Tony Pro's men were waiting. Soon Hoffa was dead. According to an FBI informant, Hoffa's body was stuffed in a fifty-gallon oil drum and transported by truck to a junkyard where it was crushed in a steel compactor.

The FBI has kept the Hoffa disappearance case open for eighteen years. The official viewpoint of the FBI on the case is that Teamsters president, Frank Fitzsimmons, conspired with Anthony Provenzano and others to kill Jimmy Hoffa, to permanently thwart a bid by Hoffa to regain the presidency of the Teamsters.

Jimmy Hoffa was the first of Frank Ragano's three alleged Kennedy assassination conspirators to die. Santos Trafficante was next. As we know he died in 1987 after making a startling confession to Ragano.

Trafficante had prospered greatly in the years following the assassination of President Kennedy. It wasn't long after Kennedy's death that the FBI ceased harassing Trafficante's huge Florida gambling network. The force behind that harassment had been Bobby Kennedy and when he resigned as attorney general his successor had other priorities.

Trafficante had a brief brush with the law in 1966 when he was arrested along with Carlos Marcello and other mobsters for attending what appeared to be a mob conclave at the La Stella Restaurant in Queens, New York. Charged with "consorting with known criminals" he was released on $100,000 bail and nothing came of the charges. A photograph of a luncheon at La Stella held a week later, after a Queens grand jury hearing, showing Trafficante and Frank Ragano in the company of Carlos Marcello and his lawyer Jack Wasserman, and other gangsters, which was published in *Time* magazine and subsequently flashed around the world, did, however, bring Trafficante much unwanted notoriety. A reserved, taciturn man, Trafficante preferred to dwell in the shadows.

We have already mentioned that in 1968 and 1969 Trafficante journeyed to Saigon to make arrangements with Corsican drug dealers to ship Indochinese heroin to the United States.

After Jimmy Hoffa was released from prison in 1971 and returned to Detroit he soon became aware that Frank Fitzsimmons, his handpicked successor as head of the Teamsters, was not going to step aside and let Jimmy have back his old job. Consequently Hoffa asked Frank Ragano to approach Trafficante and ask him to have Fitzsimmons killed. After thinking it over Trafficante told Ragano he thought it would be too risky to hit Fitzsimmons because several of Trafficante's more powerful friends in the mob wanted Fitzsimmons to remain in power. Out of fear of what they would do, Trafficante declined to issue the contract on Fitzsimmons.

In the early seventies Joe Hauser and Irving Davidson persuaded Trafficante to attempt to garner lucrative labor union insurance for them by offering certain Teamsters officials he knew huge kickbacks. But the FBI had been closely watching Trafficante since the La Stella sitdown and he and Hauser and Davidson soon found themselves charged with pilfering large sums from the Teamsters Southeast States Health and Welfare Fund. All three were indicted but the charges against Trafficante and Davidson were eventually dropped.

Trafficante's next brush with the law came in 1976 with the brutal murder of his friend and former partner in the CIA-Mafia plots to assassinate Castro, Johnny Rosselli.

It will be recalled that Rosselli had been telling a Senate committee what he knew about the Kennedy assassination, putting forth the idea that Trafficante and Cubans loyal to Fidel Castro were behind it. That had apparently been enough for Trafficante. To prevent Rosselli from running off at the mouth again before the Senate Committee, Trafficante allegedly had Rosselli killed. At least that is what a reliable informant told *New York Times* reporter, Nicholas Gage, who reported the informant's suspicions in his paper. However, Dade County [Florida] detectives, who had the responsibility of investigating Rosselli's murder, were never able to convincingly link Trafficante to the crime.

In 1986 the Justice Department indicted Trafficante on a racketeering charge under the RICO statute and the seventy-two-year-old godfather, who was suffering from a heart ailment, went on trial briefly in Tampa. Frank Ragano represented him so successfully that a mistrial was declared and all charges against Trafficante were dropped.

A suspect in many serious crimes, including the murder of the president of the United States, Trafficante nevertheless was extremely successful in avoiding charges and convictions. He had been arrested more than twenty times in his long criminal career, but had never spent a day and night in a U.S. jail, and he was convicted only twice: for evading a federal subpoena, for which he received probation for a year, and for drunken driving, for which he was fined $250. Today Frank Ragano takes justifiable pride in his twenty-seven years of service to the Tampa godfather.

There is some evidence that Trafficante became very worried after the imprisonment of Carlos Marcello in 1983 that his fellow conspirator in the Kennedy assassination plot might crack under the pressure of confinement and reveal the details of the plot to obtain his release from prison. I was told by Texarkana prison officials in 1987 that they believed Trafficante had put out a contract on Marcello's life and the officials feared the murder would be carried out at Texarkana.

For this reason Marcello was being held in the most secure area of the prison, the nine hundred inmate level-three main institution in the Texarkana compound rather than the level-one "satellite camp" holding 233 inmates in a small, wide-open complex outside the main institution's walls.

According to Frank Ragano, after the evening of November 22, 1963, Trafficante never talked with him about the assassination again until approximately two weeks before his death on March 17, 1987.

Trafficante's health had begun to deteriorate in 1986. His kidneys had failed, he had heart disease, and he was due to undergo triple bypass surgery at the Texas Heart Institute in Houston. Trafficante knew he was dying by March 1987 and so he summoned his attorney for twenty-seven years to his side for a series of final conversations. After all, Trafficante was a Catholic and, despite his criminality, remained a Catholic all his life, attending mass with his family on Sundays and bringing his children up to be Catholics. Catholics, even Catholic gangsters, believe in confessing their sins. For several days the two men reminisced about the past. Santos had some regrets about several of his murder victims. He had made the mistake of getting too close to some of his victims' family members. Trafficante spoke at length about Robert Kennedy's investigations of his gambling operations and of his rude intrusions into his personal and family life. It was obvious to Ragano that Santos was still bitter over what Kennedy had done and had threatened to do to him. He had been convinced that Bobby would not rest until he put him away for the rest of his life. As Santos rambled on about the Kennedys in a hoarse and failing voice Ragano was suddenly taken aback when the dying Mafia prince began talking about the Kennedy assassination. For almost twenty-five years Ragano had stayed clear of the dread subject, never mentioning the issue again after Trafficante had triumphantly raised his glass to Kennedy's death at Tampa's International Inn the evening of November 22, 1963.

Now, as he felt his life draining away, Santos returned to the climactic event of his criminal career, and the darkest secret of his life. As Ragano held his breath, Trafficante began talking in a hoarse whisper about certain mistakes that had been made, mistakes that he blamed on Carlos Marcello.

Trafficante looked at Ragano with a pained expression in his eyes. "You know, Frank," he said, "Carlos screwed up. We should have killed Bobby, not Giovanni."

Ragano, speechless, simply nodded his head. It was only then that he finally realized who was behind the events of November 22, 1963.

CHAPTER 17

Counterplot:
Oliver Stone's JFK

Oliver Stone's forty-million dollar film on the Kennedy assassination, *JFK*, released by Warner Brothers in December 1991 was, despite its historical distortions and inaccuracies, an important development in the Kennedy assassination case. For the first time since Kennedy's murder in November 1963 vast numbers of Americans were introduced to some of the mysteries and enigmas and horrors of what had come to be known as the "Crime of the Century."

Before Stone's film, knowledge of the Kennedy assassination case was limited to a few hundred private investigators, writers, and "buffs," who had devoted five, ten, twenty years to the study of the crime, and to the staff members of the Warren Commission and the House Select Committee on Assassinations. Now, with the appearance of *JFK,* large masses of people became exposed to the national disgrace of this still unsolved murder. At last a significantly large constituency had been formed that could conceivably help influence public policy in regard to the case.

However, as we shall see, Oliver Stone found himself committing the same "capital mistake" Sherlock Holmes had warned against, that of theorizing "before one has data." "Insensibly one begins to twist facts to suit theories," said Holmes, "instead of theories to suit facts . . . " Just as J. Edgar Hoover was guilty of theorizing before he had data that Lee Harvey Oswald, acting alone, had assassinated President Kennedy, and was compelled to twist facts to suit his theory, so Oliver Stone was guilty of theorizing before he had data that a vast conspiracy, comprised of high-ranking officials of the military-industrial complex, the Joint Chiefs of Staff, the CIA, the FBI, and the White House had arranged to have Kennedy killed so that the war in Vietnam, which Stone claimed Kennedy had wanted to put an end to, could be escalated. As we shall see, to arrive at this essentially preposterous conclusion, Oliver Stone was compelled to twist even more facts to suit theories than J. Edgar Hoover had.

Oliver Stone had served in the U.S. Army and had seen action in the Vietnam War. The horror and madness of the fighting, which he so brilliantly portrayed in his film *Platoon*, was the defining event of his adult life. He had been wounded twice in battle. When he returned home in 1968 he was consumed with rage against a government that could have brought about a disaster of such magnitude: 57,939 Americans killed in action, one million Vietnamese dead, and the loss of South Vietnam to the Communists.

For years Stone ruminated on the Vietnam catastrophe. As he embarked on his career as a film director, memories of the obscene carnage of the war haunted him. Who was ultimately to blame for this unimaginable calamity? John F. Kennedy had been a hero of his as a senior in prep school. Kennedy's assassination, coming in the early stages of the Vietnam conflict, had deeply shocked him. Who killed Kennedy? Gradually Stone formulated an opinion that was more grounded in wishful thinking than in historical reality: *The Vietnam War was escalated by the cabal that arranged the assassination of John F. Kennedy.* Now all he had to do was to find and twist data to suit his theory. The result was *JFK.*

But a film dealing with a subject of this magnitude needed a hero. Oliver Stone found that hero in a man of decidedly dubious reputation: the six-foot-six Jim Garrison, former Orleans Parish district attorney, who had reinvestigated the assassination of President Kennedy in 1967 and 1968 and had, in 1969, unsuccessfully prosecuted a retired New Orleans businessman, and notorious homosexual, by the name of Clay Shaw, for conspiring to assassinate Kennedy.

What attracted Oliver Stone to Garrison was a book Garrison had written in 1988, *On the Trail of the Assassins,* in which Garrison vividly portrayed, in often flowery prose, his crusade against enormous odds to get to the bottom of the assassination. When

Oliver Stone read the book, he was relatively new to the tangled web of the Kennedy assassination case. He was therefore easily seduced by Garrison's style and content. "Jim Garrison opened my eyes," Stone asserted, swallowing Garrison's assassination scenario hook, line, and sinker.

That scenario posited a vast conspiracy, with a cast of plotters in the hundreds, a coup d'etat organized and carried out by "a shadow government consisting of corrupt men at the highest levels of the Pentagon, the intelligence establishment and the giant multinational corporations," masterminded by, of all people, the retired managing director of the New Orleans International Trade Mart, Clay Shaw, who was known in New Orleans as a wealthy refined aesthete, with homosexual leanings, who had lovingly restored many buildings in the French Quarter to their original eighteenth-century state, and was writing a book on Louisiana's first Spanish governor. It was also rumored that Shaw had some sinister connection to the CIA. (That connection, it was later determined, was quite innocent. Shaw was not an agency employee but a CIA contact, one of twenty-five thousand Americans who were annually debriefed by the CIA on their overseas travels.)

Entirely overlooked by Stone and Garrison was the fact that Clay Shaw had absolutely no motive whatsoever to have Kennedy killed. He had everything to lose and nothing to gain by participating in a plot to assassinate JFK.

Oliver Stone was apparently unaware of the shadier side of Garrison's reputation at the time he was seduced by his book. While Garrison was in the army he was diagnosed as unstable and was discharged because Army doctors had determined he was in need of long-term psychotherapy. It was also well known that he did business with organized crime, and had, in fact, accepted many favors from members of the Marcello organization in return for looking the other way when confronted with evidence of their crimes.

A year after the acquittal of Clay Shaw, Garrison was still insisting that organized crime in New Orleans did not exist and that Carlos Marcello was a respectable businessman. However, in that same year, 1970, three members of the Marcello organization—Sam DiPiazza, Eugene Nolan, and Frank Timphony—were indicted for illegal gambling in Houston and New Orleans. Writing in *Life* magazine, Pulitzer Prize-winning investigative journalist, David Chandler charged that from 1965 through 1969 Garrison chose not to prosecute eighty-four cases against members of Marcello's organization: twenty-two on gambling charges, one for attempted murder, three for kidnapping, and one for manslaughter. Chandler also revealed that in 1969 a notorious Marcello bagman died of a heart attack during a mysterious meeting in Garrison's home.

Before long an organized crime strike force under Justice Department district attorney John Wall arrested Jim Garrison, charging him with taking payoffs from Marcello gamblers through Pershing Gervais, Garrison's former chief investigator who had become, after the Shaw trial, his bagman. One such payoff—for $1000—was found in a drawer in Garrison's desk. At trial seventy recorded conversations between Garrison and Gervais were played that clearly indicated Garrison was regularly accepting $1000 bribes from Marcello gamblers.

Yes, Jim Garrison was doing business with the mob. According to a CIA inspector general's report of 1967 while Garrison was conducting his investigation of the Kennedy assassination, Garrison met with CIA-Mafia plotter, Johnny Rosselli, in Las Vegas. We do not know what the meeting was about, but Rosselli was making his own allegations about the assassination at the time, namely that Santos Trafficante, in association with pro-Castro Cubans, was behind the Kennedy assassination.

Eventually Oliver Stone was made aware of Jim Garrison's failings and the shabbiness of his case against Clay Shaw, but that did not prevent him from depicting Garrison as the hero of the Kennedy assassination case. In the film, *JFK*, Jim Garrison, played by Kevin Costner, was transformed from the volatile, flamboyant, unscrupulous, frequently irresponsible egomaniac, and publicity hound that he was into the quiet, serious, low key, crusading strait arrow that Oliver Stone made him out to be.

This portrayal was bound to irk seasoned assassination researchers and writers who had spent a good portion of their working lives on the case and they were quick to voice their condemnation of the entire Stone project.

Harold Weisberg, the irascible twenty-six-year veteran of Kennedy assassination research, author of many books on the assassination, including three that effectively demolished the credibility of the *Warren Report*, got hold of a pirated early version of the screenplay and quickly opined publicly that "As an investigator Jim Garrison could not find a pubic hair in a whore house at rush hour." As for Oliver Stone, filmmaker, Weisberg dismissed him by saying publicly: "I think people who sell sex have more principle."

Weisberg then sent the pirated early draft of the screenplay to George Lardner, Jr., of the *Washington Post*, who knew what he was talking about since he had covered the Garrison investigation for his newspaper. "DALLAS IN WONDERLAND: OLIVER STONE'S VERSION OF THE KENNEDY ASSASSINATION EXPLOITS THE EDGE OF PARANOIA" screamed the headline of his article on the film.

But unquestionably the most violent attack on the film came from Jack Valenti, the president and chief executive of the Motion Picture Association of America and a former top aide to President Lyndon Johnson, who branded Stone's film a "hoax" and a "smear" and "pure fiction" that "rivalled the Nazi propaganda films of Leni Reifenstahl."

In his statement to the press Valenti said *JFK* was a "monstrous charade" based on the "hallucinatory bleatings of an author named Jim Garrison, a discredited former district attorney in New Orleans."

Does any sane human being believe that President Johnson, the Warren Commission members, law enforcement officers, C.I.A., F.B.I., assorted thugs, weirdos, Frisbee throwers, all conspired together as plotters in Garrison's wacky sightings? And then for 29 years nothing leaked?

"In scene after scene Mr. Stone plasters together the half true and the totally false and from that he manufactures the plausible. No wonder that many young people, gripped by the movie, leave the theater convinced they have been witness to the truth.

In much the same way, young German boys and girls in 1941 were mesmerized by Leni Reifenstahl's "Triumph of the Will," in which Adolf Hitler was depicted as a newborn God. Both "J.F.K," and "Triumph of the Will" are equally a propaganda masterpiece and equally a hoax. Mr. Stone and Leni Reifenstahl have another genetic linkage: neither of them carried a disclaimer on their film that its contents were mostly pure fiction.

What was "pure fiction" in Oliver Stone's film?

The actor Joe Pesci's characterization of David Ferrie for one. Aside from the fact that the real David Ferrie was tall and grotesque in appearance, looking nothing like Pesci, David Ferrie's principal occupation during the spring, summer, and fall of 1963 was investigator and general assistant to Carlos Marcello's lawyer, G. Wray Gill, not a Kennedy assassination conspirator in league with Clay Shaw, certain Cuban exiles, and the CIA. Ferrie was at Marcello's headquarters in the Town and Country Motel at least three times a week conferring with Gill and Marcello on Marcello's forthcoming trial, and we believe conspiring with Marcello in a plan to assassinate Kennedy. Furthermore, on the two weekends prior to the assassination Ferrie was conferring with Carlos Marcello at the Farmhouse of his swampland property, Churchill Farms, not hanging around the bars of the French Quarter with assorted CIA types and homosexual acquaintances of Clay Shaw as depicted in the film.

One of the most outrageous elements of the Stone-Pesci portrayal of Ferrie was the vituperative anti-

Kennedy outburst delivered by Ferrie about halfway through the film:

> *See what Kennedy done. With Kennedy a guy should take a knife, like one of them other guys, and stab and kill the fucker, where he is now. Somebody should kill the fucker. I mean it. This is true. Honest to God. It's about time to go. But I tell you something. I hope I get a week's notice. I'll kill. Right in the fuckin' in the White House. Somebody's got to get rid of this fucker.*

These words, as we know, were actually spoken by mobster Willie Weisburg to his boss, Angelo Bruno, head of the Philadelphia Cosa Nostra family. They were secretly recorded by an FBI listening device on February 9, 1962. To put the words of a Cosa Nostra capo in the mouth of a purported CIA operative pushes the limits of poetic license. Besides, no evidence has ever been uncovered indicating Ferrie ever worked for the CIA.

The depiction of Ferrie's death in *JFK* also differs greatly from the reality of what happened. According to Coroner Nicholas Chetta's autopsy report Ferrie died of natural causes, specifically from a cerebral hemorrhage caused by a "berry aneurysm" or weak point on a blood vessel at the base of the brain. Ferrie's cerebral hemorrhage, Dr. Chetta had speculated, had probably been brought on by stress over Garrison's impending indictment of him. Although the New Orleans Metropolitan Crime Commission director, Aaron Kohn, suspected that Ferrie was murdered, there is no evidence that he was attacked by the two killers who brutally assailed him in Oliver Stone's film. Until the cause of Ferrie's death is proved to be murder, the death struggle of David Ferrie in *JFK* remains pure fiction.

In fact, much of the ending of Oliver Stone's film is fictional. The last important scene of *JFK* is the finale of Garrison's trial of Clay Shaw: the prosecution's summation in court followed by the jury's verdict. Kevin Costner, impersonating Garrison, presents the prosecution's summation, in a long peroration that synthesizes Garrison-Stone's view of the Kennedy assassination case. The trouble with this scenario is that Garrison never gave the prosecution's summation at the Shaw trial. His two assistant district attorneys, James Alcock and Alvin Oser, presented the summation. Garrison himself just presented a brief closing statement to the jury. In the film that statement turned out to also embody snippets from a July 1967 *Playboy* interview of Garrison and from some of Garrison's public lectures. Therefore Kevin Costner's remarks in the courtroom are essentially meaningless in terms of the trial. They are nothing but propaganda for the Garrison-Stone theory that President Kennedy was killed as a result of a 'coup d'etat' organized by the highest levels of the U.S. government in league with the military-industrial complex so that the war in Vietnam could be escalated.

But the fictions delivered by Ferrie-Pesci and Garrison-Costner in *JFK* are minor compared to those enunciated by a character called "Mr. X" in a climactic scene on the Capitol Mall between Garrison-Costner and "Mr. X," who was loosely based on a retired Air Force colonel named L. Fletcher Prouty, and was played in the film very convincingly by the actor, Donald Sutherland. In this scene—which Oliver Stone admits never took place—the central idea behind Stone's conspiracy theory is stated most forcefully.

Who is Colonel L. Fletcher Prouty? He is a retired Air Force officer who served as chief of special operations for the Joint Chiefs of Staff from 1955 to 1964. Since his retirement he has been touting himself as an insider to the machinations within the halls of the Pentagon and CIA headquarters that resulted in the assassination of President Kennedy. The author of *The Secret Team: The CIA and Its Allies in Control of The United States and the World*, published by Prentice Hall, and numerous articles for the magazine *Gallery*, Prouty's credentials to write about the Kennedy assassination have been regarded as suspect by most serious students of the case. He is given little credence by such experts on the Kennedy assassination as Paul L. Hoch, who has been on the case for twenty-five years, James Lesar, president of the Assassination Archives and Research Center, and G. Robert Blakey, former chief counsel of the House Select Committee on Assassinations, among others.

Prouty has kept some dubious company since his retirement. He was reportedly involved with the rabidly anti-Semitic, racist Liberty Lobby, has been a featured speaker at the lobby's annual convention, and was a contributor to its national radio program and newsletter. Among the newsletter's articles have been "The Diary of Anne Frank is a Fraud" and "The White Race is Becoming an Endangered Species." Along with a Mississippi Ku Klux Klan leader, Prouty

was named to the advisory board of the lobby's
Populist Action Committee.

The Liberty Lobby has a history of allegiance to
racist and anti-Semitic causes that attract a large following of lunatic-fringe adherents. Its founder was
Willis Carto, an ex-John Birch Society member who
preached that the Jews were America's public enemy
number one. Prouty's reprint publisher, Noontide
Press, had published a book claiming that the
Holocaust was a Jew-sponsored hoax.

Colonel Prouty, given the cold shoulder by many of
the serious Kennedy assassination writers, took up
with one of the most contentious assassination investigators, Harrison Livingstone, author of two books
on the assassination, *High Treason I* and *High
Treason II*. Both books pointed to another megaconspiracy à la Oliver Stone. Livingstone was the first
writer to publish the lurid Kennedy autopsy photos.
After associating himself with kindred spirit Fletcher
Prouty, the latter hinted that McGeorge Bundy,
Kennedy's good friend and national security advisor,
was a possible conspirator, probably the most unlikely
conspirator anyone had ever dreamt up. Eventually
Stone got into a disagreement with Livingstone and
Livingstone retaliated by vilifying Stone to the press.

Yes, Oliver Stone surrounded himself with a
strange assortment of Kennedy assassination buffs.
Conspicuously absent from his entourage were the
seasoned veterans of the case, men such as Harold
Weisberg, Josiah Thompson, Richard Popkin, and
Anthony Summers, who had made a genuine contribution to our understanding of the crime.

In weighing the veracity of Oliver Stone's pivotal
scene on the Capitol Mall between Garrison-Costner

and "Mr. X," it should be borne in mind that what "Mr. X" tells Jim Garrison is pure propaganda. How much of it is true?

As part of the plot to assassinate Kennedy, "Mr. X" tells Garrison that for some mysterious reason he was sent to the South Pole a few days before the assassination. After the assassination "Mr. X" suspected that the reason why he was sent to the South Pole was to prevent him from arranging for additional security along the motorcade route during Kennedy's visit to Dallas. "We'd've put at least 100 to 200 [military intelligence] agents on the sidewalks *without question*," exclaims 'Mr. X.' Instead the 112th Military Intelligence Group at Fort Sam Houston, Texas, was not ordered to Dallas on November 22, they were told to "stand down" [i.e., not go].

First of all, orders to a military intelligence group to go to Dallas to provide additional security for the president's visit would have been given weeks before November 21. Such orders would have been given by "Mr. X" long before he was suddenly dispatched to the South Pole.

Second, the House Select Committee on Assassinations in its 1979 final report stated that Lieutenant Colonel Robert E. Jones, operations officer to the U.S. Army's 112th Military Intelligence Group, Fort Sam Houston, Texas, testified that there were from eight to twelve military intelligence agents performing liaison functions with the Secret Service in Dallas the day of the assassination. Jones gave no testimony that an order had been given them from the office of the Joint Chiefs to "stand down."

"Mr. X" goes on to tell Garrison that "at 12:34 P.M.

the entire telephone system went dead in Washington for a solid hour," as if the conspirators had engineered this "to keep the wrong stories from spreading if anything went wrong with the plan. *Nothing* was left to chance." Not true. Telephone circuits were understandably overloaded in the wake of the assassination and many people were unable to reach their parties. No order was given to the telephone company to cut off telephone service in Washington the day of the assassination. As for "Mr. X's" remark "*Nothing* was left to chance," was it part of the conspirators' plan to have Oswald captured by the Dallas Police and subsequently shot dead in the basement of police headquarters?

To reinforce the conspiracy scenario, "Mr. X" tells an increasingly gullible Garrison that "word was radioed from the White House Situation Room to Lyndon Johnson [On *Air Force One*] that one individual performed the assassination."

This information had been known ever since William Manchester reported it in his *Death of a President* in 1967. It was, of course, J. Edgar Hoover busily at work trying to lay the blame for the assassination on Lee Harvey Oswald, acting alone, for his own unworthy reasons.

We come to the National Security Action memos, the NSAMs. "Mr. X" appears to place great significance on these NSAMs to make his case for megaconspiracy. He tells Garrison that six weeks before the assassination, President Kennedy signed NSAM 263 endorsing recommendations to pull one thousand military advisors out of Vietnam by the end of 1963 and providing for a complete withdrawal from Vietnam by the end of 1965. In measured, ponderously serious tones "Mr. X" tells Garrison: "Once NSAM 263 was signed Kennedy was, for all intents, a dead man." In other words, Kennedy was a victim of the military-industrial establishment. To cap his case "Mr. X" brings up another NSAM, one signed by President Johnson four days after the assassination, NSAM 273, that made no mention of withdrawing any military advisors from Vietnam but provided plans for an escalation of the war instead, including preparations for attacking North Vietnam.

To the character based on "Mr. X," these two NSAMs provide the why for the conspiracy to kill Kennedy. Kennedy wanted to pull out of Vietnam, Johnson wanted to escalate the war. Case closed. Kennedy was killed by the military-industrial complex because he wanted to pull out of Vietnam. This theory was indeed music to Oliver Stone's ears.

This simplistic explanation of the assassination made sense to both Stone and Garrison. Now they knew who the bad guys were. But the inescapable fact is that despite NSAM 263, John Kennedy had no intention of pulling out of Vietnam in the near future and all his closest aides were well aware of it.

We now know that it is highly unlikely that Kennedy would have pulled out of Vietnam by the end of his first term. Kennedy intended to pull one thousand troops out before the 1964 election as a political gesture, to temporarily appease the antiwar factions and as a means to bring pressure on the South Vietnamese government to be more self-reliant. Kennedy's apparent intentions as expressed in NSAM 263 were contradicted by what Kennedy was going to say in the speech he was going to deliver at the Dallas Trade Mart after the motorcade. In that speech, which he did not live to deliver, he was planning to reaffirm his Vietnam stand. He was planning to refer to America's "painful, risky, and costly effort in Southeast Asia," declaring "but we dare not weary of the task," and announcing "we have increased our counterinsurgency forces which are now engaged in South Vietnam by 600 percent." "Our mission in the world," he was going to say, "is to carry the message of truth and freedom to all the far corners of the earth . . . We in this country are—by destiny rather than choice—the watchmen on the walls of world freedom."

And, as we all know, Bobby Kennedy continued to support the war for three years after his brother's death, believing he was furthering his slain brother's policies. In fact, when asked in the fall of 1964 whether his slain brother believed it was worthwhile not to abandon Vietnam, Bobby replied: "He reached the conclusion that probably it was worthwhile."

Oliver Stone was so anxious to pin the blame for the assassination on Kennedy's pro-Vietnam War enemies in the military-industrial complex that he even recruited a scholar to research John F. Kennedy's Vietnam policies and the question of whether he would continue to prosecute the war in Southeast Asia. His name was John Newman and he was an army major doing research for a Ph.D thesis on Kennedy and the Vietnam War. Soon he became an advisor for the film, *JFK,* and Stone found him a publisher for his thesis. The book was published by Warner Books under the title *JFK and Vietnam: Deception, Intrigue and the Struggle for Power.* In his review of the book in the *New York Times,* Arthur M. Schlesinger, Jr., remarked that there was a gulf between Kennedy's rhetoric on Vietnam and his actions. "Unfortunately Kennedy's contradictory legacy on Vietnam," Schlesinger wrote, "permitted Lyndon Johnson to plunge into the escalation and Americanization of the war honestly believing that he was doing what Kennedy would have done."

It is impossible to say whether John F. Kennedy would have pulled out of Vietnam by the end of 1965 or not. My own belief is that he would not have pulled out until it was too late, until there were many casualties, for every fiber in Kennedy's being would have prompted him to persevere. For John F. Kennedy was the archtypical Cold Warrior, driven by the Kennedy family ethos to win at all cost.

Kennedy first became deeply involved in the Vietnam War when he endorsed the findings in November 1961 of his special military advisor, General Maxwell Taylor, and one of his national security advisors, Walt Whitman Rostow, that called for an initial U.S. troop commitment to South Vietnam of eight thousand men, with the possibility of escalating to 200,000.

Before sending Taylor and Rostow off to Vietnam to evaluate the situation Kennedy hinted that he wanted them to recommend a stronger commitment by telling them: "There are limits to the number of defeats I can defend in one twelve-month period. I've had the Bay of Pigs and the pullout at Laos and I can't accept a third."

As it turned out, Kennedy could not help himself. As a believer in the policy of containment and the so-called domino theory, and as a Kennedy, he could not withdraw from the fight in South Vietnam. And so he ordered the Department of Defense to prepare for the introduction of combat troops into South Vietnam. All this was done as secretly as possible, for, as with his

Operation Mongoose, Kennedy did not want the American people to have any inkling of the extent of his commitment in Vietnam.

Defending his brother's commitment to South Vietnam, Robert Kennedy in a speech from Hong Kong in the spring of 1962 said: "The solution of the war in South Vietnam lies in our winning it. We are going to win it, and we are going to stay here until we win."

On July 17, 1963, President Kennedy held a press conference during which he made what was to be his last public utterance on the Vietnam situation. In response to a reporter's questioning about his administration's commitment to South Vietnam, he said: "We are not going to withdraw from that effort. In my opinion, for us to withdraw from that effort would mean a collapse not only of South Vietnam, but Southeast Asia. So we are going to stay there."

Kennedy took a crucial step toward Americanizing the war in Vietnam when he countenanced the coup d'etat of November 1, 1963, against the South Vietnamese government led by President Ngo Dinh Diem and his eccentric brother, Ngo Dinh Nhu. The two brothers were brutally murdered in the ensuing civil war. It is worthwhile noting that Vice President Johnson and General Maxwell Taylor voted against the coup.

After the downfall of the Diem government, the war in South Vietnam, for all intents and purposes, became an American War.

John F. Kennedy had called a conference on Vietnam for Monday, November 25, over which President Lyndon Johnson eventually presided. Johnson held the conference on Sunday, November 24, and it was attended by all those Kennedy appointees who had helped lead Kennedy into the war: McNamara, Rusk, Bundy, McCone, Henry Cabot Lodge and General Maxwell Taylor. The question was should they persist in the war or not. After the conference was over Lyndon Johnson told press aide, Pierre Salinger, to announce to the press that he would "continue John Kennedy's policy." The war would go on.

Years later it was asserted in a Pentagon study of the war that it had been John F. Kennedy who had transformed the "limited risk gamble" of the Eisenhower administration to a "broad commitment to prevent the communist domination of South Vietnam."

John F. Kennedy was the first of the four U.S. presidents involved with Vietnam to actually go to war in Indochina. His handpicked vice president continued the war, escalating it step by step, just as he had done. Most important, the cabinet officers and White House aides Kennedy had picked vigorously urged on the war under Lyndon Johnson. Not one of them ever thought they were not continuing John F. Kennedy's Vietnam policy in energetically pursuing the war.

But the most convincing evidence of all that John Kennedy would have pursued the war in South Vietnam had he lived was the fact that his brother Bobby continued to support the war on the floor of the Senate for a full three years after his brother's death, believing he was furthering his dead brother's policy.

Years later, in his excellent book, *Why We Were in Vietnam*, Norman Podhoretz wrote, "He [Kennedy] steadily expanded the size of the U.S. Military Mission, sent combat support units, air combat and helicopter teams, still more military advisers, and 600 Special Forces Green Berets to train and lead South

Vietnam in antiguerrilla tactics." For all intents and purposes, Podhoretz concluded, under John F. Kennedy "America went to war in Vietnam."

For Kennedy aide Harris Wofford, "Vietnam had become the fire in which the President was determined to prove he was made of steel."

In *JFK*, after "Mr. X" walks away into the sunset and Garrison-Costner is shown contemplating the eternal flame on Kennedy's tomb in Arlington, Virginia, the action shifts back to New Orleans and Garrison's preparations for the impending prosecution of the hapless Clay Shaw.

We see on the screen a smoke-filled room full of Garrison-Costner's assistants. Paperwork is stacked in the corners almost to the ceiling, there are coffee cups and doughnuts on the desk. The staff working on the Clay Shaw prosecution numbers some eleven people. We sense that the trial is drawing closer.

One of the assistants, Bill Boxley, tells Garrison-Costner:

> *We should be investigating all our Mafia leads here in New Orleans—Carlos Marcello, Santos Trafficante—I can buy that a hell of a lot easier than the government. Ruby's all Mob, knows Oswald, sets him up. Hoffa-Trafficante-Marcello, they hire some guns and they do Kennedy and maybe the government doesn't want to open up a whole can o' worms there because it used the Mob to get Castro. Y'Know, Castro being assassinated sounds pretty wild to John Q. Citizen. So they close the book on J.F.K. It makes sense to me.*

To which Garrison-Costner responds:

> *I don't doubt their involvement, Bill, but at a lower level. Could the Mob change the parade [motorcade] route, Bill, or eliminate the protection for the President? Could the Mob send Oswald to Russia and get him back? Could the Mob get the FBI, the CIA, and the Dallas police to make a mess of the investigation? Could the Mob appoint the Warren Commission to cover it up? Could the Mob wreck the autopsy? Could the Mob influence the national media to go to sleep? And since when has the Mob used anything but .38's for hits up close? The Mob wouldn't have the guts or the guns or the power for something of this magnitude. . . . This was a military-style ambush from start to finish . . . a coup d'etat with Lyndon Johnson waiting in the wings.*

The members of Garrison-Costner's staff are rendered speechless by this torrent of questions all begging the answer: "No, the Mob, couldn't have possibly arranged that."

First the parade [motorcade] route. Could the mob have been able to change the motorcade route at the last minute to provide for the dogleg turn off Houston Street onto Elm Street, which would slow the presidential limousine down to a crawl and bring it into the vicinity of an ambush as it passed first, right beneath Oswald's Book Depository window, and next, the slope leading to the grassy knoll? Answer: probably not. But the evidence shows that nor did any other conspirators change the motorcade route.

The record indicates that the original motorcade

route through Dealey Plaza via Main Street, which was vulnerable also to gunfire from the Book Depository and the grassy knoll, was chosen by Governor John Connally in consultation with the White House. Would Connally, who was sitting next to Kennedy in the presidential limousine, have deliberately placed himself in the line of fire? Connally's chosen route was then modified slightly on Monday, November 18, by Secret Service agent, Forrest J. Sorrels, special agent in charge of the Dallas Secret Service office. It provided for an abrupt dogleg turn to the right in Dealey Plaza from Main Street onto Houston Street and then another abrupt turn, this time to the left, onto Elm Street. This would bring the presidential motorcade right under the Book Depository window where Oswald worked and within spitting distance of the picket fence on the grassy knoll. The change Sorrels made in the motorcade route deviated from Secret Service regulations because it made the president vulnerable to a sniper attack from a tall building and from curbside onlookers. It also forced the motorcade to slow down. Why did Sorrels make the change? In his testimony before the House Select Committee on Assassinations, Sorrels said since he was under considerable White House pressure to make sure President Kennedy received maximum public exposure, he changed the route slightly to allow the presidential limousine to pass closer to curbside onlookers than would have been the case had the motorcade proceeded down Main Street.

Not wholly convinced by this explanation, the Assassinations Committee launched an investigation of Sorrels' post-assassination life to see if he profited in any way from changing the motorcade route. The Committee found that Sorrels' standard of living, and bank account, showed no significant improvements in the years following the assassination. The committee then concluded that it had found no evidence that "the selection of a motorcade route involved Secret Service complicity in a plot to assassinate the President." Sorrels was cleared.

Could the mob have been able "to eliminate the protection of the President?" Answer: yes and no.

The House Select Committee on Assassinations concluded that "the Secret Service was deficient in the performance of its duties," but uncovered no evidence that it had been influenced in any way by individuals conspiring to assassinate President Kennedy.

As for possible mob influence on the Secret Service, there is some evidence that it could have indirectly influenced the performance of certain Secret Service agents in the presidential motorcade.

In November 1988 it was revealed by Washington columnist Jack Anderson in a ninety-minute television documentary *American Expose: Who Murdered JFK?* that nine Secret Service agents had stayed up through the early morning hours of November 22 attending a raucous all-night drinking party at Pat Kirkwood's Cellar Door club in Forth Worth. And who were the sexy girls who were plying the Secret Service agents with alcohol? According to Pat Kirkwood, who was present at the party, they were strippers sent over from Jack Ruby's Carousel Club for the express purpose of getting the agents drunk. As it turned out when the shooting broke out in Dealey Plaza the reactions of several agents were noticeably slow. If we believe that mobster Jack Ruby was part of the conspiracy to assassinate Kennedy, we can answer Oliver Stone's question about whether the mob could have eliminated Secret Service protection with a qualified "yes." Not "eliminated," but influenced.

Could the mob have sent Oswald to the Soviet Union and brought him back? No. And nobody knows for sure whether anybody, or any agency, sent Oswald to the Soviet Union and brought him back. For all we know Oswald probably sent himself to the Soviet Union and brought himself back. Whatever the case, the issue is not relevant to the conspiracy to assassinate the president.

Could the mob get the FBI, the CIA, and the Dallas Police to make a mess of the investigation? A complex question, the answer to which is yes, in regard to the Dallas Police, and a guarded, qualified yes in regard to the FBI and the CIA.

It was well known in the underworld and must have been known to J. Edger Hoover, that the Marcello organization had much of the Dallas Police force in its pocket.

FBI informants William Abadie and Bobby Gene Moore had told the bureau after the assassination that Joseph Civello, Marcello's deputy in Dallas, was seen making payoffs to Dallas police officers and local judges. Jack Ruby, who, it must be borne in mind, worked in Dallas at the sufferance of Carlos Marcello, had scores of Dallas police officers in his debt. He made them low-interest loans. He gave them free drinks at his nightclubs and had his strippers provide them with sexual favors. Twice a month he would turn the entire Carousel Club over to the Dallas Police force allowing the officers to frolick all night for nothing. Jack Ruby expected these favors to be returned and they were. And bear in mind that

Sergeant Patrick Dean who was in charge of basement security when Ruby shot Oswald, was close to Joe Civello and had even dined with him when the mobster returned to Dallas from the Apalachin, New York, Mafia conclave of 1957. Would Dallas police officers be likely to do favors for Marcello men involved in the conspiracy to kill President Kennedy? The answer is definitely yes.

What about the FBI? Did organized crime exercise any power over it? I believe the answer is yes, in many subtle and indirect ways. We know that high-ranking mobster Frank Costello in a sense controlled J. Edgar Hoover. And we know that Frank Costello was very close to Carlos Marcello. It will be recalled that Costello had given Marcello his big chance in 1940 when he chose him to help distribute his slot machines in Louisiana and took him in as a partner in the Beverly Country Club gambling casino. Would Hoover turn up the heat on Marcello if Costello warned him not to? It is highly unlikely. Would Hoover let Marcello get away with conspiring to assassinate President Kennedy? For reasons that have already been discussed here, yes.

But why would the CIA want to cover-up a plot between Jimmy Hoffa, Santos Trafficante, and Carlos Marcello to assassinate Kennedy? Answer: to protect the secrecy of the infamous CIA-Mafia plots to assassinate Fidel Castro. Remember that Trafficante was one of the conspirators the CIA had hired to kill Castro and according to FBI informant Joe Hauser, Marcello admitted he was also in on the plot. It seems obvious that the CIA would never move against Marcello and Trafficante for fear the CIA's darkest secret, the CIA-Mafia plots to assassinate Castro, would come to light.

Could the mob appoint the Warren Commission to cover it up?

Unlikely. But the question is irrelevant. The members of the Warren Commission certainly did not conspire to kill President Kennedy. Nor did they conspire to cover-up the conspiracy behind the assassination. As we know, they were manipulated by FBI Director J. Edgar Hoover who selectively withheld vital information from the commission.

Could the mob have "wrecked the autopsy?" Of course not. Again the question is irrelevant. The autopsy surgeons were not involved in a conspiracy to assassinate Kennedy nor were they involved in a conspiracy to cover-up a conspiracy to assassinate him. The autopsy doctors at Bethesda Naval Hospital were simply bunglers who had never done an autopsy on a victim of gunshot wounds. And the record clearly shows they were taking orders from Jacqueline and Robert Kennedy, and the Kennedys' surrogate in the autopsy room, Admiral George C. Burkley, the slain president's personal physician and a close friend of the Kennedy family.

Could the mob influence "the national media to go to sleep?" Of course the answer is that the mob exerted no direct influence over the media. Nor, for the matter, did any other conspirators exercise such influence. The media, in the end, was influenced by ignorance and too much respect for the government's investigative agencies. Remember that J. Edgar Hoover, the indomitable G-man, was a sacred cow, a national icon, in 1963. His FBI could do no wrong. And remember that no one in the media knew the slightest thing about the CIA's plots to assassinate Castro in alliance with the Mafia in 1963. To the media, the FBI, the CIA, and the Warren Commission were pillars of law and order; they epitomized the Establishment. Anyone who challenged the conclusions of the FBI or the Warren Commission was suspect. We know better now.

"The mob wouldn't have the guns or the guts or the power for something of this magnitude." Wrong. The mob killed the chief of police of New Orleans in 1890 provoking an international incident between Italy and the United States that was finally resolved by President Benjamin Harrison. The mob killed Anton Cermak, mayor of Chicago, in 1933, in the presence of President-Elect Franklin D. Roosevelt. It is believed that the president of the American Federation of Labor, John Kilpatrick, was killed by the mob in 1961. The mob killed Colombo family boss, Joe Colombo, before a crowd of 65,000 in Columbus Circle, New York in 1971.

On December 14, 1985, Paul Castellano, boss of the Gambino crime family, was ambushed by eight Gambino gunmen under orders from John Gotti in midtown Manhattan during the Christmas season rush hour, a rubout witnessed by some ninety bystanders. In 1992 and 1993, two heavily guarded high-ranking Italian magistrates were killed in Mafia ambushes on the outskirts of Palermo, Italy. Yes, the mob had the guns and the guts and the power to do whatever it liked. If Jimmy Hoffa, Santos Trafficante, and Carlos Marcello concluded that President Kennedy had to go they most certainly had the guns, the guts, and the power to get the job done.

Oliver Stone directed a magnificent film in *JFK*. From a cinematographic standpoint, the film was a near masterpiece. The scene of the shooting in

Dealey Plaza and Garrison-Costner's debunking of the "magic-bullet" theory was extraordinarily well done. But the film did not advertise itself as essentially a work of fiction. It implied it was historical fact. It therefore misled thousands, if not millions, of Americans, particularly young Americans, as to what precisely happened in Dallas and the nation on November 22, 1963.

Videotapes of Stone's *JFK* are now being purchased by high schools across the nation to be used in U.S. history courses. Soon significant numbers of young Americans will come of age under the delusion that their own government shot and killed President John F. Kennedy.

In July, 1992, I received a phone call from a young Kennedy assassination buff who, I quickly learned, had been deluded by Oliver Stone's *JFK*. I had been in sporadic contact with him—he was a college student—since my book *Mafia Kingfish* came out in 1988.

"Mr. Davis," he gushed, "I just saw you on a TV program with Frank Ragano agreeing with everything the creep said. Don't you know Ragano was *paid* to come out with the fantastic stuff about the Mafia plotting to kill Kennedy? You realize Ragano's allegation was made only three weeks after Oliver Stone's film was released? Ragano made it to discredit Stone."

"Who do you thing paid him?" I asked.

"Simple. The *real* conspirators. The Military-industrial-governmental complex. They gave Ragano enough money to settle his debt with the IRS. They wanted to introduce a false sponsor for the assassination to discredit Oliver and his film."

CHAPTER 18

Frank Ragano:
The Issue of Credibility

If Frank Ragano is telling the truth his allegation that Hoffa, Trafficante, and Marcello plotted the murder of John F. Kennedy is the most important development in the Kennedy assassination case since the House Select Committee on Assassinations issued its final report in 1979. For Ragano has provided the much needed corroboration of the Assassinations Committee's conclusions. But is Ragano believable?

Frank Ragano has been a mob lawyer all his professional life. G. Robert Blakey once testified at a trial that Ragano was "house counsel" to the Trafficante crime family. As we know mob lawyers are routinely required to lie on behalf of their clients. And occasionally they are forced by their clients to perform questionable functions. For example, in 1967, it will be recalled that the "save Hoffa" forces had induced Jim Garrison to attempt to discredit Edward Grady Partin, the chief prosecution witness against Hoffa, by implicating him in the Kennedy assassination. Frank Ragano was involved in that corrupt endeavor. Partin testified: "Frank Ragano called me and said he could get Garrison off my back. In return he wanted a signed affidavit from me saying that I lied in Hoffa's trial. Naturally I didn't sign."

But if mob lawyers lie and cheat in behalf of their clients does it mean they necessarily do the same outside their professional life?

In 1967 Frank Ragano got into some trouble as a result of a lawsuit he brought against Time Incorporated over the photograph it published of the luncheon at La Stella Restaurant attended by Carlos Marcello, Santos Trafficante, and their lawyers. *Time* magazine had captioned the photograph "Top Cosa Nostra Hoodlums." But Frank Ragano and Jack Wasserman were lawyers, not hoodlums. Taking offense to the caption's implied characterization of him as a hoodlum, Ragano sued the magazine's owner, Time Incorporated, for libel demanding $2.5 million in damages. During the course of the trial it was revealed by the defense that Ragano had received a five-million dollar "loan" from a Teamsters pension fund that he had not declared as income to the IRS. In the end Ragano lost his libel suit and was subsequently convicted of income tax evasion for which he received a suspended sentence and was forbidden to practice law in Florida for five years.

At his libel trial Ragano was represented by Melvin Belli who had defended Jack Ruby in his trial for the murder of Lee Harvey Oswald. Ragano has stated he was under explicit instructions from Trafficante not to discuss the Ruby trial with Belli.

In 1990 Frank Ragano was again convicted of tax evasion. This time he failed to report income from a film on the life of Jimmy Hoffa he had been working on. The case is currently on appeal.

Certainly these blots on Ragano's escutcheon do not say much for his honesty toward the IRS. But are they relevant to an evaluation of whether or not Ragano is telling the truth about the Kennedy assassination?

In making an assessment of Frank Ragano's credibility a number of questions must be asked.

Were Hoffa, Trafficante, and Marcello close enough to Frank Ragano and trusting enough of him to confide something as momentous as a plan to assassinate the president of the United States to him?

G. Robert Blakey pondered this question and concluded that Hoffa, Trafficante, and Marcello had no reason not to trust Ragano. Hoffa had grown very close to Ragano during the Kennedy years and believed Ragano hated Bobby Kennedy every bit as much as he hated him. Ragano himself confirmed this. Hoffa's battles with Kennedy were his battles he has said. He admits he was elated when he first learned of President Kennedy's assassination. Trafficante also grew very close to Frank Ragano, regarding him as his best friend in addition to being a much valued house counsel to his crime family.

Trafficante was absolutely sure Ragano would not betray a confidence.

But what about Marcello? The man who had "THREE CAN KEEP A SECRET IF TWO ARE DEAD" tacked on his office door? Ragano was not an attorney for Marcello, only an acquaintance.

Marcello was too close to Santos Trafficante not to trust Frank Ragano. For years the two godfathers had done mutually profitable business together. Their interests were intertwined. Carlos and Santos were the Cosa Nostra in the South. Their territory stretched from the Florida Keys to Dallas and also embraced the Caribbean. If Trafficante trusted Ragano that would have been good enough for Marcello. He would have no doubts about him.

This is not to say that Blakey accepts Frank Ragano's allegation in its entirety. For instance, Blakey does not believe that Hoffa was in a position to order Trafficante and Marcello to do anything. Rather he believes that "it is far more likely that Ragano conveyed Hoffa's concurrence in the plot to kill the President, perhaps responding to prior communications to which Ragano might have been privy."

We come to the question of why Frank Ragano would concoct his conspiracy allegation if it was untrue. What would be his motive to lie?

Certainly making his conspiracy allegation would not affect the status of his tax-evasion case. The IRS would have little interest in it and would certainly not grant Ragano any leniency because of it. The government has a history of not reacting favorably to Kennedy assassination conspiracy allegations.

Ragano concocted his Kennedy assassination conspiracy allegation to spice up his forthcoming memoirs. Unlikely. When an author has some sensational revelation to make he keeps it to himself until his book is published. No one holds his cards closer to his chest than a writer in possession of secrets. Frank Ragano went public in January 1992 almost two years before his memoirs were scheduled to be released. He has even appeared on national television shows in connection with his conspiracy allegation. No author would divulge a major revelation from his book on national television long before his book was due to come out. Publishers usually wait until full national distribution of a book is achieved before they schedule an author for an appearance on a television or radio show.

Robin Moore, author of *The French Connection*, has raised the issue of Ragano's credibility in connection with a film on Jimmy Hoffa he was writing a screenplay for in 1981 and 1982. While writing the screenplay Moore was in constant touch with Ragano, who was a paid consultant on the film, and Ragano never once mentioned the Kennedy assassination plot during their discussions. And, Moore observes, Hoffa's involvement in a Kennedy assassination plot would have certainly spiced up the film *Hoffa*. The answer to Moore's observation is that, for obvious reasons, Frank Ragano could not have revealed his knowledge of the plot to assassinate Kennedy until Santos Trafficante was dead. Ragano worked on the film script with Moore in 1981 and 1982. Trafficante died in 1987.

Frank Ragano has expressed a willingness to appear before a committee of the U.S. Senate to testify, under oath, about his knowledge of the plot to assassinate President Kennedy. It is highly unlikely that he would take the risk of perjuring himself by telling a monstrous lie to the United States Senate.

No, it appears that the reason why Frank Ragano made his allegation is to get his knowledge of the Kennedy assassination plot off his chest. Ragano is seventy years old and in failing health. He wants to make amends. There have been some things in his life he has not been especially proud of and his role in the Kennedy assassination plot is one of them. When he dies he wants to be at peace with himself. And he believes it is about time the American people knew who was responsible for the assassination of President John F. Kennedy.

During the 1980s several people confessed to playing a role in a plot to assassinate President Kennedy but none of them had the credentials of Frank Ragano. One of them was Thomas Easterling, a Mississippi hardhat who told author Henry Hurt in 1981 that he was a low-level conspirator intimately involved in certain plans that led to Kennedy's murder. An emotionally unstable man, who did time in several mental institutions, his testimony has been authoritatively discredited. In the mid-eighties two convicted French drug smugglers, Christian David and Michel Nikoli, told author Steve Rivele that Kennedy had been shot by three men belonging to the Marseilles-Corsican Mafia on orders from certain unspecified organized crime leaders in America, possibly Carlos Marcello or Santos Trafficante. David and Nikoli even named the president's assassins. They were French contract killer Lucien Sarti, now dead, and drug-smugglers Roger Bocognani and

Sauveur Pironti. While it is not far-fetched to associate Santos Trafficante with Corsican drug-smuggler killers, for, as we know he did considerable business with Corsican drug dealers, Rivele's scenario is based solely on the highly questionable testimony of two notorious French criminals and therefore must remain, at best, a conjectural hypothesis. Then, in 1990, an unemployed electrical worker, Ricky White, the son of a Dallas police officer, Roscoe White, who was on the Dallas Police force at the time of the assassination, came forth and asserted on national television that, primarily on the basis of a now-missing diary written by his father (which had allegedly been confiscated by the FBI), he was convinced his father was the grassy knoll gunman. White's allegation has since been convincingly discredited, principally by JFK assassination investigator, Paul L. Hoch, who subjected White's purported documentary evidence to rigorous scientific analysis.

It will be noted that in contrast to the allegation of Frank Ragano, the questionable allegations of Thomas Easterling, Christian David, and Ricky White were made by low-level individuals with no apparent knowledge of the plot to kill President Kennedy. Which brings us to an important point. Frank Ragano is the highest-level person to claim knowledge of the conspiracy to assassinate Kennedy. As one of the nation's top criminal defense attorneys for the past thirty years, who was closely associated with Jimmy Hoffa, Santos Trafficante, and Carlos Marcello, his allegation deserves an added measure of respect.

Finally, from a purely personal standpoint, I was impressed by Frank Ragano when I first met him and his wife and found nothing in their attitude or demeanor that told me they were not sincere. That impression was further confirmed by Jack Newfield who, during his series of conversations with Frank Ragano in January 1992, in Tampa, found him so trustworthy and believable he decided to stick his neck out and write a series of positive articles on his allegation for the *New York Post*.

The allegation of Frank Ragano now has an impressive list of supporters: House Assassinations Committee chief counsel G. Robert Blakey, writers Nick Pileggi and Jack Newfield, and former Kennedy aides Frank Mankiewicz, Adam Walinsky, and Richard Goodwin.

Although there still remain many unanswered questions about the assassination, I believe it is now reasonable to affirm that thirty years after the murder in Dallas we at last have an inkling who was ultimately responsible for the crime. The conclusions of the House Select Committee on Assassinations in 1979 have at last been confirmed by a witness to the plot.

SOURCES

I. The Allegation of Frank Ragano

Articles

Newfield, Jack. "Hoffa Had The Mob Murder JFK." *New York Post,* January 14, 1992. (The original allegation.)

Newfield, Jack, and Mel Juffe. "Top JFK Prober Backs Hoffa Story," *New York Post,* January 15, 1992. (Robert Blakey, Frank Mankiewicz, Adam Walinsky, and Nick Pileggi endorse Ragano's allegation.)

Newfield, Jack. "'I Want Kennedy killed!' Hoffa Shouted. An Eyewitness Account." *Penthouse,* April 1992, (An elaboration of original allegation.)

Book

Blakey, G. Robert, and Richard N. Billings, *Fatal Hour: The Assassination of President Kennedy by Organized Crime.* New York: Berkeley Books, 1992. (Reissue of 1981 book, *The Plot To Kill The President,* with a new Introduction endorsing the Ragano allegation).

Television Documentaries
> *The Kennedy Assassinations.* George Paige
> Associates, Los Angeles. Syndicated. Television
> interview with Frank Ragano and others. July 7,
> 1992. (Ragano answers questions on his allega-
> tion and is endorsed by host and guests on the
> show.)

> "JFK, Hoffa, and the Mob," *Frontline* PBS.
> Interview with Frank Ragano. Discussion of his
> allegation. November 17, 1992.

Informal Conversations with the Author
> Frank Ragano, Los Angeles, July 6, 7, 1992.

II. Carlos Marcello

PRIMARY SOURCES

Federal Bureau of Investigation, File on Carlos
Marcello. Most of the FBI file on Carlos Marcello
that was turned over by the FBI to the House Select
Committee on Assassinations in 1978 is on file at the
Assassinations Archives and Research Center, 918 F
Street, Washington, D.C. 20004.

Federal Bureau of Investigation, Freedom of
Information Act Releases.
> 1. The Allegation of FBI Informant SV T-1 Gene
>   Sumner. FBI File N. 44-24016-254. Freedom
>   of Information Act Release.
>   • SAVANNAH TELETYPE 11/26/63. To Director

and SACS, New Orleans and Dallas. Page 1. The original allegation by SV T-1, Gene Sumner, to Glynn County police officer, Lt. Johnny Harris, stating he saw someone resembling Lee Harvey Oswald accepting a payment in the Town & Country Restaurant, New Orleans, from the restaurant owner (Joseph Poretto).

•NEW ORLEANS AIRTEL, 11/27/63. FROM SAC, New Orleans, to SACs, Dallas and Savannah. Pages 1, 2. Re: Savannah teletype 11/23/63. Informing Dallas and Savannah that Town & Country Motel and Restaurant "is a known hangout of the hoodlum element" and is owned, in part, by Carlos Marcello and managed by Joseph Poretto, who has a criminal record.

•NEW ORLEANS REPORTS OF INVESTIGATION OF THE SV T-1 SUMNER ALLEGATION CONTAINED IN THE SAVANNAH TELETYPE OF 11/26/63. REPORTS DATED 11/27/63.

  •Interview of Joseph Albert Poretto by Special Agent Reed Jensen. Dictated 11/27/63.

  •Interview of Mrs. Ella Frabbiele by Special Agent Reed Jensen. Dictated 11/27/63.

  •Interview of Anthony Marcello by Special Agent Reed Jensen. Dictated 11/27/63.

•SAVANNAH TELETYPE, 11/29/63. To Director and SACs, Dallas and New Orleans. Pages 1–3. Re: Savannah teletype of 11/26/63. Reinterview of SV T-1 by Lt. Johnny Harris identifying informant as Gene Sumner, a businessman from Darien, Georgia. Sumner expands on allegation and mentions names of individuals he was with at Town & Country Motel when he saw someone resembling Oswald receive a payment from the owner, who he now identifies as having been "in the rackets" in Chicago.

•NEW ORLEANS TELETYPE, 11/30/63. To Director and SACs, Dallas and Savannah. Re: Savannah teletype of 11/29/63. SAC, New Orleans, observes that Oswald was not supposed to have been in New Orleans when SV T-1 allegedly observed him in the Town & Country Motel.

•REPORTS OF SPECIAL AGENT JOHN P. MCGUIRE, FBI, SAVANNAH ON ALLEGATION OF SV T-1, GENE SUMNER, 12/2/63. Reports of McGuire's interview of SV T-1, Gene Sumner, in which Sumner reiterates his original allegation, is shown a photo of Oswald, and asserts it resembles the individual he saw accepting a payment at the Town & Country Motel.

2. The Allegation of FBI Informant Eugene De Laparra. FBI File N. 62109060. Freedom of Information Act Release.

•PHILADELPHIA TELETYPE, 11/28/63. To Director and SACs, New Orleans and Dallas. Pages 1, 2. The original allegation by De Laparra suggesting existence of a plot to assassinate President Kennedy "when he comes south." Concludes with "copy Newark."

•NEW ORLEANS TELETYPE, 11/29/63. To Director and SAC Dallas. Pages 3, 4. Response to Philadelphia teletype of 11/28/63. Notes that De Laparra has provided reliable information in the past to New Orleans "regarding gambling activities." Refers to a New Orleans teletype of 11/28/63. Ben Traegel [sic] listed as "suspect" in the Kennedy assassination.

•PHILADELPHIA TELETYPE, 11/29/63. To Director. Page 1. Refers to Philadelphia teletype of 11/28/63.

•NEW ORLEANS REPORTS OF INVESTIGATIONS OF THE DE LAPARRA ALLEGATION CONTAINED IN PHILADELPHIA TELETYPE OF 11/28/63. REPORTS DATED 11/30/63.

•Interview of Bernard Alfred Tregle by Special Agent Reed W. Jensen. Dictated 11/29/63.

•Interview of Norman Joseph Le Blanc by Special Agent Reed W. Jensen. Dictated 11/29/63.

•Interview of Mrs. Bernard Tregle by Special Agent Ronald Hoverson. Dictated 11/29/63.

•Statement by Special Agent Regis L. Kennedy that he was in U.S. District Court, New Orleans, at trial of Carlos and Joseph Marcello on Nov. 22, 1963, and observed Vincent Marcello attending the trial. Dictated 11/27/63.

•NEWARK TELETYPE 2/23/67. To Director and Dallas. Pages 1,2,3. De Laparra's second allegation suggesting existence of a plot to assassinate President Kennedy. Made the day after death of David Ferrie. Asserts that it was Tony (Anthony) Marcello who told Ben Tregle and others in Tregle's Bar that "the word is out to get the Kennedy family."

●NEWARK AIRTEL 2/27/67. To Director. Page 1. Refers to Newark teletype of 2/23/67.

●NEWARK LHM, 2/27/67. Page 1. Summarizes Newark teletype of 2/23/67.

●NEW ORLEANS TELETYPE 8/8/67. To Director and Dallas in response to Bucall's [telephone call from FBI headquarters] to New Orleans of 8/7/67. Page 5 refers to Special Agent Jensen's interview of Norman Le Blanc of 11/29/63. Page 6 refers to Special Agent Jensen's interview with Bernard Alfred Tregle of 11/29/63 and requests Dallas review in files to determine report in which FD 302s of Norman Joseph Le Blanc and Bernard Alfred Tregle were reported "and furnish identity of report to bureau."

3. U.S. Senate, Kefauver Hearings. Special Committee to Investigate Organized Crime in Interstate Commerce. Hearings in New Orleans, Jan. 25, 26, and Feb. 7, 1951. Interrogation of Carlos Marcello, Anthony Marcello, and Joseph Poretto.

4. U.S. Senate, Kefauver Reports. Special Committee to Investigate Organized Crime in Interstate Commerce. Second Interim Report. Feb. 28, 1951. Third Interim Report, May 1, 1951.

5. U.S. Senate, McClellan Hearings. Select Committee on Improper Activities in the Labor and Management Field. Hearings in Washington, Mar. 23, 24, 25, 1959, and Aug. 28, 29, 30, 31, 1961. Testimony of Aaron

Kohn. Interrogations of Carlos Marcello, Vincent Marcello, Joseph Marcello, and Joseph Poretto.

6. U.S. House of Representatives. Organized Crime Control Hearings. May 20 to Aug. 5, 1970. Testimony of Aaron Kohn (in *Congressional Record*). Interrogation of Carlos Marcello.

7. U.S. House of Representatives. House Select Committee on Crime. Organized Crime in Sports (Racing). Hearings, May 9 to Jul. 27, 1972. Interrogation of Carlos Marcello.

8. Federal Trials (excluding BRILAB)
•U.S. District Court, New Orleans. *The United States v. Carlos Marcello and Joseph Matasa*. Transcript of trial record. Oct. 4, 1964 to Aug. 17, 1965.

9. U.S. Department of Justice-Immigration and Naturalization Service. Hearings, Deportation Proceedings, Carlos Marcello, New Orleans, Louisiana. Jun. 27, 1972; file N. A2-669-541. Transcript of hearings, 453 pages. In this document Marcello related to the immigration officers the story of his 1961 "kidnap-deportation" and exile in Central America.

10. U.S. House of Representatives. Select Committee on Assassinations (HSCA). Investigation of the Assassination of President John F. Kennedy. Final Report. 95th Cong. 2d sess., Washington,

D.C.: 1978–79. Carlos Marcello is guardedly named a suspect in the assassination.

11. U.S. House of Representatives. Select Committee on Assassinations (HSCA). Investigation of the Assassination of President John F. Kennedy. Appendix to Hearings. Vol. 9. Organized Crime. Staff Report on Carlos Marcello, pages 61–92.

12. U.S. House of Representatives. Select Committee on Assassinations (HSCA). Investigation of the Assassination of President John F. Kennedy. Outside Contact Report. I. Irving Davidson. Nov. 22, 1978.

13. The BRILAB Operation and Trials. The BRILAB Tapes.
•U.S. District Court, Eastern District of Louisiana. *United States v. Carlos Marcello, I. Irving Davidson, Charles E. Roemer, Vincent A. Marinello.* Indictment for (1) conspiracy to participate, through a pattern of racketeering activity, in the affairs of an enterprise, the activities of which affect interstate commerce; (2) a substantive violation of such participation in the affairs of that enterprise; (3) interstate travel in aid of racketeering; (4) wire fraud; and, (5) mail fraud, June 17, 1980. 25 pages. Contains a brief history of the BRILAB undercover operation, with some quotations from BRILAB tapes. Marcello and Roemer were convicted. Davidson and Marinello were acquitted.

•U.S. District Court, Eastern District of Louisiana. In the Matter of the Application of the United States of America for an Order Authorizing the Interception of Wire Communications. Affidavits. Feb. 8, 1979 to Jan. 1, 1980. These contain a summary of Joseph Hauser's career as an insurance operator, his troubles with the law, his relationship with Davidson, his relationship with Marcello before Feb. 8, 1979, and a running history of the BRILAB undercover investigation of Marcello from Feb. 1979 to Feb. 1980. In addition, the affidavits contain many verbatim transcripts of taped conversations between Carlos Marcello, the undercover agents, Irving Davidson, Vincent Marcello, and others.

•U.S. District Court, Eastern District of Louisiana. *United States v. Carlos Marcello, I. Irving Davidson, Charles E. Roemer, Vincent A. Marinello.* Crim. A No. 80-274. Transcript of record of trial at Federal Records Center, Fort Worth, Texas.

•U.S. District Court, Central District of California. *United States v. Carlos Marcello, Samuel Orlando Sciortino, and Phillip Rizzuto,* Crim. No. EJD-81-720. Transcript of record of trial at Federal Records Center, Laguna Niguel, California.

• *United States v. Carlos Marcello et al.* 508 F. Supp. 586 (1981), 637 F. Supp. 1364 (1982, F31 F. Supp. 1113 (1982), 537 F. Supp. 399 (1982), 568 F. Supp. 738 (1983), 731 F. 2d 1354 (1984). These contain summaries of the New Orleans and Los Angeles BRILAB undercover

operations, commentary on the trials, and
many verbatim transcripts of taped conversations between Carlos Marcello, the undercover agents, and others.

•The BRILAB Tapes. United States District
Court For the District of Columbia. *John H.
Davis v. U.S. Department of Justice.* Civil
Action N. 88-01330(TPJ). Freedom of
Information Act lawsuit to secure release of
the approximately 160 reels of taped conversa-
tions between Carlos Marcello, the under-
cover agents, and others, recorded during the
FBI undercover investigation of Carlos
Marcello, February 1979 to February 1980
that were admitted into evidence at the two
BRILAB trials in New Orleans and Los
Angeles. Approximately 1,400 reels of
Marcello's conversations were recorded.
Among these were three tapes of Marcello's
conversations about the John F. Kennedy
assassination and the House Select
Committee on Assassinations investigation.
These were put under judicial seal by Judge
Morey Sear.

•U.S. District Court, Eastern District of
Louisiana. *United States v. Carlos Marcello et
al.* Criminal case N. 80-274 Section "G"
Proffer. The Defendant Carlos Marcello
Should Be Allowed To Demonstrate to the
Instant Jury Any Prior And Present
Government Bias Against Him Which May
Have Prejudicially Influenced the Conduct of
the FBI Investigation in this Case Against
Marcello. (An excellent summary of the INS

deportation case against Carlos Marcello, presenting the irregularities and illegalities of the government's case.)

• U.S. District Court, Eastern District of Louisiana. *United States v. Carlos Marcello et al.* Criminal Case N. 80-274 Section "G" Motion to vacate Conviction Pursuant to 28 USC 2255. October 7, 1987. (Marcello's appeal of his mail and wire fraud conviction. Contains a concise history of the BRILAB operation and trials).

Secondary Sources

Books-General

A selected list of books in which Carlos Marcello is prominently mentioned.

Chandler, David Leon. *Brothers in Blood: The Rise of the Criminal Brotherhoods.* New York: Dutton, 1975. (Book Four).

Davis, John H. *The Kennedys: Dynasty and Disaster.* New York: McGraw-Hill, 1984. (Parts 3, 4, 5).

Dorman, Michael. *Payoff.* New York: Berkley, 1972. (The Marcello-Halfen connection.)

Moldea, Dan E. *The Hoffa Wars: Teamsters, Rebels, Politicians, and the Mob.* New York: Paddington, 1978.

Reid, Ed. *The Grim Reapers: The Anatomy of Organized Crime in America.* Chicago: Henry Regnery, 1969. (Chapter 9).

Schreiber, G.R. *The Bobby Baker Affair.* Chicago: Henry Regnery, 1964.

Sheridan, Walter. *The Fall and Rise of Jimmy Hoffa*. New York: Saturday Review Press, 1972.

Books-John F. Kennedy Assassination.
A selected list (in order of publication) in which Carlos Marcello is mentioned as a possible suspect.

Noyes, Peter. *Legacy of Doubt*. New York: Pinnacle Books, 1973. (The first book on the Kennedy assassination to name Carlos Marcello as a possible suspect in the crime.)

Anson, Robert Sam. *They've Killed the President—The Search for the Murderers of John F. Kennedy*. New York: Bantam Books, 1975.

Fensterwald, Bernard, Jr. *Coincidence or Conspiracy?* New York: Zebra Books, 1977.

Kantor, Seth. *Who Was Jack Ruby?* New York: Everest House, 1978.

Summers, Anthony. *Conspiracy. Who Killed President Kennedy?* New York: McGraw-Hill, 1980.

Blakey, G. Robert, and Richard N. Billings. *The Plot to Kill the President*. New York: New York Times Books, 1981.

Scheim, David E. *Contract on America: The Mafia Murder of President John F. Kennedy*. New York: Shapolsky Books, 1988. (Originally self-published, 1983.)

Davis, John H. *Mafia Kingfish: Carlos Marcello and the Assassination of John F. Kennedy*. New York: McGraw-Hill, 1988. NAL/Signet, 1989.

North, Mark. *Act of Treason: The Role of J. Edgar Hoover in the Assassination of John F. Kennedy.* New York: Carroll & Graf, 1991.

Rappleye, Charles and Ed Becker. *All-American Mafioso: The Johnny Rosselli Story.* New York: Doubleday, 1991.

Morrow, Robert D., *Firsthand Knowledge: How I Participated in the CIA-Mafia Murder of President Kennedy.* New York: S.P.I. Books, 1992.

Newspaper and Magazine Articles.

A selection of key articles representing major milestones in the acquisition of information on Carlos Marcello. Most of the hundreds of articles generated by the House Select Committee on Assassinations investigation and BRILAB operations and trials are omitted.

"Abscam (cont.). Mafiosi Call Off a Summit." *Time,* February 25, 1980.

Amoss, Jim, and Dean Baquet. Articles on the BRILAB undercover operation and trials. *New Orleans Times-Picayune,* 1980, 1981, 1982, 1983.

Amoss, Jim, and Dean Baquet. "Carlos Marcello." A three-part series in *Dixie Magazine, New Orleans Times-Picayune,* February 1982. Based on over 100 interviews. Interviews with Carlos Marcello conducted through one of his attorneys, Provino Mosca.

Anderson, Jack. "Assassinations Committee Is Checking Mafia Plot." United Feature Syndicate, January 4, 1979.

Anderson, Jack. "Carlos Marcello . . . Mobster." United Feature Syndicate, July 13, 1979.

Anderson, Jack. "House Panel Traces Mobster's Strings." *Washington Post,* July 12, 1979.

Atkinson, Jim. "Who's Behind the Mafia in Dallas?" *Dallas Magazine,* December 1977.

"Carlos Marcello: Cosa Nostra Boss." *Wall Street Journal,* October 14, 1970.

Chandler, David Leon. "The `Little Man' Is Bigger Than Ever. Louisiana Still Jumps for Mobster Marcello." *Life,* April 10, 1970.

Crewdson, John M. "Ex-Immigration Official is Said to Have Assisted Crime Figure." *New York Times,* February 11, 1980. (About Irving Davidson, Carlos Marcello, and Mario Noto.)

Davidson, Bill. "New Orleans: Cosa Nostra's Wall Street." *Saturday Evening Post,* February 29, 1964.

Dorman, Michael. "Jack Halfen and Lyndon Johnson." *Ramparts,* 1968. (The Marcello-Halfen-Johnson connection.)

Fithian, Rep. Floyd J. "A Challenge for America, from the House Assassinations Committee Probe." *Indiana Law Enforcement Journal,* Spring 1979.

Golz, Earl. "Marcello Listens as Damaging FBI Tapes Unwind." *Dallas Morning News,* May 30, 1981.

Lardner, George, Jr. "Investigator Detailed Mafia Leaders' Threat Against Kennedy." *Washington Post,* July 21, 1979.

Lardner, George, Jr. "U.S. vs Marcello. Reputed Rackets Chieftain Eludes Federal Prosecutors for 30 Years." *Washington Post,* February 19, 1980.

"The Marcello-JFK Connection?" *Gris Gris,* New Orleans, January 15–21, 1978.

Marshall, Jonathan. "Requiem for a Mobster." *Inquiry,* September 1, 1981.

"The Rise of Carlos Marcello." *Los Angeles Times,* September 4, 1970.

"The Mob," (Part I.) *Life,* September 1, 1967.

"The Mob," (Part II.) *Life,* September 8, 1967.

Maxa, Rudy. "Confessions of a Political Dirtmonger. Ed Becker`s World of Suspicions and Surmises." *Washington Post,* April 17, 1980.

Oglesby, Earl and Jeff Goldberg. "Marcello-Oswald Connection Possible." *New Orleans Times-Picayune,* February 25, 1979.

Selcraig, Bruce. "Marcello Spins Web in Dallas." *Dallas Morning News,* March 9, 1980.

"Summon Marcello, JFK Probers Urge." *Washington Post,* April 1, 1977.

Taylor, Jack. "FBI Quiz Thwarts Multi-Million Dollar Mafia Plot." *Sunday Oklahoman,* February 24, 1980.

New Orleans Times-Picayune. Articles on Carlos Marcello deportation case, 1953–1988.

Goldfarb, Ronald. "What the Mob Knew about JFK's Murder. The Death of Racketeer Carlos Marcello Raises Important Old Questions. *Washington Post,* March 14, 1993.

Files of the Metropolitan Crime Commission, New Orleans.

Extensive thirty-year file on Carlos Marcello, his brothers, and associates largely compiled by Aaron Kohn when he was managing director.

The New Orleans Times-Picayune Collection.

Extensive file on Carlos Marcello and his family and associates. Several thousand pages of articles and documents including the *Times-Picayune's* 100 interviews for its three-part *Dixie Magazine* series on Carlos Marcello and an extensive interview with Carlos Marcello through his intermediary, Provino Mosca.

Formal Interviews (taped)
(Listed by date)

August La Nasa, Dec. 23, 1986. New Orleans attorney.

Aaron Kohn, Jan. 7, 11, Feb. 4, 5, Mar. 31, 1987, and Jan. 20, 1988. Former FBI special agent and assistant to J. Edgar Hoover; former director New Orleans Metropolitan Crime Commission. Investigated Carlos Marcello for over twenty years.

Harold Hughes, Jan. 18, Feb. 13, and Apr. 1, 1987. Former FBI special agent, chief of Organized Crime Strike Force, New Orleans, coordinator of the New Orleans BRILAB investigation of Carlos Marcello. Covered Carlos Marcello for thirteen years.

Richard Angelico, Feb. 9, 12, 1987, and Apr. 1, 1988. Investigative reporter, WDSU-TV

New Orleans. Covered Carlos Marcello for twenty years.

Jim Amoss, Feb. 4, 1987. Metro editor, *New Orleans Times-Picayune*.

Charles Turnbo, Feb. 10, 1987. Warden, Federal Correctional Institution, Fort Worth, Texas.

Alvin Beauboeuf, Feb. 11, 1987. Friend of David Ferrie.

Edward Becker, Feb. 18, 1987. Private investigator, Las Vegas.

Courtney Evans, June 10, 1987. Former assistant director, FBI. Liaison between J. Edgar Hoover and Robert F. Kennedy.

Joseph Hauser, Jul. 15, 21, and Aug. 5, 1987. U.S. government informant, BRILAB investigation of Carlos Marcello.

G. Robert Blakey, Aug. 7, 1987. Former chief counsel, House Select Committee on Assassinations.

Larry Montague, Dec. 11, 1987, and Jan. 21, 1988. FBI special agent, undercover agent, BRILAB investigation of Carlos Marcello.

Bruce Kelton, Jul. 22, 1987, and Jan. 22, 1988. Former assistant U.S. attorney, Los Angeles. Assistant prosecutor, Los Angeles BRILAB trial of Carlos Marcello.

Michael Wacks, Jan. 24, 1988. FBI special agent, undercover agent, BRILAB investigation of Carlos Marcello.

Walter Sheridan, Jun. 9, 1988. Former head of labor racketeering unit of the organized crime section, Justice Deaprtment, under Attorney General Robert F. Kennedy.

William G. Hundley, Jun. 16, 1988. Chief, organized crime and racketeering section, Justice Department, under Attorney General Robert F. Kennedy.

Morgan Goudeau, Aug. 9, 1988. District attorney, St. Landry Parish, Lafayette, Louisiana.

Collections

The Papers of Paul L. Hoch, press clippings, magazine articles, FBI documents, made available to the author by Mr. Hoch.

The Papers of Anthony Summers. Press clippings, magazine articles, notes for The Grim Reapers by Ed Reid, miscellaneous allegations, FBI reports, Secret Service reports, on Carlos Marcello and David Ferrie, made available to the author by Mr. Summers.

Informal Interviews (not taped)

Paul L. Hoch. Numerous occasions, 1987–88. Coauthor of *The Assassinations: Dallas and Beyond.*

Bernard Fensterwald, Jr. Numerous occasions, 1987–88. Author of *Coincidence or Conspiracy?*

Peter Noyes. Author of *Legacy of Doubt.*

Written Interviews

Joseph Hauser, Aug. 3. 1987. Mr. Hauser's answers to twenty-two questions put to him by the author.

Films (in which Marcello is represented)

The Two Kennedys. Rome, 1976. Italian documentary film on the Kennedy assassinations. WHS edition, Ben Barry Associates Productions, 1976.

The Kwitny Report on the Assassination of John F. Kennedy PBS, 1988.

III. James R. Hoffa

PRIMARY SOURCES

1. U.S. Senate. McClellan Hearings. Select Committee on Improper Activities in the Labor or Management Field Hearings. February 26, 1957 to September 9, 1959.

2. U.S. House of Representatives. Select Committee on Assassinations (HSCA) Investigation of the Assassination of President John F. Kennedy. Final Report pp. 174, 176–179. (Summary of the evidence against Hoffa.)

SECONDARY SOURCES

Books

Davis, John H. *Mafia Kingfish: Carlos Marcello and the Assassination of John F. Kennedy.* New York: McGraw-Hill, 1988. Updated paperback edition, NAL/Signet, 1989.

Fensterwald, Bernard, Jr., *Coincidence or Conspiracy?* New York: Zebra Books, 1977.

Kennedy, Robert F. *The Enemy Within*. New York: Harper Bros., 1960.

Moldea, Dan E. *The Hoffa Wars: Teamsters, Rebels, Politicians, and the Mob*. New York: Paddington, 1978.

North, Mark. *Act of Treason. The Role of J. Edgar Hoover in the Assassination of John F. Kennedy*. New York: Carroll & Graf, 1991.

Sheridan, Walter. *The Fall and Rise of Jimmy Hoffa*. New York: Saturday Review Press, 1972.

Sloane, Arthur A. *Hoffa*. Cambridge, Mass: The MIT Press, 1991.

IV. Santos Trafficante

PRIMARY SOURCES

1. U.S. House of Representatives. Select Committee on Assassinations (HSCA) Investigation of the Assassination of President John F. Kennedy. Final Report pp. 151–154, 172–175, 179. (Summary of evidence against Trafficante.)

2. U.S. House of Representatives. Select Committee on assassinations (HSCA) Investigation of the Assassination of President John F. Kennedy. Vol. 5: Testimony of José Alémán, pp. 301–324. Testimony of Trafficante, pp. 346–377.

3. Federal Bureau of Investigation. File on Santos Trafficante. File N. 92-2781. Most of the FBI file on Santos Trafficante, Jr. that was turned over by the

FBI to the House Select Committee on Assassinations in 1978 is on file at the Assassination Archives and Research Center, 918 F Street, Washington, D.C. Files are heavily censored.

SECONDARY SOURCES

Books

North, Mark. *Act of Treason: The Role of J. Edgar Hoover in The Assassination of John F. Kennedy.* New York: Carroll & Graf, 1991.

Rappleye, Charles, and Ed Becker. *All-American Mafioso: The Johnny Rosselli Story.* New York: Doubleday, 1991.

Fensterwald, *Coincidence or Conspiracy?;* Moldea, *The Hoffa Wars;* Blakey and Billings, *The Plot To Kill The President;* Scheim, *Contract on America.*

V. The Assassination of President John F. Kennedy

PRIMARY SOURCES

Federal Bureau of Investigation. Files on the John F. Kennedy Assassination. Approximately 221,000 pages have been released. These may be consulted at the FBI Freedom of Information Acts Reading Room, FBI Headquarters, The J. Edgar Hoover Building, Pennsylvania Ave., Washington, D.C., and at the libraries of several universities, such as the University of Wisconsin, Stevens Point, Wisconsin, and at the Southeastern Louisiana University at Hammond. Also available privately from: Harold Weisberg, 7627 Old Receiver Rd., Frederick, MD 21701.

National Archives and Records Services, General Services Administration. Records of the President's Commission on the Assassination of John F. Kennedy (the Warren Commission). Record Group 272. National Archives, Washington, D.C. The Warren Commission documents, known as CDs, including many FBI reports that were not published in the Warren Commission's twenty-six volumes of *Hearings and Exhibits (*see 4 below).

The *State of Louisiana v. Clay L. Shaw,* Criminal District Court, New Orleans (the Garrison Investigation). Forty volumes. The Linus A. Sims Memorial Library, Southeastern Louisiana University, Hammond.

President's Commission on the Assassination of President John F. Kennedy (the Warren Commission). *Hearings and Exhibits.* 26 vols., 1964.

President's Commission on the Assassination of President John F. Kennedy. *Report* (the Warren Report). 1964.

U.S. House of Representatives. Select Committee on Assassinations (HSCA). Assassination of President John F. Kennedy. Final Report. 95th Cong., 2d sess., 1979.

U.S. House of Representatives. Select Committee on Assassinations (HSCA). Investigation of the Assassination of President John F. Kennedy. Hearings and Appendixes to Hearings, 12 vols. 95th Cong., 2d sess., 1978–79.

U.S. Senate. Select Committee to Study Governmental Operations with Respect to Intelligence Activities (the Church Committee). Book V. The Investigation of the Assassination of President John F. Kennedy: The Performance of the Intelligence Agencies (the Schweiker-Hart Report). 94th Cong., 2d sess., 1976.

Central Intelligence Agency. Papers on the Assassination of President John F. Kennedy. 15 vols., 3847 pages. Linus A. Sims Memorial Library, Southeastern Louisiana University, Hammond.

SECONDARY SOURCES

Books
    A selection of the seminal books (*in order of publication*) on the assassination, excluding those identifying Carlos Marcello as a prime suspect. For these see the preceding section.

    Joesten, Joachim. *Oswald: Assassin or Fall Guy?* New York: Marzani & Munsell, 1964.
    Lane, Mark. *Rush to Judgment: A Critique of the Warren Commission's Inquiry into the Murders of John F. Kennedy, Officer J.D. Tippit, and Lee Harvey Oswald.* New York: Holt, Rinehart, & Winston, 1966.

Popkin, Richard H. *The Second Oswald.* New York: Avon/New York Review of Books, 1966.

Epstein, Edward Jay. *Inquest: The Warren Commission and the Establishment of Truth.* New York: Viking, 1966. Bantam, 1967.

Weisberg, Harold. *Whitewash: The Report on the Warren Report.* Hyattstown, Md.: H. Weisberg, 1966. (Followed by Vols. II, III, IV, 1967–74.)

Meagher, Sylvia. *Accessories after the Fact: The Warren Commission, the Authorities and the Report.* Indianapolis: Bobbs-Merrill, 1967.

Thompson, Josiah. *Six Seconds in Dallas. A Micro-Study of the Kennedy Assassination.* New York: Bernard Geis Assocs., 1967.

Garrison, Jim. *A Heritage of Stone.* New York: Putnam, 1970.

Weisberg, Harold. *Post-Mortem. JFK Assassination Cover-Up Smashed.* Frederick, Md.: H. Weisberg, 1975.

Hoch, Paul L., Peter Dale Scott and Russell Stetler. *The Assassinations: Dallas and Beyond. A Guide to Cover-Ups and Investigations.* New York: Random House (Vintage Books), 1976.

Scott, Peter Dale. *Crime and Cover-Up: The CIA, the Mafia and the Dallas-Watergate Connection.* Berkeley, Calif.: Westworks, 1977.

Evica, George Michael. *And We Are All Mortal: New Evidence and Analysis in the*

Assassination of John F. Kennedy. West Hartford, Conn.: University of Hartford Press, 1978.

Lifton, David. *Best Evidence: Disguise and Deception in the Assassination of John F. Kennedy*. New York: Macmillan, 1980.

Kurtz, Michael. *Crime of the Century: The Kennedy Assassination from a Historian's Perspective*. Knoxville: University of Tennessee Press, 1982.

Hurt, Henry. *Reasonable Doubt. An Investigation into the Assassination of John F. Kennedy*. New York: Holt, Rinehart, & Winston, 1985.

Marrs, Jim. *Crossfire: The Plot That Killed Kennedy*. New York: Carroll & Graf, 1989.

Summers, Anthony. *Conspiracy: The Definitive Book on the JFK Assassination*. Updated and Expanded Edition. New York: Paragon House, 1989.

Crenshaw, Charles A., with Jens Hansen and J. Gary Shaw. *JFK: Conspiracy of Silence*. New York: Signet Books, 1992.

Shaw, J. Gary, with Larry R. Harris. *Cover-Up: The Governmental Conspiracy to Conceal the Facts About the Public Execution of John Kennedy*. Cleburne, Tex.: Shaw, 1976. Reissued in 1992.

Unpublished Manuscripts

Hoch, Paul L. "The Oswald Papers: The FBI versus the Warren Commission." Copyright © Paul L. Hoch, 1974.

Hoch, Paul L., Peter Dale Scott, Russell Stetler,

and Josiah Thompson. "Beyond Conspiracy." Copyright © Hoch, Scott, Stetler, Thompson, 1980.

Newspaper and Magazine Articles (Selected)

Alavarez, Luis W. "A Physicist Examines the Kennedy Assassination Film." *American Journal of Physics,* 44, 1976, 813–827.

Branch, Taylor, and George Crile III. "The Kennedy Vendetta." *Harper's,* 251, August 1975, 49–63.

Donahue, Howard. "Evaluation of the Pathology of the Wounding of John F. Kennedy." *Biological Aspects of Forensic Science.* April 26, 1982.

Kurtz, Michael. "Lee Harvey Oswald in New Orleans: A Reappraisal." *Louisiana History,* 21, 1980, 7–22.

Lowenstein, Allard K. "The Kennedy Killings." *Argosy,* February 1976, 28-33, 86.

Malone, William Scott, and Jerry Policoff. "Fear and Loathing on the Assassination Trail." Unpublished article. (On The House Select Committee on Assassinations' investigation of the JFK assassination.)

Malone, William Scott, and Jerry Policoff. "A Great Show, A Lousy Investigation." Special Report. *New York Times.* September 4, 1978. (On the House Select Committee on Assassinatins' investigation of the JFK assassination).

Reppert, Ralph. "Kennedy Assassination: A Different View." *Baltimore Sun Sunday Magazine,* May 1 and 8, 1977.

Sliva, Helga. "Fear of Mafia and Future Led

Aleman to Fatal Finale." *Miami Herald,* August 2, 1983.

"Special Gallery Report. The JFK Assassination," *Gallery* magazine. July 1979.

Wecht, Cyril H. "Pathologist's View of JFK Autopsy: An Unsolved Case." *Modern Medicine,* November 27, 1972, 28–32

Wecht, Cyril H., and Robert P. Smith. "The Medical Evidence in the Assassination of President Kennedy." *Forensic Science,* 3, 1974, 105–128.

York, Marva. "Exile Tormented Before Fatal Spree." *Miami News,* August 1, 1983. (Death of José Alemán).

Reviews and Newsletters

a. *The Third Decade: A Journal of Research on the John F. Kennedy Assassination.* Published bimonthly at State University College, Fredonia, NY 14063. Editor and Publisher: Professor Jerry D. Rose.

b. *Echoes of Conspiracy.* A newsletter on research, investigations, and writings pertaining to the assassinations of John F. Kennedy, Martin Luther King, Jr., and Robert F. Kennedy, and related subjects. Editor and Publisher: Paul L. Hoch, 1525 Acton Street, Berkeley, CA 94702.

Bibliographies and indexes

a. Guth, DeLloyd J., and David R. Wrone. *The Assassination of John F. Kennedy—A Comprehensive Historical and Legal Bibliography, 1963–1979.* Westport, Conn.: Greenwood Press, 1980.

b. Meagher, Sylvia, in collaboration with Gary Owens. *Master Index to the J.F.K. Assassinations Investigations: The Reports and Supporting Volumes of the House Select Committee on Assassinations and the Warren Commission.* Metuchen, N.J.: Scarecrow Press, 1980.

c. Duffy, James P., and Vincent L. Ricci. *The Assassination of John F. Kennedy. Dates, Places, People. A Complete Book of Facts.* New York: Thunder's Mouth Press, 1992.

Note: See bibliographies on the John F. Kennedy assassination in Kurtz, *Crime of the Century,* 1982; Blakey and Billings, *The Plot to Kill the President,* 1981; Davis, *The Kennedys: Dynasty and Disaster,* 1984; Hurt, *Reasonable Doubt,* 1985; and Scheim, *Contract on America,* 1988. These bibliographies take up where Guth and Wrone left off.

Interviews

G. Robert Blakey, former chief counsel, House Select Committee on Assassinations, September 8, 13, 19, 1983, and January 3, 1984.

Nicholas Katzenbach, former attorney general of the United States, Sept. 23, 1983.

Edward Becker, February 18, 1987.

Anthony Summers, June 15, 1988.

Collections

The Papers of Paul L. Hoch. Extensive collection of papers and official documents of the John F. Kennedy assassination, and the FBI,

Warren Commission, and House Select
Committee on Assassinations investigations,
made available to the author by Mr. Hoch.

The Papers of Anthony Summers. Research notes
for Mr. Summers' book, *Conspiracy: Who
Killed President Kennedy?* and subsequent post-
publication research notes on Lee Harvey
Oswald's visit to Mexico City, September 27—
October 3, 1963, including notes on the work-
ing papers of the House Select Committee on
Assassinations 300-page classified report on
Oswald in Mexico City which Mr. Summers
obtained from a committee investigator.

VI. General Bibliography

Note: Limited to books and articles used as
sources of information for this book.

Bernstein, Carl, and Bob Woodward. *All the
President's Men.* New York: Simon &
Schuster, 1974.

Cohen, Mickey, with John Peer Nugent. *In My
Own Words.* Englewood Cliffs, N.J.: Prentice-
Hall, 1975.

Davison, Jean. *Oswald's Game.* New York: W.
W. Norton, 1983.

Demaris, Ovid. *The Last Mafioso.* New York:
Times Books, 1981.

Flammonde, Paris. *The Kennedy Conspiracy: An
Uncommissioned Report on the Jim Garrison
Investigation.* New York: Meredith, 1969.

Haldeman, H.R., with Joseph DiMona. *The Ends of Power.* New York: Times Books, 1978.

Kelley, Clarence M., and James Kirkpatrick Davis. Kelley. *The Story of an FBI Director.* Kansas City: Andrew, McMeel & Parker, 1987.

Kennedy, Robert F. *The Enemy Within.* New York: Harper Bros., 1960.

Lukas, J. Anthony. *The Underside of the Nixon Years.* New York: Viking Press, 1973.

Maas, Peter. *The Valachi Papers.* New York: Putnam, 1968.

Marchetti, Victor, and John D. Marks. *The CIA and the Cult of Intelligence.* New York: Knopf, 1974.

Morgan, John. *No Gangster More Bold. Murray Humphreys: The Welsh Political Genius Who Corrupted America.* London: Hodder & Stoughton, 1985.

Navasky, Victor. *Kennedy Justice.* New York: Atheneum, 1977.

Schlesinger, Arthur M., Jr. *Robert Kennedy and His Times.* Boston: Houghton Mifflin, 1978.

Schorr, Daniel. *Clearing the Air.* Boston: Houghton Mifflin, 1977.

Sullivan, William, with Bill Brown. *The Bureau. My Thirty Years in Hoover's FBI.* New York: W.W. Norton, 1979.

Summers, Anthony. *Goddess: The Secret Lives of Marilyn Monroe.* New York: Macmillan, 1985.

Teresa, Vincent, with Thomas C. Renner. *My Life in the Mafia.* Garden City, N.Y.: Doubleday, 1973.

VII. Miscellaneous U.S. Government Documents

Federal Bureau of Investigation

David William Ferrie. New Orleans Field Office file 89-69A-100 to 3299.

Joseph Albert Poretto. New Orleans Field Office file 62-9-33-411.

Internal Memorandum. From Assistant Attorney General, Criminal Division to Director, FBI, June 7, 1978. Re: House Select Committee on Assassinations. (Justice Department's recommendation that Assassinations Committee's request for FBI's Dallas and New Orleans Field Office files on the John F. Kennedy assassination be denied.)

File on Joseph Francis Civello. N. 92-2824. Assassination Archives and Research Center, Washington, D.C.

File on Jack Leon Ruby. Assassination Archives and Research Center, Washington, D.C.

•The Allegation of William Abadie, 12/7/63, Los Angeles, Calif. Los Angeles file 44-895. In which Abadie asserted Jack Ruby was involved in gambling in Dallas and maintained a slot machine and juke box "warehouse shop" and a bookmaking establishment often frequented by the Dallas Police. Ruby described by Abadie as a "a quiet, intense racketeer, gambler, and hustler."

•The Allegation of Bobby Gene Moore, 11/27/63, Oakland, Calif. File SF 44-494,

DL 44-1639. In which Moore asserted Jack Ruby was associated with Dallas Mafia boss Joseph Civello and was "connected with the underworld in Dallas."

U.S. District Court, Eastern District of Louisiana

Affidavits in support of applications of the United States of America for an order authorizing the interception of wire communications. Misc. N. 2142, 1986, 1987.

  • 352 pages of affidavits of FBI special agents executed throughout 1986 and 1987 revealing extent of the infiltration of crews of the Bruno/Scarfo and Gambino crime families in various rackets in New Orleans once controlled by the Marcello organization.

United States v. Carlos Marcello et al. Criminal Docket N. 80-274. Section "G," Government's Memorandum of Law Concerning the Sufficiency of Evidence to Convict Defendant Vincent A. Marinello on Counts 1, 2, 11, and 12 of the indictment. (15-page memorandum giving concise history of the BRILAB bribery scheme.)

United States v. I. Irving Davidson et al. Criminal Action N. 80-274, Section "C," Defendant Davidson's Proffer Regarding Challenges for Cause to the Prospective Jurors, Severance, and Change of Venue.

U.S. Secret Service

Investigation of David W. Ferrie, November

24–29, 1963 by Special Agent in Charge, John W. Rice and Special Agent Anthony E. Gerrots. Report dated 12/13/63. File N. CO-2-34, 030.

U.S. Senate

1. U.S. Senate, Select Committee to Study Governmental Operations with Respect to Intelligence Activities (the Church Committee). Interim Report: Alleged Assassination Plots Involving Foreign Leaders, Nov. 20, 1975, 94th Cong., 1st sess., 1975.

2. U.S. Senate. Select Committee to Study Governmental Operations with Respect to Intelligence Activities (the Church Committee). Final Report, Book V: The Investigation of the Assassination of John F. Kennedy: Performance of the Intelligence Agencies. 1976. 94th Cong., 2d sess., 1976.

VIII. Oliver Stone's JFK

Books

Stone, Oliver, and Zachary Sklar. *JFK—the Book of The Film. The Documented Screenplay.* New York: Applause Theatre Book Publications, 1992.

Prouty, Leroy Fletcher. *The Secret Team: CIA and Its Allies in Control of the United States and the World.* Englewood Cliffs, N.J.: Prentice Hall, 1973.

Newman, John W. *JFK and Vietnam: Deception,*

Intrigue, and the Struggle for Power. New York: Warner Books, 1991.

Garrison, Jim. *On the Trail of the Assassins.* New York: Sheridan Square Press, 1988.

Articles

Lardner, George, Jr.: "On the Set: Dallas in Wonderland. How Oliver Stone's Version of the Kennedy Assassination Exploits the Edge of Paranoia." *Washington Post,* June 2, 1991.

Anson, Robert Sam. "JFK the Movie—Oliver Stone Reshoots History," *Esquire,* November 1991.

Video

JFK (Directors Cut). Parts 1 and 2. Warner Home Video, 1991.

INDEX

301

JOHN H. DAVIS is the author of several bestselling books, including *The Kennedys: Dynasty and Disaster, Mafia Kingfish: Carlos Marcello and the Assassination of John F. Kennedy, The Guggenheims,* and *The Bouviers.* A graduate of Princeton, he studied in Italy on a Fulbright scholarship and served as a naval officer with the Sixth Fleet in the Mediterranean. Davis has been a student of the Kennedy assassination case for fourteen years and is on the Board of Advisors of the Assassination Archives and Research Center in Washington, D.C. He lives in New York City.